# Considering Parenthood

# Considering Parenthood

## Cheri Pies

## SECOND EDITION, updated

spinsters book company
San Francisco

Second Edition

10-9-8-7-6-5-4-3

Spinsters
P.O. Box 410687
San Francisco, CA 94141

Cover Art, Section Art, Cover Design and Text Design: Pam Wilson Design Studio
Interior Drawings: Marcia Quackenbush
Typesetting: Jean Swallow and ComText Typography, Inc., San Francisco
Production: Kathi Jaramillo, Jennifer Hoff, Martha Davis, Debra DeBondt, Fran Taylor
Index: Sayre Van Young


Printed in the U.S.A.


Library of Congress Cataloging-in-Publication Data

Pies, Cheri, 1949-
        Considering parenthood.

        Bibliography: p.
        Includes index.
        1. Lesbian mothers. 2. Motherhood. 3. Choice
(Psychology) I. Title.
HQ75.53.P54 1988        306.8'743        88-29463
ISBN 0-933216-13-0

*For Lynn C. Campbell*
*1955–1984*

# Acknowledgements

Even before I was seriously into writing this book, I started imagining what I would say in the acknowledgments — who I would thank, how I would describe all the time and effort that had gone into writing this book, and where my experiences of writing the book had taken me. I thought this would be the easiest part. Now, as the book nears completion, I find it very difficult to capture in words the enormous amount of thanks and appreciation I feel for so many people who helped to make this book a reality.

First, I want to thank all the women who participated in my groups in the Bay Area, as well as the women who corresponded with me over the years, most of whom I have never met, but who generously shared the intimate details of their decisions concerning parenting.

I am grateful to the many people who assisted me with this book at different steps along the way. Each contributed a great deal — some through actual work on the manuscript; others by sharing their thoughts and ideas with me at lesbian mother events, over a meal, or even while taking a run; and still others through their friendship, heartfelt emotional support and loving attentiveness.

I am especially grateful to the many women who spent countless hours working on the manuscript, offering their comments, sharing their thoughts and redirecting me when I needed it — *Cathy Cade, Nancy Carleton, Debra Chasnoff, Wendy Cutler, Pat Hastings, Diane Jones, Denah Joseph, Linda Jupiter, Kim Klausner, Joan Nackerud* and *Sholey McGaffie*. Each of these women deserve my most sincere praise for their time, energy, and thoughtfulness.

I was very lucky to find *Nancy Adess,* a superb editor and long-time friend, who took my words and ideas and skillfully shaped them to clearly convey what I wanted to say.

*Deborah Kelley* and *Ricki Bodin* gave me the ideas and material for the chapter on disabled lesbians. *Deborah Kaplan* challenged my thinking and helped me formulate my ideas about prenatal screening. *Helen Keller, Nancy Kelley, Elaine MaGree, Lisa Wagner,* and *Gretchen Welsh* provided me with the framework for the chapter on single parenting. *Nancy Powell* thoughtfully compiled the annotated bibliography. *Barbara Raboy* took time to educate me on some of the fine points about fresh and frozen sperm. *Esther Levine* was an excellent resource concerning fertility and infertility. *Laurie Hauer* and *Lyn Paleo* developed an excellent resource on Women and A.I.D.S. which they generously allowed me to include in this book. My therapy group gave me loving attention and positive energy week after week to see to it I got this book done. And, the staff and volunteers at I.C.I. - A Woman's Place Bookstore in Oakland consistently encouraged me during the three years it took to write this book.

There are a number of women to whom I want to extend my very special thanks:

*Cheryl Jones* for sharing in the conception of this project with me, serving as a constant sounding board, and carefully explaining her thoughts and experiences so that I could accurately reflect them on paper;

*Molly McCourt* for patiently teaching me how to use a computer and then generously making her computer available to me at my convenience;

*Donna Hitchens,* a pioneer in the field of legal rights for lesbian mothers, for being an inspiration and a powerful reminder of the importance of this work;

*Roberta Achtenberg* for her sparkling sense of humor at a time when I really needed it, and for believing in me and the work I was doing;

*Cathy Cade* for spending hours working on the manuscript, and reassuring me when I needed it the most;

*Sandy Boucher* for consistently reminding me I could actually write a book;

*Barbara Safran* for being in my life, mobilizing my creative energies, and being a constant source of nurturance and hopefulness week after week;

*Kim Chernin* who set me on the right track very early on in this project, probably without realizing it;

*Nancy Bereano* who was one of the first to get excited about the original manuscript;

and especially *Sherry Thomas* for getting me over the final hump so that I could finish the book, for sharing her ideas and prodding me to expand several sections of the book in ways I hadn't even thought about, for sensitively and tenderly guiding me through the publishing process, and for her professional commitment to the fine art of feminist publishing.

I am very fortunate to have many dear and devoted friends who saw me through perhaps the hardest year of my life, stood by me as I continued writing this book and believed I could finish it when even I wasn't sure that I could — to these friends I extend a heartfelt thanks that written words cannot adequately convey. They were my lifeline. And, I am especially thankful for the good cooking of *Carol Lefkowitz* and *Ellen Oppenheimer*, the uplifting spirit of *Louise Music*, and the youthful exuberance of *Caitlin Sierra Jones*.

I feel lucky to be able to thank my family for their interest and support in my work on this book. I am sorry my father is not alive to share in this achievement. He taught me to reach for the stars, and both he and my mother gave me the courage to fight for the issues and causes I believe in.

In addition, I feel deeply indebted to *Lynn Campbell's* family, her parents *Mary and Warren*, and her sisters *Alice and Jill*. They contributed so much in the way of their time, talents, and emotional support which added significantly to the completion of this book.

*Liz Hendrickson* deserves an extra special word of thanks. Without her, I never would have been forced to think about these issues and find my own answers. During the past year, she read every version of the manuscript, patiently listened to me read selected paragraphs during late night and early morning phone calls, and lovingly stood by me and supported me in ways that I will treasure always. And, also deserving of special thanks is *Bridgette Beckner*, whose very existence is the reason this book was written.

Finally, my deepest thanks are to *Lynn Campbell*, whose eternal love and belief in me and my ideas were a guiding light in my darkest hours.

Lynn Campbell died on April 21, 1984 of cancer after an intense and courageous five year struggle. She was twenty-eight years old. The list of Lynn's accomplishments is long, and will probably never be complete, given that the activism she generated in the world has become ingrained in us — in our living history. She was a lesbian feminist whose contributions to, and visions for, the movement have been on the vanguard of lesbian and gay rights organizing.

Her history covers much of the best radical activism in this country's past fifteen years. Her life work included community organizing with the United Farmworkers in California as well as with Women Against Violence in Pornography in San Francisco and New York City. She was the Assistant Director of the National Committee on Household Employment for the National Urban League. Later she became the Program Coordinator at the Funding Exchange, a national network of 14 foundations that fund community organizing projects. She also fought passionately to bring the existence of lesbian and gay organizing to the national attention of fundraisers and foundations.

Lynn was an incredible woman with a warmth and hopefulness that drew people to her. She had a vibrant spirit, a sharp wit, and tenacious reasoning powers. Above all, Lynn Campbell was my best friend, my first editor, my life's companion and my lover. She was there for me through the hard times and shared my joys through the good ones. I have felt her with me during this past year as I worked on completing this book. When I couldn't find just the right word, she would bring it into my head; when I couldn't get a thought just right, she helped me work it through. This book is really her book. I finished it for Lynn. I wrote it so I could dedicate it to her and to the glorious life she was able to live.

Lynn Campbell you will be remembered always.

# TABLE OF CONTENTS

## APPENDICES, BIBLIOGRAPHY AND INDEX

# Considering Parenthood

# PREFACE TO THE
# SECOND EDITION

Since this book was first published in 1985, there have been a number of events which have profoundly affected the course of the lesbian and gay parenting movement. Most obviously, we can no longer ignore the presence of AIDS in our community and our lives. It has taken a tremendous toll on our efforts to form families. While we are birthing our children, we are burying our brothers and sisters. AIDS has wrought pervasive grief, presented us with repeated losses, and created a powerful bonding in our community. AIDS is having an effect on our lives that we cannot yet measure or even fully begin to imagine. For some lesbians and gay men considering parenthood, it has brought an abrupt end to many plans, hopes and dreams.

Because of the AIDS epidemic, I became involved in a study designed to determine whether lesbians who had used alternative fertilization between 1979 and 1987 had been exposed to the AIDS virus through this procedure. My interest in doing this study was purely personal. I felt a responsibility to those women who had attended my groups, read my book and with whom I had talked over the years and encouraged to use gay donors. I did not believe that just because someone was gay he was infected. But I was concerned that alternative fertilization may have put some women at risk of infection, and I wanted to find out if that was true.

At the same time as this study began, four women from Australia were found to be infected with the AIDS virus following insemination with semen from an asymptomatic virus carrier. This information made it clear that artificial insemination could serve as a mode of transmission for the AIDS virus. Although the results of the study we did in the Bay Area and other parts of California demonstrated that none of our participants were infected, this does not mean that alternative fertilization is safe. You will want to read the updated AIDS chapter in this new edition to learn how to prevent infection when using alternative fertilization techniques.

AIDS may be the most obvious occurrence that has affected the lesbian and gay parenting movement, but it is not the only one. If we date lesbian and gay parenting as a *movement* from the early 1970s, we have a movement now in its adolescence. The first children born to parents actively identifying as gay men and lesbians are growing up. They are growing into inquisitive, curious young people. Sometimes they want to know answers to questions we cannot answer. Some want to know who their father is. Others want to know why some kids have one mom, some two or more. Still others want to know what will happen if our relationships and families break up. I do not mean to suggest that all children are asking these questions, or that they are only asking those specific questions. But believe me—they are asking.

One issue that has commanded a great deal of attention lately in the San Francisco Bay Area has to do with the use of anonymous donors. A wide range of thoughts, feelings and ideas have been expressed and discussed at public forums, in the gay media and among friends. Many of the concerns are focussed on the children and their responses to their mothers having chosen unknown and possibly untraceable donors. Some people straightforwardly state that it is unfair to create a situation in which the child may never know her/his biological father. At the other end of the continuum are those who question whether it is necessary to insure that children with unknown donors be able to trace that donor. In many situations, the discussion has turned to the question of what, if any, similarities can be drawn between having an anonymous donor and the experience of adult adoptees.

There have been many changes in the last twenty years in how mainstream culture views single parents, "unwed" mothers, and the family unit. As is stated repeatedly in this book, both in the text and in the exercises, each person is being asked to make decisions that they can live with for a very long time. Ultimately, however, the children are the ones who will be steering the course of this issue. We will need to listen to them, and, as best as we can, try to hear what they are asking for and what they need. Many of us want to believe that our children will feel "wanted" by a biological parent and a social parent and not have that vague "need" to know their other biological roots. My guess is that some will and some will not. If you are considering the use of an unknown donor, take time to talk with lesbian parents to learn more about what their children are saying. If possible, and when appropriate, talk with the children themselves as well.

If I could add more exercises and activities to this book, I would include one that suggests questions to ask of lesbians and gay men who are now parents. I cannot emphasize enough the importance of talking with other parents about their experiences while you are making your parenting decisions. Attend public forums on lesbian and gay parenting if these are available to you. Subscribe to lesbian/gay publications that include articles on parenting. Gather as much information as you can while you are in the process of making your decision. It may not help you avoid the pitfalls, but you may end up feeling a bit more prepared.

I continue to urge you to spend time with children. And, if you are considering parenthood with another person, be sure that the two of you spend time with children together. It is best if it can be an uninterrupted block of time—a whole day, an overnight, a weekend. Notice how it feels to be with the child, and to be with your partner and the child. Most importantly, talk about the array of thoughts, feelings, fears, and issues that come up for you during the time. Think of this as "grist for the mill."

As we all are acutely aware, it is impossible to predict the future and even more impossible to predict how having a child will change your life, your perception of yourself, your identity in the world, and your relationships. People make parenting arrangements and agreements that they intend to keep when they are made. Somewhere down the road they may want to change those agreements. We must find ways to negotiate these changes. We can't predict the problems, but we can at least plan for the process.

I would be remiss if I were to avoid the subject of break-ups and separations in our families. One thing I have learned over the past few years is that anything can happen. That means that sometimes our families don't make it through the stresses and strains of parenthood. Parenthood is stressful. Life as a lesbian or gay person is stressful. People change and grow, and sometimes that growing means they grow apart. In the past few years I have seen a number of lesbian families split up as a result of the adults needing to end their intimate relationship. In some situations, the non-biological parent or the non-adoptive parent has lost custody or been denied access to the child altogether. As a community, we must begin discussing how we will resolve our differences and where we will arbitrate these changes in our families, before the differences become problematic. We must resolve our differences in ways that promote the *best interests of the child.* As individuals, it is important to talk frankly with one another long before conflict arises about how you want to proceed in the event of differences, disagreements, and a possible break-up. Talking about it doesn't make it happen. In fact, the more we can talk honestly with each other, the better chance we have of either preserving our relationships or ending them in ways that take care of everyone involved.

I was at a lesbian parenting conference recently in Orange County, California, and someone asked me what I thought was the single most important factor in causing relationships to change and end. My answer popped out even before I realized it—"not enough clear and honest communication." Telling the truth and talking to one another about what is happening in your life (not just the day-to-day life with baby, child or teenager) is critical. We are not *only* parents once we have children. We're still lovers, partners, companions, co-workers, and more. It is absolutely essential that we keep those parts of our lives active and alive and that we talk about them, especially to our intimate partner(s). Above all, talking about feelings, fears, and personal changes is important. It promotes closeness and trust, two important elements in a healthy relationship.

The political nature of the choice to parent is another topic which has prompted considerable discussion in the last few years. Some lesbian and gay activists believe that parenting is taking lesbians and gay men out of the movement and putting them into the home and in front of the TV. However, being a lesbian or gay parent is a public act. What for most people is a private choice (having a child) becomes for the lesbian or gay parent a public one. It is hard to be invisible once you are out in the world as a parent.

Some people think that being a parent makes it easier to "pass" in the world. People assume you are straight, and then relate to you as straight. What happens next is that they begin to ask an array of probing personal questions. Does your child look like her/his father? What does your husband do? Are you a single parent? Which one of you is the mother? These questions, based on the assumptions that one is straight, lead to endless opportunities to come out. When we begin to answer these questions, if we answer them, what will our children hear us saying? Are we proud of our lesbianism or homosexuality at home, but protective of it out in the world? And if so, how *do* we explain that to our children?

Some women may not want to think of themselves as having made a political choice. However you feel about being a parent, it inevitably involves taking the private into the public arena. And so, as you consider parenthood, consider that too. For many, being a lesbian or gay parent is a source of pride. For others, terror grips their hearts when they think of their child's schoolmates "finding out." These, too, are important things to think and talk about.

The lesbian and gay parenting movement is a fluid, changing entity. Parenting and children are becoming an integral part of the broader gay/lesbian community. We are all a part of it, whether or not we are parents and whether or not we have children in our lives. We must continue to discuss and debate the issues, push each other to think about and sort through the hard questions, and be respectful of one another as we pursue this uncharted course.

During the past few years, the number of resources available to lesbians and gay men choosing to become parents has multiplied many times over. There are a number of excellent films and videotapes now available, among them, "Choosing Children," "Not All Parents Are Straight," and "We Are Family." There are also some new books addressing the complexity of issues faced by lesbians and gay men who are parents. The movement is flourishing despite some serious setbacks. In fact, in some cities, organizations are springing up to provide services and educational programs for lesbians and gay men considering and choosing parenthood. In the San Francisco Bay Area we are lucky enough to have two such groups, as well as the Lesbian Rights Project, a legal organization whose primary efforts have been directed towards securing the rights of lesbian and gay parents. In Long Beach, California, there is a Lesbian Mothers Support Group. In Seattle, Washington, there is the Lesbian Mothers National Defense Network, and throughout the Northeastern part of the United States there are a variety of groups in large and small communities sponsoring events for lesbian parents. I am certain that in many cities across the U.S. there are groups for lesbians considering parenthood and groups of lesbian mothers gathering together to talk about their lives, their children and their struggles.

Thank you for reading this book and sharing it with others. As more and more people consider the choices, the possibilities multiply. Remember, this is a book about *considering parenthood*. The questions and activities are designed to give you more to think about in a structured way. Be gentle with yourself and allow yourself to enjoy the process.

Cheri Pies
September, 1988

# INTRODUCTION

The day Bridgette came home from school crying that she didn't like our family, I was stunned. She was nine at the time. With tears in her eyes she asked me, "Why can't our family be normal like other families I know?"

I felt awful. I wondered to myself, "Is she upset because we're lesbians?"

I managed to contain myself long enough to ask calmly, "What do you mean by a 'normal' family?"

She turned to me and emphatically replied, "I wish we ate meat or went to the drive-in once in a while like my friends' families do."

The process that led me to write this workbook began in 1977 when my lover decided to become the legal guardian of a child we both knew. We had been together about eight months. Liz was actively involved in a part-time arrangement of parenting the two children of a friend and at that time offered to assume more permanent responsibility for one of them. Much to my surprise, I was suddenly in a relationship with a woman who had a seven-year-old child.

Up until that time, I had never planned on having children of my own. I was friends with many children, and I liked kids a lot, but actually having a child had never been a compelling desire of mine. Then suddenly, I was a parent.

Liz and I never talked deliberately about raising a child together. The situation presented itself; we discussed it rather superficially, and then it happened. My decision to parent was made with very little forethought or conscious consideration. As those who know me would affirm, this was hardly characteristic. Here I was in a relationship with a woman I cared for deeply, and she wanted to raise a child. I liked Bridgette, but had not given much thought to the possibility of a long-term commitment to her, especially one of parenting. I felt caught and intensely ambivalent. Somewhere in my heart, I knew that my relationship with Liz couldn't work unless I made the commitment to co-parent. I knew also that I wanted to continue the intimate relationship we had with one another, and I wanted Bridgette to have a healthy and emotionally supportive home. But I wasn't sure I wanted to take on the role and responsibilities of co-parenting. Feeling I had no alternatives, I decided to be an equal co-parent and committed myself to the experience of raising and sharing responsibility for Bridgette.

As the years went by, parenting proved to be a tremendous strain on my relationship with Liz. Creating a family took time, energy, commitment, consistency, and a sense of humor about ourselves. Eventually, I felt an unusual sense of isolation from myself, my lover, and my friends. Friends without children did not know how to cope with our situation. We knew only a few lesbian parents then, and they were sometimes very helpful. However, because of the uniqueness of our situation, we had to make many difficult decisions alone.

During those years I sometimes wondered whether we would have avoided some of the problems we faced if we had spent more time discussing and seriously considering our decision to parent. At least we might have done things a bit differently. The fact that we hardly discussed this significant transition before it happened points to how little we knew about what we should even be thinking about. Even today Liz and I — no longer co-parents or lovers — marvel at how cavalierly we made this decision. We spent little time talking about the possible ups and downs, or the potential changes parenting would bring to our individual lives and to our relationship. We never once talked about how we thought our families would respond or how we would tell people at our jobs that we were now parents. As we look back on that time, knowing what we know now, we can hardly believe we ever lasted as a family for as long as we did.

Through coming to terms with my own parenting, I became convinced that lesbians considering parenthood needed support to sort out their feelings, questions, and concerns about becoming parents. During the years with Liz and Bridgette, I had been working as a health educator at Planned Parenthood. There I facilitated groups for heterosexual couples and single heterosexual women considering parenthood. One day it dawned on me that I could be leading similar groups, with some modification, for lesbians.

This new direction was an outgrowth of my personal experiences as a lesbian parent, my work as a health educator, and my political commitment to the lesbian community. Another woman and I then planned to offer a six-week workshop for lesbians considering parenthood. We put up a few fliers at the local women's bookstore, the women's center, and a popular women's restaurant hoping that people would show up. Twenty-five women came to that first meeting held in my living room in the fall of 1978. It was incredibly exciting. Some of the women were in couples, others were single. All were struggling with the questions of considering parenthood as lesbians. That first meeting made it clear to me that there *was* a need for groups such as this one to support lesbians considering this option and to give them the information necessary to make an informed and responsible choice.

Since 1978, more than 300 women have attended my groups. There are usually between eight and fifteen lesbians in each group. Some are in couples, others are single lesbians, and a few have come with two other people with whom they plan to parent. The groups last for six weeks, after which each group decides whether to continue meeting on its own. Many of the groups do continue meeting to discuss the issues raised, to support one another during the process of trying to become pregnant, to support those who make the choice not to parent, and to serve as an on-going network for each other. About 15 percent of the women in my groups have decided to have children. Others have either decided not to have children, or have not yet made a final decision.

The groups have provided me with an enormous amount of insight concerning how lesbians decide whether to become parents. Through sharing their lives with me, openly expressing their feelings, dreams, and concerns, the women in the groups have helped me understand the many compelling and confusing issues involved.

The groups have also reinforced my belief in every woman's right to choose the best course for herself. Choice has no meaning without the right to elect one of several free options. Parenting is a difficult occupation, earning little support or validation. A woman's feelings about herself and her potential child are strongly affected by her sense of certainty about her choice to parent. Just as women need to be free to decide not to be homemakers and/or wives, they must also be supported in their choice whether or not to be parents, regardless of their sexual preference. Furthermore, if women must live with the consequences of their decisions, they must have the best tools with which to make responsible and informed choices.

Just as important as the right to free choice is the issue of equal access to resources that will allow each woman to exercise that choice. Many women lack the financial resources necessary to become pregnant or adopt children through traditional channels, often due to the racism and sexism prevalent in many institutions in this country today. Low-income women and women of color are repeatedly subjected to discrimination in jobs, education, and health care services. We must recognize that choice lacks any real meaning until access to resources is equitable for all women.

During the past eight years, I have talked with hundreds of lesbians considering parenthood, both individually and in small groups. I have seen many children born, have watched with delight as they grow up, and have shared in the experience of parenting. I feel privileged to be so intimately involved in this movement and marvel as the number of lesbians choosing to have children increases.

But let us not forget that there have always been lesbian mothers. I am often reminded of those who came before us, who became parents while in heterosexual relationships. They fought for their children and their sexuality, and have made it possible for us to consider parenting today. Many of us have been raised by grandmothers, mothers, aunts, or sisters who were lesbians but were unable to share the depth of that secret with anyone. Many women who were lesbians chose to get married to have children because that was the only way they knew to bring children into their lives, despite what may have been their primary sexual preference. These women paved a path down which others of us are now walking, blazing new trails of our own with few role models and many difficult turns.

Now, thanks to our own cunning and know-how, we can have children as we choose — as lesbians, on our own, with our lover and/or extended families, with or without a man. There are lesbians all over the world having children, adopting, and raising children as "out" lesbians. As a lesbian considering whether to be a parent, you are not alone. You are part of a movement of women which continues to grow, supporting the right of any woman to choose whether she wants to be a parent.

I am repeatedly asked, "What is so different for a lesbian considering parenthood? What makes her choice any different from that of a heterosexual woman?" Plenty!

Profound and significant differences make this a unique decision for lesbians. Most people are unaware of the many issues we need to deal with in the course of deciding whether or not to parent. Many women today are finding the parenthood question an increasingly perplexing one. For lesbians making this decision, however, there are several added dimensions which make this choice even more difficult and complicated. It is not a simple, straightforward choice, and the complexity of the concerns can be both challenging and overwhelming.

To begin with, society has traditionally viewed us merely in terms of our sexuality, rather than in terms of our skills, capabilities, and personal qualities. Judgments about our abilities to be good parents have often been obscured by deep-seated prejudice against homosexuality. As a result, there is a prevailing societal attitude that lesbians could not make good parents. Because of this, many of us think we must be more than simply "ordinary" mothers.

Secondly, for a lesbian who wishes to bear a child, just the logistics of getting pregnant are tricky, not to mention the intricate planning that must take place before even beginning to try. We must decide, for example, whether to inseminate or have sexual intercourse to become pregnant and whether to have a known or unknown sperm donor. We must understand the legal risks of knowing our donor and must locate relevant health information about him. Then, we must consider whether to provide the child with access to the sperm donor in years to come and, if so, what kind of relationship the child may have with him.

Any potential parent considering adoption or foster parenting must wade through the bureaucracy of the local social service agencies. Lesbians, however, are also confronted with the institutionalized homophobia of these agencies which do not recognize us as credible or desirable parent material. The question of whether to "come out" to social service personnel in this situation must be carefully weighed. Will coming out jeopardize the chances of being an adoptive parent? Will not coming out jeopardize one's position as an adoptive parent if the truth were to be learned later in the adoption process?

Finally, a lesbian can be a non-biological mother to a child, either as a single parent, with her lover, or with a friend. Some of us may find ourselves in this role by sheer coincidence – our lover decides she wants to have a child or we become involved with women who already have children. Some of us choose this option by adopting or by co-parenting with another woman. Regardless of the situation, society gives little credibility to the parent who cannot demonstrate some biological or legal connection to the child. Even the lesbian community is guilty of a lack of recognition of lesbians who are not biological parents. The ongoing struggle to change people's ideas about families and family structures involves a good deal of energy and a commitment to educate others through actions.

Regardless of how you choose to become a parent, you will also need to learn and understand the relevant laws in your state in order to protect yourselves and your rights as a mother, the rights of your co-parent(s), and those of your children. Attorneys have developed some guidelines for protecting the lesbian parent. Nevertheless, potential legal problems can be frightening. As Donna Hitchens, founding attorney for the Lesbian Rights Project, notes, "The situation of lesbians choosing to become mothers creates new and unique problems. Because lawmakers never anticipated it, very little law or legal precedent exists that enables lawyers to provide sound advice." The added stress posed by potential legal problems makes it imperative that lesbians considering parenthood understand the legal ramifications of our choices.

From leading my groups, I have also realized that lesbians need to be prepared for the numerous personal and sometimes offensive questions from people who know we are thinking about this issue. Health care providers, lawyers, teachers, co-workers and employers, family members, and friends are all likely to ask questions you wouldn't expect even a best friend to ask. The most common questions seem to be:

- How will you do it?
- Why do you want to have children?
- Isn't this going to be hard for a child?
- How can you deny your child a father?

- What right do you (as a lesbian) have to be a parent?
- How can you bring a child into this kind of family?

Heterosexual women are rarely, if ever, asked such personal and demanding questions. Nevertheless, lesbians are expected to have coherent answers, and we are expected to be able to explain our choices both articulately and convincingly. Inevitably, if you decide to be a parent, you will be asked questions like these throughout your child's life. The challenge will be to find a response that feels good to you and is respectful of your child.

As a lesbian mother you will frequently be called upon to educate others about your life choices, your parenting, and the reasons for your choices. You will be expected to be articulate about your parenting style. Be aware that at each turn you may be judged by your child's behavior and your own actions as a parent. The individual lesbian mother often becomes a prototype for other lesbian mothers, with the assumption that she is an example of all lesbian mothers.

Parents and other family members are usually among the first to ask some of the more difficult questions. If you have not "come out" to your family, the issue of your lesbianism may surface simultaneously with that of being a parent, creating even more tension. The combination of these two issues can be explosive and stressful for many families. And, even if your family has accepted your lesbianism, you may be faced with new judgments and with the possibility of little or no support if your family does not accept the idea of you as a mother.

Parents often worry, too, about how they will explain the arrival of a grandchild to their friends and other relatives. They may be wondering, "Do we now have to 'come out' as the parents of a lesbian with a child?" For them, the question of how they can comfortably talk about this grandchild may be uppermost in their minds. For many family members, this kind of parenting seems untenable, making it difficult for them to be pleased, excited, or even supportive of the decision.

Explaining a pregnancy or new child to an employer or co-workers can also be an awkward, if not impossible, task for any potential lesbian parent. This is true whether you are to be the biological or non-biological mother. Here again, you must determine how to explain a pregnancy or a new child when the natural curiosity of co-workers arises. This means deciding whether to come out and to whom, as well as weighing whether coming out on the job could threaten your job security. At the very least, there is the loss of personal privacy as the lesbian finds herself the target for co-workers' judgments and biases about lesbianism and lesbian parenting. If as a pregnant woman you choose not to come out, you may instead be faced with people's attitudes, feelings, and questions about "unwed mothers."

As lesbians considering parenthood, we are challenging the traditional heterosexual nuclear family. We are saying we can do it differently and we can make it work. Having and raising children without men calls into question the heterosexual institution of marriage, the necessity of male-female sexual relations to bring children into the world, and the traditional model of the heterosexual couple as ideal parents. Since such questions threaten the very fabric of what has been defined as the family, lesbians considering parenthood face disapproval of those who do not accept alternative, non-traditional, or "different" family styles. Our definition of family is far more extensive than the commonly held one. In fact, as lesbians we are breaking new ground and creating more options, not only for ourselves, but for heterosexual single women as well.

Finally, many lesbians have said that becoming a mother seriously affected their identities as lesbians. For some, there is the unexpected sense of "heterosexual privilege" which is unconsciously awarded to women with children when one's sexual orientation is not immediately obvious. Others of us question how having a child will change our relationship to the lesbian community and our lovers. Many fear being abandoned by the community, our families, and our friends.

Of additional concern is the growing controversy within the lesbian community during the last few years concerning lesbians having children. On one hand there is a subtle pressure for lesbians to consider parenthood, reflecting society's focus on motherhood as an expected role of women. Maternalism, an emphasis on choosing motherhood, has become a strong force in some lesbian communities. On the other hand, there is fear that the growing community of lesbian mothers will deplete the ranks of lesbians who are politically active. Many lesbians are caught between these two positions and find it difficult to sort out their choices. However, there is nothing that says mothers cannot do political work: it does not have to be a choice of one over the other. For some lesbians choosing motherhood, the choice *is* a political one. However, having children does not make all lesbians political activists. It raises a multitude of political questions that as mothers we will have to respond to, but that is not necessarily the same as being a political activist.

In spite of all these varied pressures associated with considering parenthood, there *are* opportunities available to many of us. The broader realities of discrimination against all women by class and race still prevail, however, and they will continue to determine how these opportunities get acted upon and which women will have access to reproductive and child-rearing choices. Although we may face financial, social, cultural, and racial barriers, as lesbians we do have the reproductive right to have children or not have children, the know-how to conceive, and the legal right to adopt children who need good homes.

Because this is a monumental life decision, I offer this workbook as a guide to help you make your way along the path to considering parenthood. With each decision regarding your parenting choices, there is yet another to be made. This workbook can help you make informed, responsible, and honest decisions. There is no expectation that you will choose or not choose to be a parent. There is only the hope that the exercises and text will guide your thinking, present you with many possibilities, and assist you in making choices that feel right to you, the life you have chosen for yourself, and the life you hope to live.

Cheri Pies
April 1985

# Making Decisions

# GETTING ACQUAINTED WITH WHAT'S TO COME

This book is designed for use by lesbians considering parenthood on their own, with a lover or friend, with a partner who already has a child, and by lesbian families and groups of lesbians considering parenthood. In addition, it can be used by therapists, teachers, trainers, group leaders, nurses, physicians, parenting instructors, childbirth educators, clergy, and others who work with lesbians planning on, or considering, parenthood.

You do not have to use this book in any particular order. Each section is an entity in and of itself. Read the chapters in the order that suits you and your needs. Perhaps there is only one area you want to know about or only one section which is relevant to where you are in your considerations right now. Start there and move on to other chapters at your own pace. The information is organized in the order that I usually follow in leading my considering parenthood groups. The chapters do not necessarily build on one another, but the sequence makes sense in terms of what most people want and/or need to think about first, second, and so on.

I have designed this as a workbook to provide you with information about the choices available to lesbians and to give you an opportunity to think through these choices in a conscious, deliberate manner. Within each chapter there are exercises for you to complete. Doing the exercises may help you sort through your feelings, thoughts, attitudes, and ideas. You may choose just to read the exercises in one chapter, think about those in another chapter, and actually *do* the exercises in other chapters. However you choose to use this book, I think you will find that actively engaging in the exercises will give the issues new dimension and new life.

Each chapter is divided into several parts. First you will find a brief introduction explaining the purpose of the exercise and what I hope

3

you will gain from doing it. Next will be the instructions of how to do the exercise. There may be questions to answer, an activity to complete, or even a situation to remember. Some of the chapters have a section entitled "Questions to Ask Yourself." These questions are meant to help stimulate your thinking and help you sort through the feelings and thoughts that came up for you while doing the exercise. Another section is entitled "Things to Consider." This will include other aspects of the topic you may want to take into consideration as you think about this issue and determine how you feel about it.

As you probably know, the decision whether or not to parent is not necessarily a rational one. Although having all the facts may be a critical element, most women find that it is not the kind of decision they make solely by assembling necessary information. In addition, it is not a straightforward decision. Instead, it involves a variety of ingredients and the recipe is different for each of us. You will probably notice that different aspects of this decision may be made from your gut-level feelings about the issues, not necessarily your rational sense of what "should" be. Within this book you will find many things to think about which will alter or strengthen your gut-level feelings. As you do each exercise, remember that there are no right or wrong answers — there are only *your* answers.

You can do these exercises alone, with a friend, or in small groups. I feel it helps to do them with others. Having others to talk to, share ideas and thoughts with and get support from, deepens your experience of doing the exercises and broadens your perspectives. You may want to use a journal to record your responses to the exercises. You may also want to include in it thoughts, feelings, and new ideas that come up for you while using this workbook.

Throughout the book you will come across exercises in which I make reference to a "parenting partner." Some of the exercises *are* designed for people choosing to parent with someone else; in those exercises, I make reference to doing this together with your parenting partner(s). If you are planning to have a child with another person(s), you may want to have them do the exercises in the book, too. I want it to be perfectly clear I have no bias that parenting is better with one, two, or more people. I do, however, feel strongly that if you choose to parent with others, it is important, even essential, that everyone involved talk over these critical and often emotionally charged issues.

You will also notice that there are many references to "a child," "your child," "the child," and "children." Sometimes it will be obvious that I am referring to an infant or newborn; other times, I encourage you to use your imagination and visualize a child of any age. I have no expectation that lesbians will only be parenting newborns. Many lesbians become parents of toddlers, school-age children, and teenagers. Take the references to "children" and picture them as they relate to your own life and the choices you are making.

4

Set aside a specific amount of time to work on the exercises. Some will take you 30 minutes, others longer. For some of the exercises, you may even want to take a few days. You can begin an exercise on one day, give yourself time to digest feelings you are coming up with and to integrate your thoughts; then you can talk things over with the people in your life. It is often a good idea to let things sit on the back burner for a couple of days before completing the exercise. Your decision about parenting may last you a lifetime, so be sure you give yourself the time you need to make it wisely.

Above all, be gentle with yourself. Go slowly. Don't expect to finish this book and have made the "right" or perfect decision. You may not come to a final decision after finishing the book. You don't have to answer all the questions in each exercise. Do what you can now and come back to the other parts later, if you want to. Being able to do every part of each exercise is in no way a measure of how ready you are to have a child. I have designed these exercises to help you maximize your consciousness of what you know about yourself and what you want for yourself. Remember that all of this must be tempered by a loving tenderness toward yourself and others.

Talk with lesbian mothers you know who feel comfortable sharing this information with you. Make sure they *do* feel comfortable. Not everyone wants to share the intimate details of their life as a mother, so be sure you give people the room to say "no." Many of you may not know other lesbian parents to talk with about the issues included in this book. If that is the case, be sure and check the bibliography for current articles about lesbian mothers and the issues with which they are struggling.

The quotations used in the book are taken from the women who have been in my groups over the years and the lesbian mothers I have talked with about these topics. I have included them as a way of highlighting some points, presenting varying viewpoints and perspectives, and affirming that there really is a range of responses to any given issue.

Since you may not find everything you need in this book, I have also included an annotated bibliography. Seek out other sources as well as other resource people. Read whatever you can that looks like it might be useful to you.

Because I developed these materials from years of leading groups, I have also included a special section on groups. If it is at all possible for you to form or join a group of lesbians considering parenthood, or planning to begin inseminating, or trying to adopt, I urge you to do this. The stimulation of talking with others, even if they are not women you would necessarily choose as friends, will ultimately be extremely valuable.

# STARTING AT YOUR BEGINNING

Making a decision about parenting is much like doing a puzzle. It may be best to start by finding all the pieces that make up the edges to get a sense of what the area is, and how and where the other pieces might fit in. The three exercises in this chapter are all meant to help you get a clearer picture of the framework within which you will be working — in other words, the edges of your puzzle.

Knowing where you are in your considerations about parenting can be very useful before starting out on this decision-making journey. Many of you have probably come across one of those maps that has a colorful dot indicating "you are here." Identifying that "I am here," wherever that might be, can bring an enormous sense of relief. As you continue your journey, you can look back at the paths you have taken and see where you were and where you are now.

## The Map of Intention

Write a few sentences describing where you are on your journey of making this decision, how you got to this place, and where you would like to end up by the time you finish this book. You might want to include issues you have been thinking about, feelings you are having, and concerns that prompted you to pick up this book. You might even want to draw a simple map like the one below, identifying all the different avenues you need to explore before arriving at your final destination. Be sure and put a colorful dot marking the spot to indicate "I am here."

Everyone is starting at a slightly different place in this maze. But keep in mind that you are not alone in your travels. Some lesbians already know they want to be mothers but don't know whether they want

7

# THE YOU -ARE- HERE MAP

to adopt, get pregnant, or be a non-biological mother. Others are wondering how to discuss their thoughts about parenting with their parents and other relatives. Then, there are some who are concerned about money and the financial resources necessary for raising a child. Not surprisingly, most lesbians are trying to sort out many of these issues at the same time.

    **"** I've been planning this for a long time, and I am finally ready **"** to start trying to get pregnant.

    **"** My biggest question is how will I tell my family. I just don't **"** think they will understand what I'm talking about when I tell them my lover is going to have a baby and I am going to be the other parent.

    **"** I am almost 37. I am afraid my time is running out. I have to **"** decide now, or it could be too late.

    **"** We've been thinking about donors. I want to use my lover's **"** brother as our donor, but she is not crazy about the idea.

    **"** I want to have a child. I am alone and have no plans of getting **"** together with someone before I do this. I have some money saved, but I still need to think about work and how I will manage on my own.

    **"** I feel stuck. I want to have a child and my lover doesn't. We've **"** been together almost four years and don't want to split up over this.

    **"** I hope to adopt a child with a gay male friend of mine. I know **"** there are lots of things for us to discuss, and I am ready to get moving on all of it now.

Wherever you are in the process of beginning this journey, you are not alone. There are many lesbians asking the same questions and contemplating the same concerns, even if they are at different places along the paths to their decisions. Take pleasure in where you are, and remember that as you work on the exercises in this book, you will move in different directions.

## Determining Your Decision-making Style

Making decisions we feel good about takes practice. Sometimes we are better at it than at other times. All kinds of things can affect the way we make decisions — whether we are trying to please ourselves or others, whether our decisions will hurt someone we are close to if we choose what we want for ourselves, how we saw our parents or other adults make decisions, or whether we feel confident about the decisions we make. Considering whether to parent is really an involved decision-making process. This book is designed to help you make the decisions that you will need to make all along the way.

We each have an individual style of making decisions which reflects our sense of ourselves and our way of viewing the world. Whether the decision is major or seemingly simple, most people rely on their unique decision-making process, scaled to the type of decision being made. In the following exercise, you will identify your particular decision-making style, and determine how well this style works for you in reaching decisions you feel good about.

No one style is better or worse than any other. Focusing on your particular style will help you see the process you will probably be using in making decisions concerning parenthood. If you discover by doing this exercise that you are unhappy with your decision-making style, this will give you an opportunity to see which aspects of it you would like to change.

## INSTRUCTIONS

1. Recall a recent decision you had to make, large or small, regardless of the subject. Write down what you were trying to decide as clearly as you can.
2. Identify and describe the steps you took to make the decision, including the time you first realized you would have to make this decision. Be sure to include things like efforts you made to avoid making the decision, whether you made the decision and then changed your mind, to whom you talked, what factors you took into consideration, how long you took to come to a decision, and what you think was the most important factor in the decision you finally made.
3. What was your final decision? What happened after you made the decision? Did you stick with it? If not, what caused you to change your mind?

## QUESTIONS TO ASK YOURSELF

1. Were you satisified with the decision you made?
   If yes, why?
   If not, why not?
2. How comfortable do you feel with your style of making decisions?

③ As you review the steps you went through in coming to your decision, what do you notice about your style?

④ How does this particular style work in helping you make decisions you feel good about?

⑤ What do you think is good about it *for you*?

⑥ What aspect(s) of this style would you want to change?

⑦ As you look back at your process, recall how you felt when you were in the midst of trying to make the decision. Describe those feelings; how did you cope with them as you were making your decision?

⑧ What advice would you give yourself in the beginning of your decision-making process, in the middle, and at the end to help you make your decisions more effectively?

Now that you have a better idea of your particular decision-making style, respect it and follow it if you feel it works well for you. If you are not happy with how you make decisions, or with the quality of the decisions you make, get some help from friends or others skilled in this area. You will have plenty of opportunities to practice making decisions while using this book. Remember, most decisions can be changed. Furthermore, you will only be able to make some decisions now — others will come later. Decision-making, much like parenting, is an ongoing process.

If you want to read more about decision-making, check the bibliography. There are a few books listed which attempt to demystify the process and give suggestions for improving your decision-making style and increasing your satisfaction with the outcomes.

Everyone's decision-making can be strengthened by remembering a few common things. Here are a few pointers that I have found helpful both with women in my groups and in making my own decisions:

- The more clearly you define the problem/issue, the easier it will be to sort through the different choices you have to make.
- The more factors you take into consideration, the stronger your decision will be.
- Identify all the alternatives, even if they are not choices you would necessarily consider.
- Recognize and clarify your personal values on the subject. Remember that some decisions cannot satisfy all the values you have; some values may conflict with others.
- Live with a tentative decision for 6-24 hours, and see how it feels after that time.
- Stay in touch with your gut level responses; they are a keen sensor to what you may want for yourself.

11

# Childhood Memories

   This exercise will stimulate your thinking about some of the more psychological factors that often guide our decisions about becoming parents. For many of us, early childhood experiences contribute significantly to the decision we make about parenting. As part of this exercise, you will be asked to recall particular aspects of your childhood and adolescence, making these past experiences more conscious, bringing them into sharper focus, and noticing how they might influence your decisions about parenthood.

## INSTRUCTIONS

   Answer the following questions as thoroughly as you like. Do one question at a time and make notes as you are thinking about each one.

   These answers may take you some time to complete. Spend 20 minutes to start, and come back to it again later. Begin by taking a few minutes to sit quietly and remember your childhood and adolescence. You may want to recall specific situations, people, or places. In constructing a few of these memories, see what you can remember from different times during those years.

1. What do you remember liking about your childhood and your time with the adults in your life?
2. What do you remember not liking about your childhood and your time with the adults in your life?
3. In what ways do these experiences, feelings, and memories influence your thoughts/considerations about being a parent?
4. Now, describe the kind of relationship you had with your parent(s) or the person(s) who raised you. In what ways were you close? How were you taken care of? Was there laughter, fighting, quiet moments? How were you physically and emotionally intimate? What kinds of activities did you do together?

## THINGS TO CONSIDER

- What parts of this relationship would you like to keep, leave behind, change if you were to have a child?
- How would you want your parenting to be similar or different from the kind of parenting you received?

   We are all a product of the environments in which we grew up. This environment includes not only the people we were close to and our relationships with them, but also the attitudes of the community around us, our religious upbringing, cultural values, and whatever political perspective we may have been exposed to. Our decisions regarding parenthood have a lot to do with the interplay of all these elements.

12

# HOMOPHOBIA AND COMING OUT

Throughout the process of considering parenthood, you may find you are expected to repeatedly explain and discuss your sexual preference with others. You may be asked about the ways in which your parenting choices are influenced by your lesbianism. Other people may want to know why you think a lesbian should be allowed to have children. Or you may be expected to explain how a child can be well-adjusted without male role models in the home. Homophobia is everywhere in our society; sometimes it is subtle; often it is not. In the following chapter, you are encouraged to think about your internalized homophobia. In addition, you will have an opportunity to look at where you are concerning the question of "coming out" in the process of considering parenthood, as well as the issues of "coming out" as a lesbian mother.

As lesbians, we have our own assumptions about ourselves as potential and actual parents. In many ways, our mythology reflects aspects of our internalized homophobia about lesbians as parents. Many of us have taken on the fear, dislike, or judgments of our lesbianism that we identify in the world as homophobia. Internalized homophobia is made up of the criticisms and doubts we have about ourselves, our lifestyle, and our lesbian peers. It is difficult to avoid internalized homophobia in a culture which perpetuates these myths by continuing to categorize lesbians as only sexual beings. As lesbians, many of us must struggle daily to remind ourselves that we are okay. It is hard to avoid homophobic attitudes and ideas when the heterosexual lifestyle is hailed as the only acceptable choice and almost everyone is assumed to be heterosexual.

Unfortunately, homophobia can become a frightening weapon we use against ourselves, destroying our identity, our self-esteem, and our basic understanding that sexual preference is not the critical element by which to measure one's character, potential, and worth.

13

# Lesbian Myths

The myths listed below, which reflect common homophobic assumptions, were collected over the past seven years while talking with various people — lesbians considering parenthood, straight friends interested in my work in this area, media people who have asked me a variety of interesting and often outrageous questions, and other mental health and women's health practitioners with whom I have worked. You might want to add your own myths to this list, ones which reflect your own anxieties about lesbians as parents or yourself as a lesbian parent.

These myths are often assumptions stemming from heterosexually biased ideas which many of us have come to accept as true. We have been given little opportunity or encouragement to explore the options. Little validation is given to anything that in any way deviates from what the popular (i.e. heterosexual) culture judges as acceptable.

SOME MYTHS:

- A woman should be in a heterosexual relationship if she wants to have a child.
- A two-parent family means a woman and a man, a mom and a dad.
- A woman cannot raise an emotionally healthy child on her own.
- Lesbians will raise homosexual children.
- Lesbians don't know how to be good mothers.
- If a lesbian has a child, this will prove she is healthy even though she is queer.
- Every woman needs a man to help her raise a child.
- Children want to be raised by a mom and dad.
- Lesbians are not capable of raising healthy children because of their lesbianism.
- All children need a male role model in the home.
- If two lesbians have a child, one has to act like the "mother" and the other has to act like the "father" in order to raise a well-balanced child.
- It is not socially acceptable in our culture for lesbians to have and raise children, therefore they should not have them.
- Lesbians cannot have or adopt children on their own.
- Lesbians who want to have children are strange.
- If a lesbian decides to be a mother, she must be a perfect parent in all ways.
- If a lesbian's child has emotional problems, they are usually as a result of the mother's lesbianism.

Many people, including some lesbians, believe most of these statements to be true. Undoubtedly, many of us have thought at least one of these to be true at some time. There is no point in arguing whether any of these are true or false. What is important is to begin identifying some of the homophobic ideas that we may have, that others suggest to us in subtle and not so subtle ways, and that the world around us constantly reinforces as true. In this way, we can begin to notice how these statements gradually undermine our self-respect, our respect for and acceptance of one another, and our ability to see parenthood as a viable alternative for those who choose it.

## Coming Out

It is amazing to me how many times in any given week I am confronted with deciding whether to come out to someone who does not know I am a lesbian. There are countless times in which I have only a split second to determine how sharing my identity as a lesbian will affect my relationship to a particular person, their reaction to me, how I will be treated in a given situation, whether I will be regarded with scorn, how my thoughts will be heard, whether I will be respected, and on and on. It is a challenge which I know almost every lesbian faces on a regular basis.

We get a good deal of practice deciding when to come out, to whom, in which situations, and for what purpose. For lesbians considering parenthood, the decision to come out and talk about our considerations is complicated by our *own* ideas of what others think of lesbians as mothers and the blatant reality of what other people actually *do* think of this parenting choice.

Lesbians considering parenthood must decide whom to tell. You are given many opportunities to talk about it to your family, co-workers and employers, friends, and others.

> ❝ Should I tell my boss? He's fine about me being a lesbian, but ❞ frankly I don't think he is ready to accept that lesbians can have children.

> ❝ My family will freak out when I tell them I am thinking of ❞ having a kid. They are just getting used to the idea that I'm a dyke, and that's taken almost four years. This could take forever.

> ❝ Coming out as a lesbian who is thinking about having a kid has ❞ been really exciting. People aren't as negative as I thought they would be.

15

Lesbians choosing to be parents will also have many opportunities to choose whether to come out throughout their child's life, and even before a child is on the scene. No matter which method you choose for becoming a parent, the decision of whether to come out will be ever-present during the process. Lesbians hoping to adopt or be foster parents must decide whether and when to come out to the agency personnel. Lesbians becoming pregnant must decide whether and when to come out to their health care practitioner.

It is usually assumed when you have a child or children with you that you are the mother and you are straight. The choice lesbians must make is whether, and when, to talk to people about being a *lesbian* mother. For example, lesbian mothers question whether to share their lesbianism with the staff at their child's daycare center, or with a teacher at school. They fear judgment of themselves as parents, and potentially differential treatment of their child. Because of these fears, it is not unusual for some lesbians to choose not to come out, and instead settle on "passing" as heterosexual, to ensure that their children will be treated equally.

As you read each chapter of this book, I encourage you to think about your "coming out" questions and concerns as they relate to that chapter.

- ▣ Keep notes on your thoughts about coming out in reference to each issue.
- ▣ Imagine possible situations and how you might handle them.
- ▣ Recall the feelings you have experienced when coming out in different settings and what has made you feel comfortable and uncomfortable.
- ▣ Talk with others you know who are thinking about these questions.

Coming out is yet another of the many complex issues that are woven into the fabric of our decisions about parenting.

**❝** It's funny, I never really thought that I would be thinking **❞** about coming out as a lesbian mother when my son was older. Now he's eight. When we go on weekend trips and he takes a friend, I have to decide whether to tell the other child's parent(s) that we are lesbians.

**❝** When we first learned I was pregnant, we couldn't decide **❞** whether to tell the doctor that we were lesbians. Once we decided it was better to tell him, we then had to figure out *when* would be the best time. This has been a real challenge.

**❝** I was glad we came out to the adoption worker in the begin- **❞** ning. It really made everything above-board right from the start. That doesn't mean it has been easy, but we haven't been plagued with wondering when to come out.

**❝** The first time someone who didn't know I was a lesbian asked **❞** me whether my child looks like me or her father I balked. I couldn't simply answer the question without thinking whether I wanted to be out to that person.

# TIMETABLES AND A LITTLE LIFE PLANNING

This section contains four exercises to help you examine your reasons for wanting a child, your life plans and dreams, and how you currently spend your time. With each exercise you will be asked to assess your life as it is now, and to look at how it would change with or without a child.

## *All Things Considered, So to Speak*

This exercise will help you identify the factors you want to consider when making your decision about parenting. You can add to this list at any time.

INSTRUCTIONS

Make a list of all the factors you want to consider in making an informed decision about parenting. The list may include things like:

- time for myself
- time for my relationships
- my commitment to a co-parent
- how do I have a child
- adoption
- how do I get pregnant
- legal rights of a non-biological parent ·
- what do I tell my parents
- work life
- finances

- how will a child affect my relationships?
- having a "special needs" child
- age — my age and fertility
- reactions of the lesbian community to me as a mom
- any others that come to mind

Review your checklist to be sure you have included everything you can think of at the moment. Your list will undoubtedly be a potpourri of items, some of which may appear unrelated or even irrelevant when taken alone, but all of which are essential to you in the final decision-making process. You will also have the chance to consider both the rational and emotional aspects of making the decision of whether to parent.

## *We All Have Our Reasons*

**&&** Everyone always said I'd make a great mom. I love children. It **&&** doesn't make sense to give up my plan for having a child just because I am a lesbian.

**&&** I had a hard time as a kid. My parents weren't around much. **&&** I want to do it differently and really love a child and give it a good home to grow up in.

**&&** I am not sure I want to make that kind of full-time commit- **&&** ment to a kid.

**&&** I don't think I would make a good parent. My folks hated **&&** having kids and I am afraid I would just repeat that.

This exercise asks you to look at *your* reasons for wanting and not wanting a child. In completing the two sentences below, you will probably have a variety of responses for each one. Take a break after working on the first sentence in order to clear your head and refocus. You may also want to talk with friends to get different viewpoints which might help you in formulating or expanding your thoughts.

INSTRUCTIONS

Complete these sentences:

1 I want to have a child because . . .

2 I don't want to have a child because . . .

20

It can be very difficult, or more difficult than you expect, to make a list of why you would or would not like to have a child, and this can make you doubt yourself. Don't be discouraged if this exercise is a hard one for you. Because deciding as a lesbian to have a child is such a conscious choice, you can begin to feel pressure to have just the "right" reasons.

There are no right or wrong reasons. In fact, your reasons may change over time. But these are your reasons now, and it is good to acknowledge what they are. You may feel they are not the "best" reasons, or you may question your motives for wanting or not wanting children. Try to suspend judgment of your reasons. Write them down, identify what they are, and as much as possible, embrace them as yours. Each of us has unique reasons for wanting or not wanting children. Remember, you are human. In my experience of working with women who are considering parenthood, whether straight or lesbian, very few decide to have children for what the outside world would consider all the "right" reasons.

> **"** I get nervous talking about my reasons. I'm afraid my reasons **"** will be used against me. If I say I'd like the continuity of a relationship with a child, someone is sure to criticize me when I say I need space for myself.

> **"** Because I want to raise a child. I want someone like that to **"** love. I want to have a family when I am older. I hope it will happen.

> **"** I love kids but I'm not ready to have one of my own. There are **"** lots of reasons — the strongest is that I am not feeling like I need to have a child of my own. I can be active in the lives of my friend's children.

Lesbians who are considering parenthood or who decide to have children are asked many personal and sometimes offensive questions. People often feel they can ask us questions that they would never dream of asking a heterosexual woman choosing parenthood. The two most commonly asked questions seem to be: "*How* are you going to do it?" and "*Why* do you want to have children?"

> **"** If I were a straight woman, no one would be so curious about **"** why I want to have a child. They would think it was great. If a kid is wanted and will be loved and cared for, my sexuality shouldn't be an issue.

Of course, it is not necessary to answer everyone who asks why you want to have a child, or who is curious about how you plan to "do it." It is important, however, that you answer these questions for *yourself*. In this section we will be talking about the complexities of the question concerning "why" you want to have children, and we will address the question of "how" you are going to become a parent in a later section.

It is a good idea to have some idea of what *your* reasons are for choosing or not choosing to be a parent. You may find that having a list of your reasons will be of value in the future as well. Suppose you do decide to parent. One day while in the thick of mothering, you may find yourself wondering "Why did I ever decide to do this?" — a reasonable question at any time during the parenting process. This list can remind you of your reasons for wanting to have a child. Sometimes we put the reasons we have for deciding to do something out of our mind the moment we make the decision. Often, though, these reasons can be poignant reminders of what we initially wanted before circumstances changed and in some way altered our thinking.

> **❝** I grew up in a large family, oldest of six. I loved taking care of **❞** my younger sisters and brothers. I know I'd be a great parent.

> **❝** Having a child always seemed remote to me. Now that I am 36 **❞** I am feeling these biological urges and a real desire to have children in my life.

> **❝** I gave up a child for adoption when I was 16. It is a painful **❞** memory for me. Now I want another child that I will be able to keep.

Listing your reasons can also be helpful if you decide not to parent. You may find yourself reconsidering your decision at different times in your life. Looking back at this list will remind you of the initial reasons for your decision, and provide you with a basis from which to re-evaluate your thoughts on this often changing personal question. Ultimately, what matters is that you have given some thought to where you stand and that you can articulate your thoughts and feelings in ways that feel comfortable to you.

> **❝** I decided not to have a child, mostly because I didn't want to **❞** be a single parent more than anything else. Then I got involved with Ellen. She wanted to have a baby. I thought it over and realized I was willing to share the parenting with her.

> **❝** I thought I had to be in the perfect relationship. I couldn't find **❞** one and decided not to have a child. When I realized I could do it alone, I had to face the reality that I didn't want the responsibility of being a parent and that I didn't really want to have a child.

> **❝** My father died a year ago. We were very close. I got the urge **❞** to have a baby then. I thought about it a lot. I realized I was still grieving and that it really wasn't the right time to make this decision.

# Lifeline Exercise

This exercise will help you get a sense of what you want in your life in the years to come. While for some people this exercise feels too hypothetical with no basis in the changing reality of our everyday world, others find it helpful and constructive to articulate their plans in a concrete manner. Still others have said it is a privilege only a few can enjoy, to be able to actually "plan" one's life or assume there will be a choice in how things will go.

It is true that not all of us have the same degree of control over the circumstances affecting our lives, or are even interested in having much control. But we certainly all have hopes and dreams. This exercise gives you the chance to identify some of your hopes and dreams, with the clear understanding that we may not all have the power to bring them into reality.

You may have done something like this in a values clarification seminar or career planning workshop. This is the kind of exercise you might want to do every few years, just to be sure you are living the life you want to be living.

## INSTRUCTIONS

Do this exercise in sequence from number 1 to 4. You may want to have other people who are intimately involved in your life do this exercise too. You can then share and compare your lists, identifying similar or mutual goals and dreams, and those areas in which your individual plans for the future differ.

1. Make a list of all the things you want to accomplish and/or experience in your lifetime. Include things related to home life, family, finances, travel, work, relationships, etc.
2. Make a list of the things you will do during the next five years to begin moving toward some of these "life" goals.
3. Make a list of the things you will do during the next year to begin working on this five-year plan.

For the next part, you must suspend your sense of rational time, space, and thinking. It is a purely hypothetical suggestion, but do it as though you believed it to be true.

4. Suppose you find out you have only six months to live. You will continue to be in good health and can do anything you choose during these months. Make a list of all the things you would want to be sure to do during those six months. How would you spend your time? What would be your "heart's desire?"

## THINGS TO CONSIDER

Take a good look at your lists. Here are some things to think about and discuss with a friend, your lover, or anyone else with whom you did this exercise.

- ☑ How did it feel to do this exercise? Was it difficult, easy, stimulating, discouraging? What else?
- ☑ What was it like to be so deliberate about identifying your life goals? Did it seem real to you?
- ☑ How are the activities listed in Part 4 similar to or different from the activities listed in Parts 1, 2, 3?
- ☑ Where does a child fit into your life plan? Is this what you expected?
- ☑ Were there any surprises for you in doing this exercise? If so, what were they?
- ☑ How does this exercise help *you* clarify your plans or goals for the future?
- ☑ Share your responses to this exercise with any people in your life who are making this parenting decision with you. Talk about the similarities and differences in your lifetime plans, point out where you may have problems, and where you may need to compromise along the way. You don't have to solve these potential problems; simply notice them and begin to be aware of where your life plans are on a similar path and where they are not.

Take the list you made for Part 4 seriously. So often, the things we really want and yearn to do, or would choose to do when pushed up against some kind of time clock, are the things we need to be integrating into our daily lives *now*. Whether you decide to have a child or not, begin to figure out how you can make these "heart's desire" plans an integral part of your life. Much too often, we compromise what we dream of doing because of our life's pace, complexity, and intensity. You might want to make a copy of Part 4 and put it up somewhere so you can see it daily.

You might also want to keep a copy of this exercise to look back at in a few years. I have a copy of my first lifeline exercise done in 1976. Some of the things I included are still life dreams of mine; some I've accomplished or am working on, and others no longer interest me. There are even one or two things I can't remember wanting. I'm glad to have it to look back on, to update every now and then, to remind myself in a very deliberate way of the truly important things I yearn to do in my life that often get lost in the day-to-day routine of things.

# Pie Exercise – Time

Often weeks go by and we can't remember what we've done or how the time was spent. When considering parenthood, it can be helpful to look at how you like to spend your time and what you do during your week. Much of this may change if you bring a child into your life.

The next exercise will give you a chance to look at how you spend your time on a weekly basis and to imagine how your time might be spent with a child. You may want to do this exercise in two or three sittings, giving yourself a day or two to think about it. While in some ways it can be fun to do, in other ways it can be tremendously difficult.

You are going to be making two circle graphs or pie charts. The first one will help you focus on your life now, and the second will help you imagine your life with a child. Give yourself enough time to do this exercise fully. It could take from 30 minutes to one hour. You can be creative; use coloring pencils or pens if the spirit moves you.

PIE #1

1. Taking what seems like an average week for you, make a list of all the activities you do during the week. Include sleeping, eating, working, time spent alone and with friends, exercising, etc. Think about how much time you spend doing each activity and assign it an hourly amount. Some activities may have to be lumped into general categories, such as "leisure time" (time with friends, reading, movies, walking) or "household chores" (laundry, housecleaning, washing dishes, etc.). Keep a list of what you have included in each category.
2. There are 168 hours in a week. Add up the hours in your week. If you come in over 168 hours, this may be a good indication of why you feel overextended or why you feel you can't get enough done in a week's time.
3. Now draw a circle representing a week and divide it into sections proportionate to the amount of time you spend doing each activity. Once you have the circle graph made, you will have an actual picture of how you currently spend your time.

PIE #2

Now, imagine that you have a child. Be aware of the age of the child you have in mind. Because this exercise is purely hypothetical, you may ask yourself, "How can I possibly know what my life would be like with a child? Each child is so different." Of course you won't know exactly, but you can imagine how your life might be. This Pie Exercise is meant to give you a graphic idea of how you currently spend your time (something many of us have no larger picture of) and some of the activities in your life which might change as a result of having a child.

1. Imagine your week as if you had this child. Make a list of the activities that would now be in a typical week. Assign an hourly amount to each activity.
2. Draw another circle graph and divide it according to the activities you do with this child.

## QUESTIONS TO THINK ABOUT AND DISCUSS

- What did you learn about how you spend your time?
- Were there any surprises? What were they?
- How did you feel while doing this exercise?
- How did the way you spend your time change when you added a child? Which specific activities changed? What would you identify as lifestyle changes? How did it feel when you began to realize that these activities would have a different place in your week's time?
- How old is your child? Imagine how your time would be spent with an older child, perhaps eight or thirteen years old, a young child, six to ten months, and an adult child, twenty-two years old. Jot down your thoughts on how the time and energy you spend on your child at these different ages would be similar or different.

Many women doing these exercises have been surprised at how they spend their time. Others have felt clearer about their needs and priorities. Some have felt overwhelmed by the dramatic change that parenting could bring to their lives. But one problem with these exercises is that you cannot graphically represent the things you *gain* from being with a child. All too often, people simply focus on how their lives will change and what they will lose. One lesbian mother explains, "Think of it as a transformation rather than loss or even change. It is not that you don't eat or sleep, it is that the time is qualitatively transformed, not quantitatively altered." There is also much to be gained from adding a child to your life, but that is not always clear when considering issues of time and time management.

Because it is often hard to imagine the more positive aspects of having children when looking at the issue of time, one lesbian mother suggested I include another part to this exercise. Talk to a mother, lesbian or not, with similar values as yours. Ask her about how she manages her time and the different dilemmas she has with time management. It is hard to imagine the balance if you are not raising a child now. Hearing about how others do it, the rewards as well as the rough spots, will give you a more balanced perspective.

The Pie Exercises explore one aspect of time in our lives. As you do the exercises and think about the information in other parts of this book, the question of time will come up repeatedly. As you go through the list of "time related" questions below, add any others that come to mind for you. Other exercises in this book will help you come up with answers to some of these questions:

- ☐ Do I have time in my life to raise a child?
- ☐ When is the right time for me to have a child?
- ☐ Will I enjoy my time with a child?
- ☐ Is this how I want to spend my time?
- ☐ Is it fair or even safe to bring a child into the world at this time (with threats of nuclear war, increased violence, racism, sexism, etc.)?
- ☐ How much time will it take to be become a parent (adopt a child, become pregnant, for my lover/partner to become pregnant)?
- ☐ Biologically, do I still have time to have a child?
- ☐ Will there be time for *me*, my friends, my lover, my dreams if I choose to have a child?

# Exploring the Issues

# FRIENDS – BUILDING A SUPPORT NETWORK

Early in the decision making process, most lesbians considering parenthood begin exploring the idea by talking with their friends. Often, there is no deliberate reason in mind; in fact, the subject may just come up in casual conversation. Others may consciously broach the subject with friends, hoping to find support, to share the complexity of the decision, or to mull over the ambivalence. Friends can provide a good sounding board for airing the many questions and issues surrounding this decision. In the two exercises in this chapter we will talk about how your friends might respond to your thoughts about parenting, what your expectations of them might be if you were to choose to parent, and how choosing parenthood might change your relationship with them. We will also look at the importance of support networks for all lesbians considering parenthood, whether single, in a couple, or in an extended family unit. The suggestion of having and raising children sparks different reactions in people. For that reason, you may want to begin talking over your thoughts and plans early in the decision-making process.

## Opening the Subject Up for Discussion

This exercise can be done with friends, family, even co-workers. I strongly recommend you keep track of what people say, questions they ask, how you respond to these questions, and how you feel while doing the exercise. This may seem like a simple exercise, one which you have already done without the structure. I encourage you to do it again. As you raise these issues and questions with others, you will gain perspective from the different responses friends have. Their questions and concerns may help you clarify your own thoughts.

31

## INSTRUCTIONS

Select five friends with whom you will talk about your thoughts and/or plans about becoming a parent. It is best to do this exercise with no more than two people at a time. With more than two it is difficult to keep track of who said what and how you were feeling during the conversation.

Think about how you want to bring up the topic and how you want to talk about your thoughts. You can begin by telling them you are using this book, or that you are in a group for lesbians considering parenthood, or that you are just beginning to consider becoming a parent and are interested in their reaction.

Be ready to discuss the issues that come up. You will find that people have a range of positive and negative responses, some expected and others that will come as a total surprise to you. Even though this sounds simple, it can be difficult to do. You are being asked to consciously and deliberately have a conversation about a topic that not everyone is comfortable with. It is best to start with friends you know well and with whom you feel comfortable discussing difficult topics.

### QUESTIONS TO ASK YOURSELF AND TO THINK ABOUT

- Why did you select the particular people you chose to talk with?
- Think about the positive and negative things people said.
- What questions were you asked? Which ones were difficult to answer?
- How did you feel while talking with your friends? Were you relaxed? Did you become defensive?
- What topics made you uncomfortable? What about those topics made you uncomfortable?
- How did people show their support? What kinds of things did they say?
- Did some questions come up with more than one of the people you spoke with? If yes, what were they? Were you more comfortable answering these questions the more often they were asked?
- What did you imagine people would say to you? What did you imagine they would ask you? Was it at all like you expected?

Friends are often happy and excited that you are deciding whether to have children, but they may also be worried and upset that having a child will take you away from the relationship with them. The thought of bringing a new person into a relationship can be threatening to long-term friendships and cause relationships to change in a variety of unpredictable ways. Remember, you are not asking anyone to sign on the dotted line that they will be there for you if and when you have a child. You are simply opening the subject up for discussion, a discussion which will help you gain a deeper understanding about how the people close to you feel about your considerations of parenthood.

> **❝** Some of my friends were worried that I would turn into some- **❞** one who would only talk about her kids. I had to remind them I was just *thinking* about having kids at this point.

> **❝** A few of my friends are excited and very supportive. Some **❞** think I am nuts to raise a kid as a single parent. I can't wait for the perfect person to come into my life who will want to do this too. I'll do it alone, but I told my friends I hoped they would be there to help.

Reactions will vary and change over time. In addition, remember that the idea of parenting and having kids brings up different things for each person, either from their experiences as children or as parents. You can't possibly know what thoughts your plans for parenting may bring up for someone else. You may want to explore some of these things as you discuss this topic with your friends, family, and/or co-workers. I guarantee it will be an enlightening experience.

> **❝** We have a few friends who want to have children too. We plan **❞** to have an informal support group. Our dream is to raise our children in a large extended family type setting, since most of us know our families of origin won't be supportive of our choices.

> **❝** One close friend asked me a lot of good questions. Everyone **❞** else shies away from the topic. I think they are conflicted about it, about lesbians having kids, I mean.

If you get more negative feedback than you expected from your friends this could raise a whole set of other issues to think about. Is it that some do not think of children as a positive addition to one's life? Do they question your capacity for being a parent? Are they responding from a place of their own ambivalence about children? Is there some homophobia here, i.e., that lesbians should not have children? You may want to explore the reasons for their responses in more depth.

## Clarifying Your Expectations

We all have expectations of our close friends in times of celebration and in times of need. Take a moment to identify the expectations you have concerning what kind of support you will get from your friends if you become pregnant, have a baby, or adopt a child. Try not to judge these expectations; they don't necessarily have to be reasonable. Try to capture in words the kinds of things you would like to expect or think you might expect from your close friends if you choose to become a parent.

## INSTRUCTIONS

Make a list of what you expect from your friends around such issues as childcare, shared parenting, money, attitudes toward your child, emotional support, amount and quality of the time together, help with chores, support while trying to become pregnant or adopt, and concrete support after the child arrives on the scene, etc.

## QUESTIONS TO ASK YOURSELF

- ☑ Which of your expectations seem realistic to you?
- ☑ Which friends could actually meet any of these expectations?
- ☑ Identify whom you might ask for specific kinds of support.
- ☑ Which expectations could you live without? Which ones would you not want to live without?
- ☑ Set priorities for your most important expectations.

Knowing you have these expectations will make a big difference. You can begin to avoid disappointment when you are clear about what you expect and when you are willing to accept that not all your expectations will be met. People can respond honestly to you, by saying, "No I cannot do that," or "Yes, you can count on me for that." Of course, not all your needs can be anticipated, but you will be amazed at the difference it can make, both to yourself and your friends, to clarify the expectations you know of now.

> **"** My friends are excited about our adopting a child. I have asked **"** for help with things like meals, shopping, laundry, in the beginning. I can't think past the first few months right now.

> **"** I have three friends who have said they would help me raise **"** my child. To me that means many things. Some of that includes emotional support of me and the kid, concrete help with childcare, someone to talk to when I question my decision to do this, help with decisions when I need it.

> **"** My friends — the close ones — are encouraging me with my de- **"** cision. I guess that's what I expect. I expect people to support me in my choice, even if they wouldn't necessarily want the same thing for themselves. I know that is asking a lot.

**"** My friends are freaked out. There are no other kids in our **"** circle. They think it is a mistake, telling us we will lose our freedom.

**"** My friends have been great. They do wonder what I'll do if it's **"** a boy. That seems to be the biggest worry. I don't care what sex the kid is; I'll love it all the same.

**"** I am sure my circle of friends will change. Even though I **"** haven't decided yet, just talking about it with people, I can tell certain people are already backing away while others are coming closer.

**"** We are really lucky. Our friends are excited about our adopt- **"** ing this child. I feel like we will have some help when we need it. But more than help, I know we will have the support to hang in there and work things out.

## Support Networks

Many lesbians considering parenthood make plans to develop and maintain a strong support network even before beginning any other part of the process. That is one of the primary motivations bringing women to my considering parenthood groups. They want to find other lesbians interested in exploring their thoughts and feelings about parenthood and the task of parenting. For some lesbians, finding a support network could mean joining a support or discussion group. For others, it may mean consciously nurturing relationships with a few special friends you see as "family" and who are supportive of the idea of your having children and of having children in their lives. For still others, it means getting out the word that they are planning to have a child and are looking for other lesbians who have kids already or who are planning to have children. If you live in a community where there are larger numbers of lesbians with children, you may be able to attend social activities where you can meet other lesbians to talk to and with whom to network.

The response of your friends in the previous exercise may give you some indication of how much they will support you if you do choose to have a child. For some lesbians considering parenthood, this is an important aspect of their decision. As one woman described it to me, "I want to be sure I can get enough support from my friends and the people I consider my support network to make parenting a feasible choice for me in my life."

Whatever your choice, you will find that a strong support network will be a tremendously valuable part of your decision-making process and, if you decide to parent, your parenting experience.

35

## QUESTIONS TO ASK YOURSELF

- ◘ Who is part of my support and friendship network now?
- ◘ Whom can I count on if I decide to become a parent?
- ◘ In what ways can I strengthen the ties I have with the people who are important in my life?
- ◘ Do I want to form or be in a support group that meets regularly?
- ◘ What kind of support do I want now and how can I go about getting it?

It is important to remember that forming and maintaining a support network is an on-going process. There will be periods of time when things will go very smoothly and you will feel secure in the support that you are getting. There will be other periods when you will wonder why you feel all alone as a parent, where your friends have gone who were once so faithful and involved, and why you feel as though you are hustling all the time.

You will also find that people will come and go from your support network as your child grows up. Some friends will be more comfortable with younger children or some with older children. Your child will make adult friends of her/his own who may become part of your support network, and you may find yourself wanting more or less connection with others at unpredictable times throughout your child's life.

As many lesbian mothers will tell you, support networks are absolutely essential. Whatever kind of parenting relationship you are in, regardless of your family size, you will want a support network.

# YOUR FAMILY OF ORIGIN –
# PLANNING A STRATEGY

In this section you will have an opportunity to think about how you will talk with your family about the possibility of, and your thoughts on, having a child. We will focus *specifically* on families, and on the different ways of talking about the parenting issue with them. You may also want to go back to the last chapter and redo the exercises there with your family in mind. These exercises are general enough that you could use the first one for conversations you may have with family members and do the second one for clarifying your expectations of your family as you discuss your thoughts and plans about parenting and your expectations once you become a parent.

Each family reacts to talking about parenting differently depending on their own dynamics, attitudes, and uniqueness as a family unit. By "family" here, I am referring to members of your family of origin, which may include parents, siblings, grandparents, aunts, uncles, cousins, nieces, and nephews. For some, this family may no longer be functional, or even accessible. For others, these people may have varying degrees of involvement and interest in your life. Whatever your situation, figuring out how to talk with your family about your thoughts, plans, or simply considerations for having a child will take careful planning and some awareness of the kind of relationships you have with them.

This chapter contains two exercises to help you lay the groundwork for talking with family members. I've included some experiences other lesbians have had while raising this issue with their families. The information will give you ideas and suggestions for approaching this often difficult task. In the end, of course, you know your family and the kind of relationship you have with them better than anyone else, and you will make the final plan for dealing with them on this topic.

Talking with one's family can be emotionally-charged and painful. Families can be hurtful. Parents and other family members are often not as supportive and excited by your thoughts and decisions as you would want them to be. For some, negative reactions from families create an obstacle to truly embracing a decision to parent. For others, their families are genuinely supportive and delighted by the possibility of a new family member. What makes one family's reaction different from another's is hard to say. The quality of the relationships, religious values, moral rules, communication styles, family traditions – all these things and more contribute to a family's response.

For many lesbians, just the anticipation of talking with their parents about the possibility of parenthood creates tremendous anxiety. Many have told me they are certain if they were heterosexual and in a relationship with a man, their families would encourage their plans for being a parent and having a child. Lesbianism obscures people's vision of what it would mean for the individual woman to be a mother, completely separate from her sexual orientation. Negative attitudes about lesbians in general, and often incorrect assumptions about lesbians' attitudes toward children, contribute to the feelings of ambivalence around sharing one's plans with one's family.

The topic of lesbians actively choosing to have children raises all kinds of heated and volatile reactions from many people. This choice challenges the basic structure of the traditional family. And, if you are a non-biological mother, you are asking for recognition in a role that has previously gone unnoticed and largely undefined. For the lesbian planning to be a non-biological mother, lack of validation for this role often begins here, with one's own family. They may have difficulty recognizing the quality and depth of the commitment that you are willing to make despite not having a direct biological link with this potential child. It often takes considerable time and energy to educate family members to your parenting choice. You may find yourself having to answer questions that may be rude, impertinent, offensive, and remarkably personal. You don't have to answer every question asked of you. Declining to answer questions without being overly defensive is an art that many people have to practice. You might want to say, "That question seems too personal for me; I'd rather not respond to it until I have a chance to think about what I'd like to say." Or, "Questions like that are very difficult to answer. I feel put on the spot right now." However you handle these questions, if you manage to respond as honestly and calmly as possible, you may in time give family members a deeper understanding of your choice and greater empathy for your decision.

## Identifying the Relevant Issues

There are a variety of topics for you to think about as you begin planning your strategy for dealing with your family. The following issues are part of the groundwork that provides a sturdy foundation for the rest of the work you will be doing (not only with your family, but with others in your life as well).

First of all, let's talk for a moment about exactly what you plan to tell your family. Are you out to your family members as a lesbian? If not, are you planning to come out to them? If so, when? How are you planning to go about doing this?

Not all lesbians come out to their parents if they choose to have a child. In one group I led, out of 15 women from 20 to 35 years of age and from varying class and ethnic backgrounds, not one was out to her family. We spent an entire evening talking about coming out before we could get anywhere near the topic of telling their families they were considering becoming mothers.

Some lesbians do not find it necessary or even relevant to talk with their families about their sexual orientation. Others may want to discuss it. Still others may fear their family will try to take the child away if they know the mother is a lesbian. Many lesbians fear their families will take legal action or will reject them totally as a part of the family. These fears make coming out a risky and frightening aspect of telling family members about parenting plans.

If you are not out to your family, take a few moments to list the pros and cons of coming out and not coming out.

Many women in my groups have found it helpful to discuss this topic of coming out with friends. A first-hand conversation can be extremely useful in helping you clarify your thoughts and sort out what would be best for you. Don't be frustrated if you can't figure out what you are going to do about whether or not to come out. You may need time to decide just how you want to handle the situation. Furthermore, there will be many opportunities to decide about whether to come out to your family as you continue the process of deciding about parenthood.

> **66** I kept asking myself 'Why do they need to know that I am a **99** lesbian?' My parents live 2,000 miles away and have never come to visit me. They just aren't a part of my life anymore. If I have a child, I don't imagine that will change anything.

> **66** I just couldn't go on with my plans to become a parent until **99** I spelled it out to my family that I am a dyke.

> **66** I am sure my parents know I am a lesbian, even though I have **99** never mentioned that word. I always bring my women friends home for visits. Now that Janice and I are going to adopt a child I think things would be too weird if they didn't understand about our relationship.

> **66** I am giving myself time to decide about this. First, I'm going **99** to tell them I am thinking about being a parent. I'm hoping their response to that will give me some clues about what to do about telling them I am a lesbian.

If you are already out to your family, you may find that you have to come out to them again, this time as a lesbian *who is thinking about or planning to be a mother.* Just because you are out to them does not mean that talking to your family about parenting will be any easier. Certainly for some it will be, but for others it may not. It is possible that for some family members the feelings, thoughts, and attitudes they experienced upon learning that you are a lesbian may still be very fresh for them. Some may have worked through the questions and issues that were difficult for them, others may have pushed the information about your lesbianism out of their consciousness, and still others may have thought this is just a phase and will pass. Don't be surprised if you are confronted with many of the same reactions as when you first came out. Hopefully, talking to them about parenting as a *lesbian* will be easier, but you will want to be prepared for a range of possible responses.

Now let's imagine you have decided to become a parent. Will you tell your family that you are going to be a parent?

> **❝** I've been out to my folks for three years. When I mentioned **❞** I was thinking of having a child they didn't understand *how* a lesbian could have a baby. I couldn't believe that was their biggest question.

> **❝** I didn't know what to expect. Coming out hadn't been easy so **❞** I was prepared for another rough time of it. I mean months of struggle. I was right. They flipped out when I said Abigail and I were planning for a child. It's been over six months since I told them and they are still angry and upset.

> **❝** You know, I never wanted to remind my parents that I was a **❞** lesbian. Really. But I did. I explained I was going to be parenting Juleann's children with her. They tried to be cool about the whole thing. I mean, my mom just told me it is my life and I could do what I wanted with it. My dad was silent.

Let me remind you that this is a painful topic for almost everyone. I have learned that for most lesbians seriously considering parenthood and hoping to have children, deciding whether to tell their families is a difficult and wrenching decision. Not all families welcome the news with the joy and excitement that we all deserve. Below are some of the reasons one of my recent groups generated for both telling and not telling family members about their thoughts on parenthood.

I would tell my family because:
- ❏ I want them to know my child.
- ❏ We live close by, and it would be hard to hide it.
- ❏ They will be happy for me once they get over the shock.
- ❏ This is their only chance to have a grandchild.
- ❏ I want to stop hiding my life; I want them to really know me.

I would not tell my family because:
- [ ] They would never talk to me again.
- [ ] They will try to take my child away.
- [ ] They wouldn't understand that I am a non-biological mother.
- [ ] They would think it was absurd.
- [ ] I don't think I could stand another rejection from them.

Whether you tell your family about your plans to parent is another decision that can change over time. You may want to wait until you or your partner is pregnant, or until you know you have a child to adopt. Or you may want to wait until you actually have a child. Knowing your own family and how they respond to change will be helpful in deciding when or even if to tell them. There is no one answer for everyone. If you are having trouble figuring out what to do about this, talk with close friends who may know your family, or talk with a family member you feel close to and can trust. As you focus on what is important to you, you will be able to figure out whether or not to talk with other family members about your plans.

If you do decide to tell them, the next stage to consider is how you will tell them you are planning to be a parent. Here is a list of a few possibilities. What are some of the ways you've imagined? Which way feels best to you?

- [ ] a letter
- [ ] have someone else tell them
- [ ] a phone call
- [ ] an in-person visit with them
- [ ] any other way you've thought of

Finally, you will want to think about when to tell your family your thoughts concerning parenthood or your plans to be a parent. Here are a few possible times:

- [ ] while you are still considering
- [ ] once you (or your partner) have gotten pregnant
- [ ] while applying for adoption
- [ ] just before the birth
- [ ] after you learn the adoption is final
- [ ] after the birth
- [ ] never
- [ ] any other time that seems right

What do you see as the pros and cons of each of these times? Which seems like the best time to you? Which seems like the worst time? Realistically, when do you want to tell them?

Your immediate family may need a significant block of time to get used to the idea that you are going to be a parent and that there will be a new member in the family, and to sort through their own feelings, fears, and anxieties. Six months — if you can tolerate it — would not be too much time to give them. Time helps people prepare for what is often an overwhelming transition, and enables them to integrate the new information at their own pace. Perhaps pregnancy lasts nine months for many reasons. One of them, in this context at least, may be to give family members and friends a good block of time to adjust to the reality that there will soon be a new being in their lives.

> **&#x201C;** We waited until Margaret was three months pregnant to tell **&#x201D;** our folks. We were afraid she might miscarry. We just couldn't face dealing with all their stuff until we knew the pregnancy was going okay.

> **&#x201C;** My parents have known for about two years that I wanted to **&#x201D;** adopt a child. It took them time to get used to the idea of me as a mother, and me as a lesbian mother. But you know, they have been great. Now that I am in the throes of the adoption process they are being very supportive. They are even excited.

> **&#x201C;** My sister and brother know that Wilma had a baby, but I **&#x201D;** haven't been able to tell my parents yet. Gerry is three months old this week. We're supposed to go for a visit in a few months so I plan to write them the news before then.

## Planning a Strategy

With these considerations in mind, you can now plan your ideal strategy for talking with family members about parenthood. In these exercises you will practice telling them about your plans and anticipate questions they might ask. This practice will help you think through your responses to their potential questions and plan how you would like the experience to unfold.

### INSTRUCTIONS

Below I have suggested three ways to inform your family members about your parenting considerations. Feel free to expand with your own variations on the main theme. Think about each of these suggestions as a possibility. Complete the exercise for each suggestion even if you are already certain about which method would work best for you and your family. Try each one if you have the patience for it. Write it all down no matter how time consuming it seems to be. This way you can work on refining what you want to say, to be certain you are saying it the way you want.

- ▶ First, write the letter you would like to send. Begin by jotting down the main things you want to say, almost in outline form. Then expand on each area until you have included all the things you want to be sure to mention.
- ▶ Next, write your part of a phone conversation. Jot down the things you want to be sure to say. Practice saying them out loud, and imagine the response of the person at the other end.

  Would you write to them beforehand to prepare them?

  What time of day and day of the week would you make the call?

  What has to happen for you to feel good about this conversation?
- ▶ Now, do a dry run with a friend. Call her (or him) on the phone, lay out the scenario, and have the conversation you have just written.
- ▶ Finally, imagine a family visit when you will have a chance to talk with certain family members. Think about where the visit will take place (your turf or theirs?), when during the visit you will talk with them (time of day, place, etc.), whom you want to tell, and how many people you want to tell at one time. You will want to be sure your allies in the family are present, know about your plans, and/or have been prompted to help you with this talk. Plan out what you will say. Write it all down, as though you were preparing a special presentation.

For each of the suggestions above, *practice* your strategy with a few friends, or a family member who is an ally. Get suggestions for improving your presentation. Be aware of how you are feeling as you talk. Share those feelings and try to talk about them in an effort to identify what comes up for you in this kind of a situation and where you think you might "lose it."

Think about how you hope they will respond.

- What would you like them to say?
- What is your greatest fear?
- Who will be the hardest person to tell and why?
- What can you think of that would be helpful in talking with this person?

Rework your letter, phone conversation, or visit plan until it feels good to you. Even if you don't end up doing it exactly like this, you will have had a chance to become more comfortable talking about the aspects of the consideration and decision-making process that are important to you.

## THINGS TO REMEMBER

Undoubtedly you will be asked many questions to which you do not have answers. Don't panic. (Repeat that to yourself often.) You don't need to have the answers to these questions. You don't even have to answer them. You can say, "I don't know." You can also say, "I am still struggling with that issue, still thinking it over." Or you can explain, "No one really knows the answer to that question."

*How* you answer these questions is more important than *what* your answers are. Our actions serve to educate others. Often, I think our family members ask these kinds of questions because of their own growing anxiety in anticipation of coming out as the relative of a lesbian mother. They fear being asked these same kinds of questions by their peers and having no idea how to respond.

They may be thinking how will I explain this pregnancy to my friends? What will I tell them? To whom do I say the child belongs? Who do I tell them is the father? Who is the father? Their greatest fear may be having to come out as the parents (sister, aunt, etc.) of a lesbian. Will they have to defend you and your lifestyle choices to their friends? And, if you are the non-biological parent, how will your family relate to this child? Will they even recognize the child as a family member, or at the very least, you as a parent?

You don't have to be an expert on the issue of lesbians considering parenthood or lesbian parents or the mental health of children of lesbians. You simply have to be yourself. Having some information at your fingertips might be useful, or having the name of a book (if your family learns through reading) to recommend might help. But don't feel you have to have answers to all the technical and often unanswerable questions.

What you are being asked to do is role model the way to answer these personal and sometimes offensive questions so that your family members have some idea as to how they should respond when these questions are asked of them.

> **"** I got asked some really hard questions. I thought I had to **"** know all the answers or else they would think I wasn't going to be a good parent.

> **"** I was afraid of my mother's questions. The first time we dis- **"** cussed it I was a mess afterwards. I had gotten pretty upset. But the next time we talked about it, the conversation was a little easier. Now when I bring up the topic of parenthood I can see my mom bristle, but she isn't completely freaked out.

> **❝** When I mentioned I was planning on having a child my **❞**
> mother said, 'Well, if we can put a man on the moon I guess
> lesbians can have children.' I couldn't believe that's all she had
> to say. After a few months she was able to listen to my plans,
> and I was able to see how upsetting this was for her.

> **❝** No one in my family asked any questions. They didn't really **❞**
> know what to ask. They never thought I would want to be a
> mother since I was a lesbian. So I had to talk about my desires
> to be a parent even before explaining how lesbians can have
> children.

It is probably best not to expect a joyful and positive response within the first 30 minutes, unless you already know your family will be supportive. People may need time to absorb the information. Keep in mind that you have been thinking about this conversation for a while and have had time to prepare yourself for it. Give them the room to be upset, surprised, shocked, angry, scared — whatever it may be.

As lesbians, we must help our families see us as healthy, strong women who can be good and caring mothers, regardless of our sexual orientation. This is not an easy task. Educating others regarding the myths and the assumptions many people have about women who are lesbians takes time, energy, and a commitment. We are exposed to heterosexual assumptions that lesbians don't like children or they would have gotten married, hate men and won't take good care of their male children, want to raise their children to be homosexuals, and so on. We end up with the job of educating others through our actions and behavior. They learn by watching us live our lives as regular folks.

Throughout the years of doing groups, I have found that the question of whether to tell grandparents or elderly family members about one's parenting plans perplexes many lesbians. A lesbian who is not out to her grandparent(s) and yet wants to share the joy of having a child needs to evaluate her reasons for telling or not telling them. We generally try to protect others from information we think they could not hear or that would upset them. Remember, it is probably a mistake to assume that older people are any more or less homophobic than the population at large.

As you think about your family members, and who you will tell, how you will tell them, and when you will tell them, keep in mind that each person will have their own assortment of issues, feelings, and reactions. You don't have to go through a lot of changes to make it easier for your individual family members to understand your choices, nor do you have to have your thoughts and plans clearly organized before discussing them. As you begin thinking about getting the support of your family, be clear with yourself about what you need from them and, given your family history, what is reasonable to expect.

# WORK

Along with concerns about money, work is probably the most frequent worry of anyone (of any sexual preference) considering parenthood. There are many factors to be considered when you start thinking about work and parenthood — the kind of work you will do if you become a parent, how much to work once you have a child, whether to come out at work, how you will work and be a parent at the same time, how to be committed to a career and still be a good parent, and so on. This is not a topic to be taken lightly. In fact, I have found in my considering parenthood groups that the topic comes up again and again.

You will undoubtedly need time to sort out the various issues related to your particular lifestyle, career choices (or lack of them), goals, and relationship to work. You may want to do the exercises in this section several times, a few weeks apart, as a way of mulling over your answers, and in order to reassess and re-evaluate them.

Here are some of the critical questions you will consider in this section on work:

- ▶ What kind of work will you do once you have a child?
- ▶ How much time will you work at a job where you make money?
- ▶ What kind of work do you imagine you will do at different times in your child's life?
- ▶ How much of your self-image, self-esteem, and self-respect do you derive from working and seeing yourself in a paying job?
- ▶ Do you have specific career goals and plans? If so, what are they?
- ▶ If you plan to parent with someone else, will you both

47

work at jobs, will one work for a while and then the other? How do you plan to manage this?

▶ How will you explain your pregnancy or new child at work? Will you come out?

Keep these questions in mind as you read this chapter. Make note of the ones that are most pressing for you. Rank the rest according to how important they are given your life, lifestyle, work options, and life choices. You may have other issues more specific to your work situation and lifestyle. Take a moment here to formulate any pertinent questions which will be helpful in directing your thinking on this issue.

## *Worklife Fantasy*

As you work on this exercise, keep in mind that you will probably not resolve your questions surrounding this topic now. You also don't need to have all the answers to these questions before you proceed with your decision. This exercise is to help you know what you already *do* know. Whatever decisions you come to will evolve and change as your life situation changes.

### INSTRUCTIONS

Imagine that you have a child and must work. Given the skills you now have — or assuming, if you wish, you will take the time to acquire new skills prior to having your child — describe in detail your ideal working situation. This ideal may change as your child grows from infancy to toddler, then to school age and so on. Describe specifically the kind of work you imagine doing at the different stages in your child's life, how many hours you will spend at it, etc. Be realistic about how much you will have to earn, and can earn, about travel time to and from your job, and how much of your job you may have to take home with you. Be sure to include information about your career goals if appropriate to you.

### QUESTIONS TO DISCUSS

1 What kind of work would you like to be doing ten years from now? How do you plan to build toward that career goal while having a child?

2 How important is work to you? Where would you put yourself on a continuum from "not important" to "quite important" to "workaholic"?

3 Realistically, how much will you need to work at a job for money?

As you answer these questions, remember that once you have a child you will need to be flexible, and you may even choose to change your work/job plans. Many women make elaborate plans to enable them to return to work within a specific amount of time following the birth of their child and end up finding it difficult to leave their baby. Needless to say, you will be presented with a range of new decisions about work once you actually have a child on the scene. But identifying now how you would like to proceed will help keep you focused on your goals.

> **"** I had a complete plan worked out about what I would do **"** about my job before I even adopted my child. After the adoption took place the company announced they were closing down. I hadn't even anticipated that!

> **"** I thought I would want to go back to work right away after **"** having the baby. I kept putting it off. Now I work part-time and I am trying to figure a way to work at home.

> **"** For a workaholic like me, being a working mother has been **"** quite satisfying — there is always enough work to do.

> **"** I have worked in a Catholic girls' school for six years. They **"** like me a lot there. They know I am not married, but they don't know that I am a lesbian. How would I explain a pregnancy? Lie?

## Your Employer and Co-workers

There are always a good number of nervous giggles in my considering parenting groups when we plunge into the topic of employers and co-workers. Everyone has an interesting story to tell about what their co-workers think about them and their lifestyle. I am certain this is true for a large number of lesbians. Unfortunately, these stories are not always amusing; many of us must pass as straight in our jobs. This alone creates a multitude of lies and deceptions that are difficult for anyone to live with, let alone have to face everyday.

I have identified some general areas to think about in relation to co-workers and employers, as well as some hints other lesbians have suggested. It is not just the issue of talking with employers and co-workers that is in question here. It is the issue of how these people will respond to you as a lesbian, and possibly a pregnant lesbian at that, and whether or not your job will be in jeopardy because of your decision to parent.

Unfortunately, there is no foolproof way to handle this situation. You take a risk regardless of your situation. You can try to anticipate reactions and present the situation in such a way as to make it easier for yourself, but it is difficult to predict the outcome. Many lesbians choose to change jobs, yet may encounter the same problems elsewhere.

### QUESTIONS TO DISCUSS AND CONSIDER

1. Will you come out at your job? If so, when?
   when you are already pregnant
   while in the process of adopting
   while trying to become pregnant (whether it's yourself
     or your partner who is trying)
   once the child is born/adopted
   other possible times
2. Make a list of the pros and cons of telling your employer and/or co-workers about your plans to be a parent. Whom in particular would you tell?
3. How do you plan to answer people who ask you "Who is the father?" Or who say with surprise, "I didn't know you were married!"
4. As the non-biological parent, how do you plan to talk about your parenting choice and your child?
5. What choices do you have at your job about how public or private to be about your personal life?

**❝** I am not out. If anyone here knew I was a lesbian, I would be **❞** fired immediately. I have to work. I can't afford to lose this job. I'll just say I'm having a baby and leave it at that.

**❝** My boss knows I am a lesbian, and he is pretty cool about it. **❞** I don't get hassled much. But it's one thing to say 'Ok, so you're a lesbian,' it's a whole other thing to be cool about lesbians having babies.

Whatever you plan to do, have a strategy. Don't go into this particular part of the process cold. Think it through, and gather as much support in your work setting as is reasonable and appropriate. Plenty of single women today are choosing to become parents. This alone could make your choosing to become pregnant a bit easier, if you would feel comfortable "passing" as a single heterosexual woman choosing to have a baby. There is no judgment here. You must carefully evaluate your situation and come up with a strategy which will work for you.

To begin with, you might practice telling a few people at work that you are considering parenthood. Test the waters with those you trust. In addition, notice how other women who are pregnant are treated. What kinds of questions are they asked? Has your employer's attitude toward them changed since they announced their pregnancy? If so, how? How has their position at work been affected? Above all, expect the unexpected; it will be another one of those times where no amount of planning will adequately prepare you for the outcome. You may be pleasantly surprised.

> **"** I own my own business. My clients will simply have to deal **"** with it. Most of them know I am a lesbian. If I lose some business, it will have to be okay.

> **"** My co-workers know I have been living with the same woman **"** for four and a half years. Once she gets pregnant I plan to tell them, 'We're going to have a baby.' I haven't thought much past that yet. I guess I'll have to see how people respond and wing it from there.

# MONEY

Interestingly enough, friends rarely discuss money in detail with one another. In fact, for some of us, money is a much more personal and private subject than even our sex lives. There are many reasons for money being such a taboo subject. Suffice it to say that talking with others about money, how they get it and how they spend it, may be harder than you anticipate.

As women, we have fewer financial resources available to us than do men. As lesbians, those resources may be even more limited than for other women. By virtue of our sexual preference, access to higher paying jobs can be significantly affected. Homophobia in the workplace continues to plague lesbians in blue, pink, and white collar jobs. Many lesbians may be at risk of losing their jobs if their sexual preference were known. Other factors contribute as well to this untenable situation, including race, ethnic background, class background, skill levels, access to education, and number of children a woman has.

When it comes to money — earning it, having it, and spending it — the issues are complex and vary greatly, even for lesbians. Some lesbians have less access to money than others. Some seek to limit their access, while others struggle daily for whatever they can earn. Read this section on money with your own economic status and projected future status in mind. Some parts may not apply to you. Some of your financial questions may not be answered here. I have done my best to compile information which could cross class and economic lines as it relates to money and the decision to parent.

Money is often a compelling topic in my considering parenthood groups. The question always seems to boil down to "How much money will I need to raise a child?" Many women are concerned with planning for financial security for themselves and their child, while others count on things working out as time goes on. Still others have few choices where money is concerned and simply want to figure out how to hold down a job, keep the money coming in, and have a child, all at the same time. So much of your attitude about these financial questions depends on your relationship to money, how you think about it, how much you had while growing up, and how accessible it is to you now.

> **"** I could not have a baby until I knew I had enough in my **"** savings to take off six months from work and support us both.

> **"** I can't delay having a baby until I have enough money. I am **"** having a child soon. I'll make do. We won't starve.

Some women start a savings account for their child months or even years in advance of becoming pregnant. Others never save any money beforehand. For many lesbians, there is no decision to be made here. They simply do not have the luxury to decide whether or not to save money. They live on what they earn. You might find it helpful to be aware of your attitudes about money — how much you want and need, if you feel compelled to have a financial plan, what you will do if you spend all you have, etc.

> **"** My folks never had much money but we all got by. They **"** didn't let us worry about it. We never took trips or had many clothes, but we had fun. If the money isn't there, it's not such a big deal for me.

> **"** I have a bad attitude about money. I always had money. Now **"** I don't know how to manage it or plan financially. I hope I can give my kid a better education when it comes to managing finances.

> **"** When it comes to money I feel pretty clear. Money is impor- **"** tant to me and I won't hide that. We just barely survived on what my dad earned. I hated that. I won't do that to a kid.

## *Pie Exercise Revisited — Money*

In the following exercise, you will have a chance to itemize how you spend your money and construct a potential budget with a child in mind as a way of estimating how much you might spend. You may want to do some research before doing this exercise. Talk with women who have children of different ages, since the cost of raising a child changes as the child grows up. There is no need to feel that you must have a specific amount of money before having a child, but some women find it helpful to be able to predict some of the things on which they might spend money.

## INSTRUCTIONS

1. Realistically determine how much you usually spend in a month. Go through your bills, receipts, and checkbook, and itemize these expenditures accurately. Be sure to account for large expenses that may only come once or twice a year (such as car insurance premiums), and subtract a monthly portion to represent these along with your other expenses.

   Now, draw a circle and divide it into sections according to how much money you spend on particular items (i.e., household expenses, food, clothes, etc.). If you end up with a large miscellaneous category, identify what you are including here so you won't forget.

2. Imagine that you have a child of a certain age. (This will help you be more specific in identifying your potential expenses.)

   Make a list of everything you imagine that you will need to spend money on in a given month. Assign a dollar amount to each category as best as you can. (Be sure to include things such as food, medical bills or health insurance, additional costs for housing, clothes, activities, toys, etc.). You may want to be specific about the living arrangements you have in mind — will you live with your child alone, with one other person, or with other adults and possibly other children? Also, keep in mind the kind of transportation you would be using — bus, bicycle, car, a combination of all? Finally, if you plan to be working, you'll want to estimate your childcare expenses if you have a child under five, and after-school care costs for an older child.

   Draw a circle graph using these categories and sums.

3. Compare your graphs. Assess what you will have to change in your budget plan, and when the time comes, how you plan to go about making those changes.

## QUESTIONS TO CONSIDER AND DISCUSS

- How are your budget circles different?
- What changed in your lists of how you spend your money? Were there any surprises? If so, what were they?
- What kinds of feelings came up for you as you did this exercise? How was it to realize that you may have to change your patterns of spending money once you have a child?

- How do you see that your expenses would be different with an infant, school-age child, teen-ager?
- Have your parenting partner do this exercise. Compare your lists of what you spend money on and how much you spend. Then compare how your spending would change. Notice places where your values are different and where you may have some communication problems.

If you are planning to parent with another person or other people, be sure you have spent a good amount of time and energy talking about money – your attitudes about it, your early experiences, and how each of you likes to spend money. Share a checking account for a while if that seems feasible, or compare notes on your money spending behavior. This is actually a very tricky issue. Don't be fooled into thinking if you have enough money, the problems will work themselves out. Talk about money first.

**66** Money – I hate having to think about it. Now that I have a kid **99** to think about I need to know when I'll have it and where it is coming from.

**66** We each come from very different class backgrounds. My **99** lover grew up upper-middle class, always had enough money; while I grew up in a working-class family. When it comes to spending money I am very conservative while she wants our kid to never have to worry about money. It's just not realistic as far as I am concerned.

## Planning Your Financial Future

In this exercise you will be asked to think about how you plan to generate an income over the next five to ten years. Though things may change, causing you to revise your plan, it can't hurt to start off with some plan which could be helpful in alleviating initial anxiety about money.

### INSTRUCTIONS

How do you plan to bring money into your life? There are any number of combinations to consider given your type of work and how much money you think you will need at any given time. Review the following checklist and assess the pros and cons of each suggestion.

- Work full time (go back to work after _____ amount of time).

56

- ☐ Live off savings for _____ months.
- ☐ Work part time (how many hours/week, starting when?).
- ☐ Work at home.
- ☐ Go on welfare for _____ months (food stamps, AFDC).
- ☐ Work outside the home (child care arrangements?).
- ☐ Partner will support you and child for _____ number of months.
- ☐ Other financial resources (parents, income other than work).
- ☐ Continue on current income (limited, moderate, comfortable?).

Add any other items which are part of your plan. Jot down what you like and don't like about each suggestion.

- ☐ Which option appeals to you the most?
- ☐ Which seem most realistic to you given your lifestyle?
- ☐ What problems do you anticipate with your first choice(s)?
- ☐ Will your parents help you out financially and/or with large purchases?
- ☐ Who else can you count on for money?
- ☐ How important is health insurance or life insurance to you?
- ☐ Do you have any options where money is concerned?
- ☐ Will you and your child live alone or with others? What kind of living arrangements do you have in mind for yourself and your child? Will you rent or buy?

Everyone has her own way of dealing with money. This is a good time to look at how you get money, how you spend it, how you plan to get it, and how you plan to discuss issues concerning money with your parenting partner. Money takes on a highly charged nature where children are concerned. Somehow the issues become more complex, the choices are broader, and there are more options to consider.

**66** We never thought very much about our different attitudes **99** about money. It has been hard for us. I wanted to buy our daughter a bicycle, even though we don't have much extra money right now. Lori couldn't understand how I could even think of buying a bike when we are just making our bills. We have continued to struggle about these kinds of questions. I believe we can work them out.

**66** Joey is growing so fast; he needs a new pair of shoes every few **99** months. I just can't be pinching pennies when it comes to things like that. Sometimes I wish I had extra to spend on him, but I just spend what I have and refuse to let money become some big problem in our lives. There are enough other things to worry about.

Keep in mind that these exercises are purely hypothetical. They are meant to give you a sense of how you currently spend your money, how you might be expected to spend it, how you earn money now, and how you plan to bring money into your life. In no way do these exercises account for job changes, increases or decreases in your salary, having two incomes, being forced to live on a limited income, having a child with serious medical problems, becoming disabled, or being unable to work. There are any number of possibilities that can occur. What these exercises are designed to do is start you thinking and talking about these topics, with your parenting partner and with other lesbians who are considering parenthood.

# BUILDING AND SUSTAINING INTIMACY

Because there are few role models and few traditions for lesbians to embrace and follow, it is essential both for ourselves and our children that we do our best to preserve our relationships. It is also important that we learn to sustain our relationships in ways that can be modeled by our children and by other lesbians choosing to have children. Learning to maintain and sustain our relationships, both friendships and lover relationships, while we have children in our lives is an crucial, yet difficult task. Just thinking about the possibility of parenthood can be stressful for many women. And parenthood itself places enormous strains on one's time and emotions — often to the extent that other intimate relationships may not survive. We often hear of couples, both lesbian and straight, separating after trying for a while to become pregnant or to adopt, or during the first year of their child's life. Some couples are surprised by the strain trying to become parents places on them as individuals and then on their relationship as a couple. Others thought everything would go smoothly, and when it didn't, they were unprepared for the range of emotional responses they had to the situation and to each other. These situations are often more stressful and problematic than any of us care to acknowledge or admit. It is essential to recognize that it takes extra planning and finely-tuned skills to get through what has been called by many lesbian parents the hardest time for their relationships.

The exercises in this section give you the opportunity to examine how you develop and maintain intimacy in your life. Using them you can begin strengthening your intimate relationships now and practice maintaining your relationships whether or not they expand to include a child. In this context "intimacy" has to do with your emotional needs for contact with others — sharing your feelings, your inner world, sexual intimacy, quiet moments, whatever you like to do.

59

As most of us have learned, maintaining relationships is hard work. It involves understanding your own needs for closeness, knowing your particular style of solving problems, and developing skills in the art of compromise. Being flexible is, of course, critical, as is trusting that others will persevere with you to get through what may be very hard times.

## Intimacy – Having It The Way You Want It

This exercise helps you clarify what you like about your intimate relationship(s), what areas you would like to improve, and how to go about getting what you need in order to feel good about your intimate relationship(s). The term "intimate relationships" includes any emotionally close relationship, sexual or not.

If you plan to parent with someone else, have them do this exercise too. Share your responses. Talk with others. Hearing what other lesbians have to say about their intimate relationships will provide new ideas for expanding and improving your own. This is an exercise everyone in my groups groans about doing, then resists talking about what they wrote down, but in the end, everyone finds this to be enormously helpful and useful.

To do this exercise, focus on one particular relationship you are in. It can be with anyone with whom you have shared some amount of closeness. If at all possible, have that person do this exercise too. You will be asked to look at where you are with this relationship, where you would like it to go, and what you need to help you get there. Share your responses with each other at the end of the exercise.

Take a few minutes for each of the following questions. You don't have to do them in any order, and some of your answers may overlap.

### INSTRUCTIONS

Picture the person with whom you have the relationship. Take a few moments to think about this person, how you spend time together, what you enjoy, how you feel when the two of you are together, etc.

1. List at least three things you like about this relationship.
2. List at least three things you want to *improve* about this relationship.
3. List the three most important parts of this relationship to you. (There may be more than three, but just list three for now.)

60

4 List all the nonsexual ways you can think of in which you achieve intimacy in this relationship.

## QUESTIONS TO CONSIDER AND DISCUSS

- Did any of your responses surprise you? If so, which ones and why?
- What new things did you learn about yourself and this relationship?
- Give a rating to how you feel:

    _____ about this relationship

    _____ about yourself in the relationship

    _____ about the way you feel when you are with this person.

(You might want to use a scale of 1 to 10 with 10 being the highest and 1 the lowest.)

Answer the following questions with the person you had in mind:

- Of the things you like about this relationship, how are they similar or different from those your friend listed?
- How were the things you want to improve similar to or different from those your friend identified? Each of you describe how you hope to go about improving those things in your relationship.
- Look at the three most important parts of this relationship that each of you identified. Did you know that these were important to her? Make sure you understand how and why these things are important.
- Look at your lists of the ways you have for achieving intimacy that are not sexual. Discuss each one, sharing what you like best about each one. See if you can find any others when you think about it together.

Take time to talk about the issues that were raised in this exercise. It is possible that some of these issues are left over from past relationships. You may even notice concerns, thoughts, and feelings that come from your years with your family. Go over any new thoughts or realizations, and use the information you gathered to help you improve the way your relationship is working for both you and this particular person.

It is not unusual for unpredictable feelings of jealousy to surface with the birth of a new baby or with older children on the scene. Often a newborn is perceived by a co-parent or even friends as a new "lover" who demands all the mother's attention, time, and energy. Older children as well, desire time and attention, frequently forcing a mother to choose between the child and her lover. JoAnn Loulan speaks to this aspect of jealousy in her book *Lesbian Sex*. She explains, "There are few solutions to the jealously that occurs between a partner and the children. This is often just a type of stress that has to be accepted in the relationship. No one is to blame. It is the nature of loving someone that we want that person all to ourselves."

Talking about these issues and thinking about them beforehand can help. But be forewarned, you may experience feelings you never anticipated. Be prepared for the unexpected.

If you do choose to have a child in your life, recognizing and practicing ways of being intimate can help you keep your relationships sound during what is often a joyful, but inevitably stressful time. The dynamics of going from a couple of two to a family of three (or more) can be fraught with problems and changes. The best way to ensure that your relationships have a chance of enduring is to begin practicing the different ways you have for being intimate now, before a child is on the scene. Find the time to be together, sharing intimacy without having to be sexual. Stop to recognize the special moments you share over a meal or activity, celebrating the pleasures of your relationship. You may want to schedule one day or evening during the week for the two of you to be together. It might be a time when you have chores or errands, or a time for just relaxing together. Take time to be aware of what feels good about being together, when you feel comfortable, and what kinds of things help you to feel close.

Once you have a child there may be less time to be sexual. New parents often talk about being exhausted, not having the room to be spontaneous, and simply being unable to coordinate interest in sex with the times when childcare is available. If being sexually intimate has been your only way of being close, this could pose a problem once you have a child. Spend the time now, before you bring a child into your life, to find ways to achieve closeness that are satisfying, pleasurable, emotionally fulfilling for you.

> 66 When we first got together we took long drives on the week- 99 end. We would have these great talks about everything. Now that we have Lee we find we hardly talk about anything any more except him. So we've started taking long drives again. He falls asleep after a while and we have a chance to just kick back and catch up on lots of subjects.

> 66 We planned Wednesdays would be our night together. Wendy 99 would spend the night with some friends. I always want to take a long bath, crawl into bed and read. I can't always get interested in being close or sexual just because we have a whole evening to ourselves.

**❝** I think we are pretty lucky. We love doing chores and errands **❞** together, especially the laundry. So we have some quality time trying to get the basic things accomplished on the weekend. Sometimes Issac will be off playing at a friend's house and we have a whole afternoon to get things done *and* be together.

❦

# *Some of Your Individual Needs for Intimacy*

We can always learn more about what we need to be happy and how we plan to get what we need in our lives. Each of us has unique needs for separateness, autonomy, and intimacy. The next exercise looks at your individual needs for intimacy and closeness. Identifying this information is a way of preparing yourself for meeting your needs for closeness, if you decide to parent. This exercise may be easier for those of you who know yourselves fairly well and have spent time consciously thinking about what your needs for intimacy might be. You don't have to know it all now. Clarify what you can and come back to this exercise at another time if you want to.

1. In what ways do you create the intimacy you need in your life? When, where, with whom, how? How often?
2. How do you know that you need closeness or intimate time with another person or persons? What do you do when you notice these signals?
3. Imagine you have a child. Imagine a routine day. What needs for closeness and intimacy do you have? How do you get these needs met? Whom would you like to count on to meet these needs? What would you want to be able to do for yourself and what would you want other people to do for you? Really use your imagination.

As some mothers have described it, the mother-infant relationship can be so totally demanding that, whether you are the biological or non-biological mother, you may find yourself wanting "space" for yourself rather than "intimacy" with someone else. Each mother's needs and desires for intimacy may change at points along the way. Intimacy needs are often cyclical — for the biological mother they may increase during pregnancy when hormones are flowing through the system and decrease during the first few months of the child's life when she is involved in a most intense relationship. For the non-biological mother, they may increase when the child is born, or during those first few months when relationships are being reformed and redefined, and decrease as her relationship with her child intensifies and that closeness and bond form.

**“** I was quite surprised by my desires. All I wanted was for some- **”** one to take the baby and give me three hours alone.

**“** I found being with our baby satisfied all my needs for intimacy **”** during those first few months. I would be glad when Georgia would go out with friends so I could be with Robin alone. We've had to revise our expectations of how much energy we have for each other since Robin was born, and we know it will change as she gets older.

**“** I didn't expect to be jealous of a baby. We never get enough **”** sleep and there doesn't seem to be much time for sex anymore.

Whether you have a child or not, recognizing your needs for intimacy can be a valuable tool in forming and sustaining closeness with yourself, your friends, and your lovers. Take time to learn what kind and amount of intimacy is important and essential for you; create it if you can; and increase and decrease it as needed. Remember that sustaining intimacy in our relationships takes time and work. It is an on-going process which demands frequent attention.

# SOLVING PROBLEMS IN INTIMATE RELATIONSHIPS

Having a baby and raising a child is much like taking on any large project, whether you do it on your own or with someone else. There will be numerous large and small problems for you to face and deal with every day. You will be called upon to be a problem solver at a moment's notice, often when you least expect it. With this in mind, I encourage you to understand and reflect on how well your current problem-solving style works for you. Once you have an understanding of that style, you can practice changing, improving, and perfecting it until you feel most effective in handling various situations.

The exercise in this chapter will help you examine how you solve problems both on your own and with others. It will help make your particular problem-solving style more explicit and identify its inherent strengths and weaknesses.

## INSTRUCTIONS

Do this exercise on your own. If you plan to parent with another person, each of you should do this exercise alone, and then share your responses. Do your best to suspend judgment of yourself or your partner(s). Focus on the problem-solving style you are each identifying and not on the content of the particular problem you use as an example. Look at this as an exercise to understand how you handle problems on your own or with someone else. Enjoy it. Have fun. Laugh at the aspects of one another's particular style that have been known to drive you crazy. By accepting how you handle yourself in difficult and stressful situations, you can begin to look at your behaviors objectively and change them to suit your needs.

Recall a recent crisis or problem you had with your partner or a friend. This can be as straightforward as trying to decide what to do for the evening or where to go for the weekend, or it can be a larger dilemma concerning finances, relationships, parents, etc. If you are doing this exercise with your partner or a friend, agree on a past problem or situation beforehand, so that you are both recalling the same incident. It may take you some time to recall a problem: remember you can keep it simple.

Begin by writing down exactly what the situation was as *you* best remember it. Describe how it came up, who brought it up, and how long it had been brewing. Then, with as much accuracy as possible, reconstruct the step-by-step process you and your partner took in solving this problem. Take your time and do the best you can.

Even if there are confusing facts, try to put things in some chronological sequence. Be conscious of the different roles each of you may have taken on at different times. Who had the power in the situation? When or if the power balance changed, who talked more, who seemed to know the "right" way to proceed? Finally, how did the entire experience feel to you? Write about it as if you were writing a story.

## QUESTIONS TO CONSIDER AND DISCUSS

- What did you learn about your problem-solving skills as an individual? What did you notice about your problem-solving skills with another person?
- How do you feel about the problem-solving process you described?
- How well does this process work for you? How well does it work for you and your partner? Where do you see room for improvement?
- Were you satisfied with the outcome of this situation? If not, what could you have done to make it different?
- Notice how you handled your feelings. Did you do anything that you feel might undermine or "sabotage" the final decision in any way? By sabotage, I am referring to anything that would keep the agreed upon solution from working.
- What do you want to change about your problem-solving process? What things about the process does your partner want to change? How will the two of you work on these?

Reread the problem situation you described. Try to give yourself a title for each of the "roles" you took on at different times in the situation (i.e., "stubborn mule," always agreeable "compliant one," the "victim," the "heroine"). Do the same for the other person as you see her position (or his position if your friend is a man). How satisfied are each of you with

66

the roles you take on in an effort to cope with problem situations that come up?

## Changing Patterns

A problem-solving process gets established early on in a relationship, often before anyone realizes it. It's possible that neither person feels good about this process. If your problem-solving process is not working for you or your partner, you can work to change it. Sometimes the roles we assume are not the ones we want to be in and do not accurately reflect our real selves. We can change and re-establish these with practice, and with support from one another.

For each person, certain problems are emotionally charged for reasons not directly related to the issue being discussed. In reality, most problems are a combination of the current situation and a lot of past experiences that may have gone unresolved or unrecognized. There are great benefits in being able to step back and acknowledge as fully as possible what else may be going on in a particular situation. At some point after a fight or crisis has passed, it is helpful to see what was operating to make this such a charged situation.

We all have memories of old fights or of less than satisfactory ways we had of handling things with someone else. You may want to zero in on these situations now, and work on them with the help of friends or a counselor. You may not be able to make everything just "perfect," but you will have a head start on clearing away some old baggage that could make a great deal of difference if you decide to have a child in your life.

    **“** Sometimes if I've had a long day at work and I'm hungry when I **”** come home, the slightest incident will set me off. I try to avoid any serious conversations until I unwind. My other red flag is no important discussions after 10 p.m. I am always too tired and can't manage to say what I mean in a good way.

    **“** It has taken us at least six months to learn a new way to solve **”** problems that works for *both* of us. We see a good therapist and then do a lot of work on our own too.

    **“** I have many old behaviors I slip into when things get stressful **”** between us. I go into this numbed-out state, and it makes Lesley furious. I figure she doesn't want to hear what I have to say — my parents never did.

    **“** I'm delighted to say we have a great way of getting through our **”** hard problems and big decisions. We've done a lot of projects together — you know, planting a garden, building a fence, re-wiring the kitchen — those gave us real concrete tasks for practicing problem-solving.

You may have a hidden agenda of what you really want to have happen in a given situation, or unexplored needs that you want met, but are unable to verbalize clearly. I encourage you to pay attention to be able to identify these. As you practice an effective problem-solving process for yourself, or for you and your parenting partner(s), it will be helpful to know what outcome you are aiming for. Then, you can know when you have reached it, or you can decide what to do in case the outcome is dramatically different from what others want.

If you are not satisfied with a given decision, say so. Otherwise you risk undermining the decision and potentially sabotaging the solution in some way. This point is especially well taken when dealing with issues of discipline with children. If you are not happy with how you have decided to handle a given situation, chances are you won't handle it well, and ultimately you may feel frustrated by the outcome and your own behavior.

Be careful to negotiate fairly with one another so that each of you gets some of your needs met. This is crucial once you have a child. Even though children may miss the content of an argument or of a particular problem you are trying to solve, they hear the tone of the words and experience the process in their own way. They learn from this experience. They get a feeling for how each person is with the other, and ultimately they develop similar styles. Our behavior is a powerful teacher to our children. As you work on problem-solving, keep in mind the message you may be giving to your child. One important element is being sure that each person gets some need met, gets some satisfaction from working on solving a problem. That in itself is one reward for working hard on a problem, even if it doesn't turn out exactly as you want it.

There is no "right" way for solving problems or handling tough situations that come up with your friends, your partner, and/or your child. What is best is what works best for you, individually and for your family unit. You will want to embrace the process that brings you to a desired and relatively painless solution to your struggles.

Everyone has a different problem-solving style, much like our different decision-making styles. If you are parenting with someone else, you may find you each have to compromise a bit, and be creative in designing a process in which you both get to be who you fully want and need to be. I encourage you to have a sense of humor about yourself and the way you do things. Being able to laugh about how we deal with problems takes the pressure off thinking you need to be perfect in working things out.

**❝** Everyone laughs at me when I want to make a problem go **❞** away. I simply try to 'fix it' in any way at all, so I don't have to

68

think about it anymore. I know it doesn't solve it in the long run but it suits my purposes for the short run.

**“** We clash around solving problems. I take my time. I can mull **”** something over for a week. Dotty wants us to discuss it, solve it, and move on. Sometimes I think it's because I can live with the tension longer. She thinks it's because I like to think about problems and she doesn't.

**“** My parents had this great system for solving problems. Nei- **”** ther one liked awkwardness much so they agreed that each time a problem came up, they would each say what they wanted and then if possible flip a coin. Really. It worked for them, maybe their problems weren't as complex in those days.

**“** Before you get seriously involved in a relationship I think **”** there are three things you should do together: order a pizza; try to find a parking place in a busy part of town on a Saturday night; and pitch a tent in the dark.

**“** Our latest plan is to try different solutions for a few days and **”** see which one feels the best. If you have the time to do this, it can be a great solution.

## Possible Trouble Spots

Here is a brief list of some areas that can be sources of conflict for lesbians choosing to parent. It contains general areas that have been identified over and over by lesbians I have worked with. You can add to this list whatever you imagine will be problem areas for you, as well as things that lesbian mothers you know have had to face and cope with. Most of these are issues you want to be sure and discuss with your parenting partner(s). Take time to get clear about what you think and how you feel about each one. Then, set aside time to talk about them together. Give yourself room to change your mind, get new perspectives, and possibly compromise. Remember, just talking about these often emotionally charged topics won't make everything go smoothly later, but it will give you a way to cope with related issues as they come up in your parenting relationship.

- ☐ Bonding — how to make that happen for biological and non-biological mothers.
- ☐ Power balance between biological and non-biological mothers — how you will recognize it, if it's a problem, and what you can do about it.

69

- Different personal rhythms — how and when you choose to do particular activities and how that affects your parenting partner(s).
- Different lifestyle choices — how you each choose to live your life and how well those styles coexist.
- Parenting styles — your similarities, differences, conflicts, agreements.
- Individual needs for control and discipline.
- Different family backgrounds and the impact that has on parenting, managing finances, attitudes about education and leisure, etc.
- Finding enough time for yourself, your child, your partner, and your friends.

It may take you time to learn how to balance the areas where you have differences or difficulties. This is where your problem-solving skills will come in handy. Surprisingly enough, how we resolve our disagreements is another illustration of the kind of intimacy we are able to maintain and sustain with our friends and partners. Many lesbian mothers have said that as they get better at solving the many day-to-day dilemmas with which they are faced, they find the quality of the intimacy they share with others improves.

**❝** I just made up my mind I was not going to get rattled every **❞** time we had a new crisis with Yaseem. The more upset I got, the harder it was to feel close to anyone. No one could calm me down. Since I've changed my attitude I feel as though there are others who might understand me.

**❝** Raising a teen-ager has been stressful. We get in hassles all the **❞** time. I found I would be arguing with my friends too, it just spilled over. My daughter was arguing more with her friends too. We agreed to try to work things out differently. It has taken some time, but life at our house has definitely improved.

# BUILDING A FAMILY

Lesbian families take many forms. There is no typical lesbian family and there is really no way to describe all the various arrangements that lesbians have come up with over the years.

In this chapter, I will cover some of the broader topics that come up most frequently in my groups on the topic of building a family. The ones discussed are not all that you will have to consider, but they do provide you with a place to start. Be sure to read the chapters "Co-Parenting," "Single Parenting," and "Being a Non-biological Mother" as well. These contain exercises to do and issues to consider that are also part of the process of building a family.

With few role models to identify with and learn from, lesbians are faced with a unique challenge and exciting opportunity when it comes to building families. We can create the family style that suits our needs and those of the individual family members best. We can take on aspects of other families that we have liked and aspects of our past experiences in forming families that will work well. Without models, however, we are often groping for a family form that will work on both a long- and short-term basis, one that will provide each family member with the support, love, and nurturance needed and one that embodies all the qualities of a healthy and warm family for adults and children alike.

As lesbians we are constantly confronted with the public scrutiny of our families and the watchful eyes of those waiting to see where our families will fail, where our children will "act out" (presumably as a result of our lesbianism), and where our relationships will fall apart in our attempts to maintain an alternative family in the midst of a changing culture. Observers fail to remember that heterosexual families also fall apart, and that children in heterosexual households are often put through an equally tremendous amount of change when parents separate. Lesbians are under a good deal of pressure to build healthy families. Our own expectations of wanting to have a close and nurturing family which provides a good place for a child to grow are often challenged by societal expectations that our families will produce sexually and emotionally unstable children at best and a myriad of unknown problems at worst.

> **66** Sometimes I feel as though I must be the·perfect mother with **99** the perfect child. If Brady misbehaves, my family instantly points to my lesbianism as the problem *and* the fact that he doesn't have a man around. Brady is only six. All kids misbehave — it has nothing to do with my lesbianism.

> **66** We have a few other lesbian friends with children. We have an **99** on-going conversation about how each of our families work. It's pretty exciting to be building a family out of our own ideas of what we think would be great, and it's scary at the same time.

## *Your Idea of Family*

Many lesbians considering parenthood have clear ideas about the kind of family unit they hope to create; others are not as sure and need to consider all the possibilities. In the exercise below, I list a few of the wide range of possible family configurations. If I have not included one you are considering, add it to the list.

### INSTRUCTIONS

Do this exercise on your own and then again if there are others with whom you are planning to parent. Notice where your reasons are similar and different. Identify points where you have differences and may have difficulties.

For each possibility listed below, identify your reasons for choosing or not choosing that particular family form. Clarify your thoughts on both sides of the question. Even if you think you would *never* choose a particular option, fantasize about it anyway. You never know when your family configuration may change and you may find yourself in a situation that you never expected or would not have actively chosen for yourself.

- ❏ single parent with one child (or more)
- ❏ two women who are lovers with one child (or more)
- ❏ two people who are not lovers with one child (or more) (this could be the biological mother and a male or female parenting partner)
- ❏ cooperative family — two or more families living in close proximity and parenting one another's children

- extended family — single lesbian or lesbian couple with one child (or more) and other identified people actively involved on a regular basis with child and family
- three or more adults who are primary parents to one child (or more)
- extended biological family

Each possibility lends itself to a number of variations. Be sure to modify each of the suggested family forms to fit your lifestyle or particular situation. For example, suppose you want to have a child but your lover does not, and you decide to go ahead and have a baby anyway. How will that affect your family form? Or, your cooperative family may consist of other lesbian families, gay families, or straight families. Your extended family might be made up of any number of people — describe who they are. If there are two or more adults parenting, you might want to specify how much time each will be committed to the child(ren).

You may end up with an elaborate combination of some of the above. For now, identify what you like and don't like about each possibility. This will give you a chance to explore all the choices and your feelings about them. If there are reasons you absolutely could not live with one or more of the possiblities, elaborate on those.

### QUESTIONS TO THINK ABOUT

- Which family configuration appeals to you the most? Why?
- Were there any surprises for you in your reasons for liking or disliking a particular form? What were they?
- Which is your first choice of a family configuration? Is it the same as the one that appeals to you the most? Why is this your first choice?
- How will you cope with the things you identified as "not liking" about your first choice?
- Which family configuration appeals to you the least? Why?
- Imagine how you might cope if you found yourself in your least appealing family situation.
- If you do this exercise with others you plan to parent with, go through each possibility and compare your reasons for liking or not liking that particular choice.

## Where I Come From

All of us are products of our families. No matter how critical you have felt of your own upbringing, there will be tendencies to do some of the same things, and you may be surprised at how much you truly value and do not want to change. Here you will be asked to describe your family of origin. Be as explicit as possible. You want to uncover all the areas that will be of importance to you as you consider parenthood and think about building your own family. Be sure to discuss this exercise with anyone you plan to parent with. It is a great way to begin identifying how parenting styles develop and to understand the charge each person has about different aspects of the parenting experience.

INSTRUCTIONS

- ▶ Describe your family of origin. Include everyone who was in this family, even if they came in and out at different times during your life. You might also want to include descriptions of how decisions were made, by whom and how they were enforced, what meal times were like, what you did on weekends and vacations.
- ▶ What happened when there were arguments between parents and child, and between adults?
- ▶ How were children treated in your family?
- ▶ What constituted discipline?
- ▶ How did the adults spend their free time? How did the children spend free time? Describe a typical weekend and weekday.
- ▶ What were your parents' attitudes about school and educational achievement?
- ▶ How did they feel about earning, managing, and spending money?
- ▶ Did your family practice any religious or cultural beliefs? If so, what were they and how were they practiced in your household?

Take as much time as you need to reconstruct this picture. If you can, check with family members about memories. Be as vivid as possible.

This is an essential exercise to share with anyone with whom you intend to parent. As I have mentioned before, our past plays a significant part in shaping our present, even if we feel reasonably free from that past. As with other parents, lesbians with children often find themselves doing exactly what their parents did, even if that isn't always how they want things to be. I remember quite vividly a day when Bridgette was about seven and I got angry at her for something. My anger came out in a tone of voice I was sure was not my own. I almost turned around to see if my mother was standing behind me. That voice was the same voice — tone, inflection, and all — that she had used with me and my sisters in similar situations. I was startled.

Not only do our voices carry memories of our past, but also the subtle ways in which we do various family activities, such as at mealtimes, weekends, and leisure time, mirror some of our childhood experiences. Time spent reviewing all of this on your own or with your parenting partner(s) will be time well spent. If you are planning to parent with others, you do not necessarily have to resolve all your differences; chances are, in fact, that you won't be able to. Instead, the goal is to be able to recognize when things might get difficult between you and begin to plan how you will manage those situations so they don't get the better of you.

> **"** On the weekend my family stayed home; Lynora's would go **"** to the beach, the zoo, the movies, whatever. Needless to say, we are constantly trying to figure out how to spend the weekend. Over the years we've gotten better.

> **"** I come from an alcoholic family. Every day my mom would **"** get so smashed she couldn't take care of us. It's important to me that I not recreate that nightmare in some other way. I'm working on it.

> **"** Everytime we sit down to a meal together as a family I think **"** we are going to have a fight. That's how it was when I was growing up. Sometimes I even *pick* a fight. Now I can tell when I'm starting to do it and I talk about it right away.

## My Ideal Family — How I'd Like It to Be

Now, I want you to describe the family you hope to create. In this exercise, you are asked to describe what you see as *essential* for your family and what you *desire* your family to be like. You may not be in a situation in which you will have the time to be so deliberate in planning your ideal family, or have the luxury of choosing the family form you would like. Nevertheless, you may want to do this exercise to explore ways in which to change and possibly improve the family you are already building.

### INSTRUCTIONS

Describe what you see as essential elements of your "ideal" family. In other words, what would your ideal family look like, how would you spend time, how would your friends be involved, what kind of living situation would you like, etc. Go through the list and determine which of these elements are "essential" (you *absolutely* have to have them), and which are "desired" (you *want* them, but they are not essential to have a happy or fulfilling life).

Carefully review your lists. Discuss and compare your lists with others who are considering parenthood, or with your potential parenting partner(s). You might want to discuss each item, clearly stating what you had in mind. If you find there are areas in which there might be differences between you and your partner(s), don't feel compelled to remedy or resolve anything now. For the moment, simply identify where you may need to compromise or change your desires and acknowledge that together.

This is another exercise that may take you several days to complete. You may want to talk with others as you do it, remembering what you have liked about families you have known and giving yourself time to fantasize about the ideal family form for you. Most importantly, you will want to live with your ideal family picture for a few days, adding, modifying, and honestly assessing if it truly captures the kind of family you would like, and that would work for *you*.

These are hopes and plans. Though they may change, they give you a path to follow. Remember that family formation is a continuous process. What you create in the first year of life with a child may be different five years later. We all have intense feelings about family. Because of this, you will want to be prepared for unexpected storms of jealousy, possessiveness, feelings of exclusion, panic, rage — a range of unpredictable behaviors and feelings. Be honest with yourself about what you want and what would work for you, as well as for your partner(s) and child(ren). Be sensitive as well to what you will feel most comfortable with, regardless of whether it seems "right" in the eyes of other people.

> **❝** I didn't think I would want a nuclear family — you know, two **❞** parents and a child, but I do. I like how it feels. Maybe I'll change and want something different later, but I want this for now.

> **❝** I knew I didn't want to be the only parent, but I wasn't sure **❞** how I could make it different since I became pregnant as a single woman. Then I met Ellie and Jean. They are also single moms. We spend a lot of time together, eat meals together and share childcare. I never imagined I could have just what I wanted.

> **❝** I wanted a large extended family for me and Mike. We are close **❞** to another family. We take trips together, spend holidays together, and have a family dinner once a week. I wanted him to know about extended families and to learn that there were other families just like ours.

# CONSIDERING THE CHILDREN

Children are our legacy for the future. They are the foundation on which we can build our hopes for a safe and more peaceful world, a world in which people can be different and where people do not need to fit into a preconceived mold. As lesbians, many of us dream of raising children who may someday carry such a message of peace, tolerance, and acceptance to others.

Within the framework of considering parenthood, there are a range of issues to be explored concerning the children themselves. I have selected a few which come up frequently in my group discussions, but the wealth of issues on the subject of children of lesbians could fill a book in itself.

In this chapter you will have an opportunity to look at the positive aspects of having children in your life. Then, you will be asked to identify your feelings concerning the sex of your child and about raising a child of one sex versus another. I will also discuss the sexuality of our children and the feelings that come up around that issue. Then you will be asked to explore the rights of children to know their biological father and how you plan to deal with that situation. Finally, I will address some of the concerns facing lesbians who have children with special needs.

As lesbians, we often feel an intense pressure to raise perfect, all-around healthy children. Our fear, of course, is that anything less might be considered directly related to our sexual preference. Our responsibility, however, is simply to do the best we can as often as we can. That is the most any child, whether raised by a homosexual, heterosexual, bisexual, transsexual, or asexual parent, can hope for. It is not a liability to be a lesbian parent; in fact, with growing regularity I am coming to see it as an asset.

77

# Positively Positive

All too often we only focus on what is difficult about having children, failing to notice the enriching and positive aspects. For some people this orientation comes from childhood memories. For others it may come from having little or no experience with children on a regular basis, or from being afraid of children. There are enormous riches in having children in your life. The gains are different for each person and differ with the various stages of a child's development. One way to discover this for yourself is to spend time with children on a regular basis. Talk with women, lesbian and straight, who are parents. Ask them how their lives have been enriched by their children. Give them an opportunity to tell you what they gain from having children in their lives.

> **66** Audre sees things I forget to notice — bug families, rocks on **99** the ground, dogs playing together. These aren't so unusual, I'm just not looking all the time. She also makes up delightful stories that bring magic into our lives.

> **66** I love my son in a way I have never known loving before. He **99** smiles at me and I glow from way down deep inside me.

> **66** Annie has the energy of a bunch of monkeys. She's always got **99** something going. I was never like that and I get a real kick out of her excitement.

> **66** Sandy and I just sit and play together for hours. Most of the **99** times we just color and talk and act silly. Adults don't get enough chances to be playful like that. I thoroughly enjoy it.

> **66** Carly brings out parts of me that I rarely show to my adult **99** friends. We can joke around and act silly and it makes me feel terrific.

Use the next exercise to clarify what you expect will be, or have found to be, the positive and enriching aspects of having children in your life. It is designed to help you recall what you like about being with children and how you feel when spending time with kids. Of course, not all your responses will be positive and enthusiastic.

## INSTRUCTIONS

Remember the times you have spent with children or with one particular child. Take a few moments to recapture a past experience or interaction. Write down the details of that experience as though you were telling a story about it, including how it felt to you, what you enjoyed the most, what you enjoyed the least, what made the time special for you, etc.

The following questions will help you sort through your thoughts and feelings about being with children.

QUESTIONS TO ASK YOURSELF

- ☑ What did I find rewarding or enriching from the experience I am remembering?
- ☑ What was difficult about the experience for me? What was easy about the experience for me?
- ☑ What do I like about being with children?
- ☑ What do I learn about myself when I am with children?
- ☑ How do I feel when I am with children? How is that different from how I feel when I am with adults?
- ☑ What kinds of things do I enjoy doing with children that I don't do with adults?
- ☑ What qualities do children bring out in me? Which of these do I like and want to explore further?

# Pie Exercise Revisited – Children

Our childhood experiences often affect our attitudes about children and what we then identify as the positive aspects of raising children. You may notice that you are most comfortable with children of some ages versus other ages. There could be any number of reasons for this – perhaps that was an age you liked being when you were a child, or you find it easier to relate to one age group instead of another, or you are afraid of children at certain ages, and so on. Many parents have commented that acknowledging your childhood history can make a difference in helping you be a more aware parent.

The following exercise is designed to help you focus on how you feel about children at different ages. So often when we think about children, we have a certain age in mind. I remember a woman in one of my groups talking about having a baby, and as she continued to talk about raising this child, it sounded as though she thought it would always be a baby. Then there was another woman who talked about children as if they came fully clothed, walking and talking out of the womb. It's not unusual to have a certain age in mind and continually visualize that. But, as we all know, babies grow into children, who then become preteens, then adolescents, and eventually adults. As you do this exercise, you may want to notice whether you have a specific age group that feels most familiar to you.

To begin this exercise, look back at your Pie Exercise from the "Timetables and Life Planning" chapter. Review your pie chart that included a child.

- How old was the child you selected?
- What are some of the reasons you chose a child of *that* age?
- Which ages seem easier for you? What about those ages makes you think it would be easier?
- Which ages seem more difficult to you? What about those ages makes you think it would be more difficult?
- Which age(s) do you recall enjoying most as a child? Do these correspond with the ages you feel would be easier for you? Also, recall the ages you enjoyed the least. Do these correspond with the ages you feel would be difficult?

This is a good exercise to do with others, both those you plan to parent with and other lesbians who are considering parenthood. When we do this exercise in the groups, someone always observes that one age seems more difficult with a girl child than with a boy. Women also find that by sharing their reasons for liking different ages, they gain new perspectives on the range of possibilities of being with and raising children of different ages.

> **❝** Most of my friends are afraid of their teenagers. That's the age **❞** that attracts me the most. I liked being a teenager and don't have much trouble tolerating all that confused and wild energy — well, at least most of the time.

> **❝** When I think about having a child, she's eight. That is, she **❞** emerges at birth to be eight years old. I realize, of course, there are many years before that to be accounted for, but they're much more scary to me.

> **❝** I'm really into sports and I keep picturing weekends with this **❞** kid about 11 or 12. Boy or girl doesn't seem to matter. JoAnn really likes babies so maybe between the two of us, it'll work out okay.

## *You Had a Boy/You Had a Girl*

Let's turn now to a discussion of your thoughts and feelings about the sex of your child. It's still unlikely that you will be able to control whether you conceive or adopt a girl or a boy. Therefore, it helps to be prepared for either possibility. Nevertheless, chances are you have some feelings or opinions about what sex your child is. When a straight woman is pregnant, she is free, it seems, to declare quite emphatically that she hopes to have a child of one sex or the other without encountering people who judge her for honestly expressing her feelings. When a lesbian is as explicit, however (and especially if she states, "I really want a girl"), chances are she risks being judged harshly for her assumed dislike of male children. In spite of this taboo, most lesbians, like most women, do have a preference for one sex or the other, and it is *not* always a preference for girls.

> **"** I'm almost embarrassed to admit it, but I have always wanted **"** a boy. Maybe it's my own stereotyping, but I just think I would have more fun with a boy child.

> **"** A lot of my friends are afraid of raising boys because they **"** don't like men and aren't sure how to relate to boy children who one day will grow up to be men. I guess I believe that boys raised by lesbians might be different.

> **"** I feel like there is a lot of pressure to be happy with either a **"** boy or a girl. I really want a girl. I would do fine with a boy, but it wouldn't be my first choice, that's all there is to it.

In the following exercise, you will explore your thoughts and feelings, positive and negative, about what sex child you may have. You will also clarify your preference, if in fact you have one, and look at your reasons for preferring that sex.

Women in my groups either love or hate this exercise. I reassure everyone repeatedly beforehand that there is nothing psychic about this exercise — the sex child you get is not necessarily the sex child you will get if you choose to parent. This is just a hypothetical exercise. It in no way predicts what sex child you will have.

## INSTRUCTIONS

Take five small (3 x 5) pieces of paper. On two of them write "you had a girl" and on three of them write "you had a boy." (Use three because the odds are slightly greater for having a boy than having a girl.) Now, fold the slips of paper into small squares and put them in a bowl or paper bag. Select one. Read it.

Simply sit with your selection and be aware of yourself and your reactions. Don't censor anything that goes through your mind. Relax and let your mind and thoughts carry you, and notice how you feel and how the feelings change as your thoughts move along.

After a few moments, write down as many of your thoughts, feelings, and reactions as you can remember. Don't judge any of them, just identify what they are. The more you allow yourself to think and feel what you really do feel on this topic, the richer your experience will be. (If you are doing this exercise with others, take at least five minutes to think silently before discussing your feelings with one another.)

# QUESTIONS TO ASK YOURSELF

- How did you feel initially about having a child of the sex you got? As you sat with your selection longer, how did your feelings change?
- Did anything about your reactions surprise you? What?
- What did you think about as you let your mind wander?
- What would be hardest for you about raising a boy?
- What would be hardest for you about raising a girl?

**"** I'm embarrassed to admit I was disappointed to have a girl. I **"** want a boy.

**"** I had a girl in this exercise. At first I was thrilled, and then I let **"** myself think about it, really think about it. I hadn't really done that before.

**"** You know, I didn't want to open my piece of paper. All of a **"** sudden it dawned on me; I don't want a child. I bet you didn't expect to hear me say that!

There are a variety of reasons for wanting one sex instead of another. Often the reasons for preferring one sex over another have to do with difficulties you anticipate in raising a girl at a particular age or a boy at a particular age. Some lesbians have political reasons for wanting a girl instead of a boy. Small group discussions of this issue always raise some points that are new for some women. Discussing this topic with others will definitely broaden your perspective.

**"** So much came up. I need to reinforce some good feelings **"** about having a boy. I can only think it will be so hard. But then I don't really think having a girl would be much easier, it just raises different issues.

**"** I really want a boy, but the lesbian community feels like such **"** a hostile place to have boy children. I want to feel comfortable with my boy child wherever I take him. I expect him to be welcome where I am welcome.

**"** I was relieved I got a girl in this exercise. I want a girl, and no **"** matter what anyone says, I think girls are treated better in the lesbian community. I know we try to give our children equal treatment, but among the lesbians I know, they'd be happier if I had a girl.

Lesbians who have boy children have experienced a range of reactions from their friends and the lesbian community at large. Some of these reactions have been hostile and oppressive; others have been supportive and validating. In some communities, these lesbians with boy children have formed support groups for themselves and their children, have put together forums for other lesbians and lesbian mothers about the issues of raising boy children, and have written articles in local women's newspapers. In spite of this work, having and raising boy children in the lesbian community continues to be a volatile and difficult issue. I encourage you to talk with lesbians who have boy children to learn more about their experiences and the experiences of their children. Attend any community forums on this issue, or organize one in your community, giving lesbian mothers a chance to speak about their experiences, thoughts, and concerns. Finally, watch for articles in lesbian magazines and newspapers which address this subject.

> **“** I'm not around people who aren't supportive of male children. **”** I have self-selected myself into this. It took me time to realize that was what I had to do, and now I am much happier.

> **“** My child is not a future rapist, which is how some lesbians like **”** to think about boy children. The attitude in this community is oppressive and I feel antagonized by it.

> **“** My mothers' group is made up of lesbians with boys and girls. **”** We talk about the difficulty of raising boy children and I get a lot of support from this. Sure, it's hard raising a boy in the lesbian community, but I'm sure it's just as hard to raise a girl — just for slightly different reasons.

> **“** You know, having Ricky hasn't been an issue for anyone I'm **”** close to except me. I have internalized the voice of the community. Sometimes I get embarrassed about how he acts and think it reflects on me. I have to remind myself he's a child and there's no reason for me to be embarrassed just because he is a boy.

## *Your Child's Sexuality*

I am repeatedly asked by people outside the lesbian community whether lesbians want their children to grow up to be homosexual. The underlying implication seems to be that lesbians are having children simply to increase the homosexual population in the world. While, of course, this question is absurd, it is useful to think about what your reactions will be to your child's sexuality and your thoughts on how you want to respond to this question.

This may be an issue you are not able to clarify for yourself until you actually have a child and are faced with her/his emerging sexuality and all the issues that go with it. The following questions will start you thinking about this topic and set you along the path of recognizing your own feelings.

Women in my groups who have done this exercise generally agree that they have not let themselves think about this very much. There is a good deal of discussion as to whether the sexuality of one's child would really make a difference in the decision of whether to parent. Interestingly, there have been women in the groups who feel they are not ready to have a child who would choose heterosexuality (or homosexuality) and realize they need to be more comfortable with either possibility before making their decision.

## INSTRUCTIONS

In this exercise, I ask you to suspend your sense of rational time, space, and judgment. For some people, it might be easier to focus your thoughts on a child or children you already know.

Imagine you have a child, being specific about the age, sex and sexual behavior that child is demonstrating. You may want to do this exercise a few times and imagine a child of each sex and different sexual attitudes and behaviors. Or, if you do this with friends, each of you will undoubtedly pick children of different ages and orientations, and that will enrich and deepen the discussion you then have. I know that this is hard to do in the abstract, so use the questions below to help you in your reflections.

## QUESTIONS TO ASK YOURSELF

- What do you imagine would be difficult for you if your girl/boy were homosexual? What would you worry about for her/him? What would you want to tell her/him about sex and sexuality given that sexual preference?
- What do you imagine would be difficult for you if your girl/boy were heterosexual? What would you worry about for her/him? What would you want to tell her/him about sex and sexuality given that sexual preference?
- What do you imagine would be difficult for you if your boy/girl were bisexual? What would you worry about for her/him? What would you want to tell her/him about sex and sexuality given that sexual preference?
- How do you think parents influence a child's sexuality and sexual choices?
- How much control do you think parents have over the choices children make about their sexuality?

84

- What is important to you about your child and her/his sexuality and sexual choices in later life?
- What do you remember from your childhood about how your parents dealt with your emerging sexuality? How do you want that to be similar or different for your own child?

❝ I really don't care whether Verna is heterosexual, homosexual, ❞ or bisexual. I simply hope she likes herself and learns to make choices that feel good and right to her.

❝ There's no way we can control our children's sexual choices. ❞ Look at me — my parents are devout heterosexuals — they tried their best but I was too busy being myself.

❝ Teddy likes girls. He's shy to admit it, afraid I would disap- ❞ prove. But I told him, 'it makes sense you like girls. You've had some great women to learn from.'

❝ My son is questioning his sexuality now, but that's perfectly ❞ normal for a teenager. I hope he feels permission to explore the possibilities; that's more than I had. It might have made my life less traumatic if there hadn't been so many taboos on sexual differences.

❝ I know I'll hate it if my daughter is heterosexual — all those ❞ boys around the house. But other lesbian moms I know say they've gotten used to it. So, I guess I will too.

## *Rights of Children to Know Their Biological Father*

For lesbians considering biological parenthood, there are complex and often confusing issues surrounding the choice of a biological father. Reproductive technologies have catapulted us into an age where questions about biological parenthood are not as straightforward as they once were. Furthermore, the use of new technologies raises ethical questions regarding the rights of children to know their biological father. Where do lesbians considering parenthood fit into this complicated maze, and how will their conception choices, with all the accompanying ethical and moral concerns, be addressed with their children?

Do children have the right to know their biological father? Will it be damaging to a child if s/he is never able to know the biological father? What do we tell our children about how they were conceived and who their "daddy" is? And when do we talk to them about the nitty-gritty details of all of this — before we tell other adults in the community? When the children first ask? When we think they are ready?

Before turning to a discussion of some of these questions and what other lesbians are saying to their children about their biological roots, the following exercise will help you recall aspects of your own childhood which may help you find some answers.

### INSTRUCTIONS

Recall something from your childhood that made you feel angry at your parents, something that had to do with their lifestyle, religion, work, behavior, where you lived, or anything else from your life situation that was out of your control. Describe that situation in as much detail as necessary to draw a complete picture. (Here is an example from my life: One of the strongest aspects of my childhood is that I was raised in a fairly religious Jewish household. While I was in junior high and high school, we lived in a predominately non-Jewish area. I remember hating feeling different, being different, and having everybody know I was different from them. I didn't have enough self-esteem to feel good about my religious background then and was often embarrassed by it, wishing my parents wouldn't emphasize it so much.)

As you look back as an adult on the situation you have chosen, list both the things you feel you gained from this situation despite its difficulty and those things that made it particularly hard for you. From your current perspective, consider the different sides and describe how you feel about that part of your life now.

The point is to highlight some of the pros and cons of a situation which for you as a child was not in your control to change or to choose. All children, regardless of their family background, ethnic, cultural, or class situation, have had to live with some stigma.

## Some Ethically Challenging Questions

Let us now turn to some of the more perplexing and ethically challenging questions raised when choosing to become a mother through alternative fertilization. As you consider these questions, remember there are no right or wrong answers — only your answers, your thoughts, and your experiences. Talking with other lesbian mothers about these issues can be extremely helpful. In addition, you may also find that talking with women who were adopted will give you a different perspective on some of these concerns.

As lesbians considering parenthood, many of us are concerned about our responsibility to our children to ensure they know their biological father. Is there a moral imperative that if you consciously choose to become pregnant and bear a child, you must provide your child with information about her/his father? For many lesbians considering parenthood, this is an emotionally charged and morally challenging issue. I do not want to suggest that there is any easy way to come to a decision about it.

The larger question raised here has to do with whether it is acceptable to bring children into the world when they will not be able to know their biological father. Is the desire to know one's biological father the result of social pressures that make us think that no one is whole or fulfilled if they do not know each of their biological parents? Or is it a true biological desire of the individual to know their origins and therefore their biological roots? Or both?

The lesbian choosing to use an unknown donor is making a choice for her child – in all likelihood, that child will not be able to know her/his biological father. As your child gets older and can grasp the full reality of the situation, you will have to help her/him cope with what may feel like a genuine "loss." You will have to help the child understand the reasons for your choice, the way you made your decisions, and your acceptance of the possibility that s/he could be angry at you.

People who are adopted have drawn some dramatic parallels to this situation. They have expressed deep feelings that locating their birth parents can be essential for a person at some point in her life. Many adoptees feel it is a child's right to know who her/his parents are and that adults need to act accordingly.

**❝** I wish my mother and father had thought a little more about **❞** how it might be for me never to find them. They were giving me up because they couldn't care for me, but now that I am old enough I want to find them and know them, just to have a chance to see who they are. I constantly ask myself, 'Why didn't they think of how I would feel?'

## The Biological Father – An Unknown Commodity

Here is another exercise to help you explore how it might feel not to be able to ever find one's biological father. Imagine you are planning a pregnancy with a donor. Take a few minutes to think about it and then describe your responses to the following situations.

How would you feel if:

1. You could never know the man?
2. You *had* to meet the man?
3. You had a choice as to whether or not you would know this person?

87

The situations are not analogous, but this example may give you a different perspective on your thoughts.

Throughout the years of doing these groups, I have seen attitudes shift concerning whether to have a donor that a child would someday be able to contact. Years ago, most women wantéd an unknown donor. Questions concerning the legal implications of lesbians having children and the cases of lesbians fighting for custody of their children with their ex-husbands had many feeling the need to have no connection whatsoever with the donor. During the past few years, however, more lesbians are seeking a known donor. Some want their child to know whom to contact in the years to come. Others want the donor to be actively involved in the parenting process. Still other lesbians are choosing a man they do not know, but someone whom a go-between or other friend knows. In that way, their child will have some access to this man in the future.

> **❝** I grew up with kids who didn't know who their fathers were. **❞** It was hard for them. I don't want to do that to my kid if I can help it.

> **❝** My lover and I are going to raise our child together. We want **❞** to protect Laura's position as the non biological mother. That means having a unknown donor. It's a big trade-off, but I think we are making the best decision.

> **❝** *This* was the most difficult decision of all. I have to admit I **❞** didn't really make it. I just let things happen and the decision got made for me.

## *What Will I Tell My Child?*

At some point, generally after children have started pre-school or have contact with other children on a regular basis, they start asking questions about many things. One question inevitably has to do with who their father is. You may want to take some time to think about how you will respond to this question, or a similar query, when it is asked.

### INSTRUCTIONS

Answer the following questions as best as you can. Maybe you just have a few ideas right now about what you would say. That is perfectly all right. What is important is identifying the thoughts you do have, even if some of your thoughts are confused or unclear.

☐ What do you plan to tell your child about the biological father?

☐ How and when do you want to tell your child about her/his biological father?

☐ What are some ideas you have for answering the following questions:
What is a daddy?
Who is my daddy?
What is my daddy's name?
Why don't I have a daddy?
Where is my daddy's house?

## THINGS TO CONSIDER

• You may have what you consider the perfect plan for talking to your child about this topic, and s/he will ask you a question you never anticipated. Or, you will find that all the words you thought you would use to describe your actions and feelings don't adequately convey what your child wants and needs to hear. So, although it is good to have a plan, be ready to abandon it if necessary.

• Answer your child's questions, but only tell her/him as much as s/he wants to know. When your child is at an early age, you may not want to go into the specific details of why you chose alternative fertilization with an unknown donor, or why you can't locate the donor until the child is eighteen. A question such as "Who is my daddy?" may require a longer answer when your child is eight than when s/he is three.

• Validate that all families are different and that there is nothing wrong with being different. If you are someone who likes to teach children about ideas through books, look for recent children's books that describe different kinds of family structures.

• Children must be given permission, time, and space to grieve their loss, especially if there is no way that they will be able to locate their biological father. This is an important point. Whatever decision you make about your donor, there is no right or wrong choice. But each choice does have definite consequences. If you choose an unknown donor, you will be faced with your child's feelings about that choice. There is no way to be prepared for how our children will respond. But we can be ready to help them react and respond, and give them support for whatever feelings they are able to express, even if those feelings are difficult for us to hear.

• Children will have their own stories about who their "daddy" might be. As a lesbian parent, you will be given many opportunities to explore your feelings about this "story" and help your child sort through what is real and what is not.

**“** I was driving my daughter home from childcare one day. She **”** was just three. All of a sudden she said, 'Look Mommy, there's my daddy.' In spite of myself, I slammed on the brakes and turned to look. I really didn't know what to say, she took me by surprise.

❝ When my child was about three, she started asking how I had ❞ her. I told her that a very nice man helped me have her, that he gave me his seed and together with my egg she was formed. I don't think she understood what I meant. So I just said 'You grew in my belly and came out through my vagina when you were ready.' That seemed to make more sense.

❝ I told my son there are two kinds of daddies. There is the ❞ daddy who helps children be born and there is the kind of daddy who helps children grow up. You have the first kind of daddy. Other kids you know also have daddies like that. And you know kids who have the other kind of daddy too.

❝ We told our children, 'It's true, you don't have a daddy you ❞ know. Instead you have two mommies. Everyone's family is just a little different.'

## Our Children – Walking a Mile in Their Shoes

This exercise is designed for a group, but it can be done by individuals on their own. If you do not have a small group of lesbian friends to do this with, do it on your own, or with even one other person. You will still get something out of it.

The purpose of the exercise is to get you thinking about how your children might feel and what they might think about as children of lesbians. It will help you focus on what their dilemmas might be, how they might phrase the dilemmas, and most importantly, what they might want you to do to help them.

If you are doing this by yourself, take on each of the roles described and jot down the thoughts and feelings that come up for you. (If you are doing this with a group, divide yourselves into two or three small groups with at least two people in each group. Take about 20 minutes in your small group to work on this exercise and then come back to the larger group to discuss what you talked about with one another. Try to be in different rooms, or different parts of a room so you are not distracted by what the other groups are saying.)

1 Pretend that you are the child of a lesbian parent(s). Take a minute or so to imagine your life situation. You can be a female or male child. You can be any age you choose. Imagine your family. How many moms do you have? Do you know your dad? Is he involved in parenting you?

Do you know how you were conceived? Create a whole scenario for yourself, a story about your life.

**2** Write down your story and answer these questions:

What it is like to be the child of these lesbian parents?

What do you like about it?

What don't you like about it?

What do you wish were different?

What do you think is better about it than your friend's families (friends who do not have lesbian moms)?

What do you think is the same?

**3** Repeat this exercise by selecting another age, a few years older or younger. If you haven't already done so, be sure you imagine yourself as a teenager, maybe 14 or 15 — this always seems to be a difficult age, for all parents, regardless of their own sexuality.

Here are a few situations to consider:

- You are between eight and 13 years old. You want one of your friends from school to spend the night. How do you want your mother(s) to act?

- You are 15, and you and your new "best" friend are going to the movies. Your mom and her lover decide they would like to see the same film. How do you feel about that? What do you do?

- If you are in a small group, ask members of the group to suggest some other situations that they imagined.

If you are doing this exercise on your own, make a list of the different dilemmas you identified. (If you are doing this exercise in a small group, discuss these questions among yourselves.)

THINGS TO CONSIDER

- As children, you may bring up more of what is hard about being the child of a lesbian, and overlook what is really great about it. Be sure you take time to include what is good too.

- Imagine how it would be for you as a parent to hear about your child's thoughts and feelings, assuming they are similar to the ones you created.

- If you have the opportunity to do this exercise with a group of people, notice the range of ideas, responses, situations, and anecdotes that come up. You will have an opportunity to consider a wide variety of issues that are important to children, some of which you may not have thought about.

◾ Take a good look at the feelings, ideas, images, and different thoughts that came up for you. These may give you some crucial clues about how you can be helpful at different times in your child's life.

## Children With Special Needs

A child with "special needs" is one who may need additional physical, emotional, medical, or educational support. Some children with special needs are developmentally disabled, some are physically disabled (blind, deaf, paraplegic or quadraplegic, or physically challenged in some other way), some are emotionally disabled, and some have special medical conditions which may be invisible disabilities (such as partial deafness, epilepsy, chronic pain, etc.), and may require continual care or medical supervision. Whatever kind of special needs your child may have, there are some critical things to think about.

As a lesbian parent of a child with special needs, you may find yourself forced to seek help from a community which does not support or accept your life choices. One of the first things you will have to decide is whether to come out to the agency personnel with whom you will be working.

Lesbian mothers with special needs children have talked about the frustrations they experienced in working with agencies such as hospitals, schools, and other institutions, in which the staff were more concerned and curious about their lesbianism than about the child's needs. It will be important to gather the support of your close friends and support network in coping with both the care of your child and any additional problems with which you may be faced. Although the situation is not always grim, it can be a difficult one.

    **❝** I thought I would have the support of my friends when my **❞** child became disabled. I was shocked when they couldn't deal with it. I have found more support from other parents whose children are similarly disabled than from my own community.

    **❝** We decided to adopt a child with special needs. Kirsten is four **❞** and has rather severe cerebral palsy. It is good there are two of us, because her care takes a lot of time. Our families have been great. Our friends too.

    **❝** My son was born with Down's Syndrome. He is three now **❞** and I finally am over the shock. I have learned a lot and feel he has brought an enormous gift into my life. It's a joy to watch him grow and change. And it is painful to know he won't grow up to be like other children.

## INSTRUCTIONS

Consider each of the following situations, taking time to think about each one before going on to the next. Jot down your thoughts and answers, feelings, and gut-level reactions.

Imagine how you would feel if:

▣ Your child were born deaf.

▣ Your child were born with a serious visual impairment.

▣ Your child is physically disabled.

▣ Your child is developmentally disabled.

▣ You have a child who requires intensive care due to a serious problem at birth.

▣ The results of your amniocentesis show you are carrying a child with Down's Syndrome.

This is one of those exercises in which there are no right or wrong answers. These are situations to think about. Unfortunately, they are not always situations we can really plan for, but we can be alerted to the possiblity of their occurring and be conscious of how we might begin to respond.

# MEN IN CHILDREN'S LIVES

In this section, you will have a chance to begin formulating your plans for including men in your child's life. We will discuss the why's and how-to's of the issues as well as the reality of how much control you can have over this situation.

One lesbian mother I know who does a good deal of public speaking on the topic of lesbian parenting is frequently asked what lesbians are doing to include men in the lives of their children. Her response is quite emphatic: "I am more concerned that my child have people from different cultural and ethnic groups in her life. There are plenty of men around, but we live in a world made up of so many different kinds of people. Exposure to people with different backgrounds and values seems infinitely more important to me."

Some lesbians do not want men in their children's lives. Others actively choose to involve men, either by co-parenting with a man (who may or may not be the biological father) or by including male friends in the child's life on a regular basis. Still others may have no clear sense of how they want to handle this situation. Wherever you stand, exploring your thoughts and feelings fully may help you in sorting out how you want to deal with this question if you decide to parent.

    **❝** My brother is really into my having a kid. I know he will be **❞** happy to share in my child's life, and I'll be glad to have him. He's not the most perfect man in the world, but I like him.

    **❝** This question about including men is maddening. Kids don't **❞** *need* male role models to grow into adjusted adults. They need to be loved. Male energy is not what I choose for myself, so I don't plan to choose it for my kid.

How lesbians choose to involve men in their child's life has a great deal to do with how they involve men in their own lives, how they feel about men in general, and what their early experiences with men (brothers, fathers, uncles, grandfathers, etc.) were like.

Lesbians are frequently criticized for excluding men from their own lives or for having negative attitudes about men which they may teach to their children. I have heard suggestions that lesbians teach their own negative attitudes about men to their children and even deprive their children of "healthy" interactions with men. While this suggestion may be true for some lesbians choosing to have children, it is probably most accurate to assume that different women have different attitudes toward men.

> **“** Our dream is to have a duplex and live in one part with our **”** child and have these two gay men we know live downstairs. The four of us would parent as a collective family.

> **“** I frankly have no control over whether my child has men in **”** his life. I guess I just don't have time to be bothered about men. Why try to control something you can't really do much about?

There seem to be two basic assumptions that come up regarding this issue. One is that all men are good, and that knowing and relating to them is a good and essential experience for all children. We all know that is not always true. It makes sense that lesbians, like most parents, want to choose whom their children relate to and learn from. Lesbians choosing to have children also choose the kind of close relationships their children will have in the early years. The fabric of these relationships changes dramatically as children grow up and embrace their own independence.

The other assumption has to do with the importance of male role models in a child's life. The large body of psychological literature provides widely varying opinions on this topic. Be careful about what you read in psychological and social work journals — there are subtle and not so subtle prejudices against women-directed families that can undermine your confidence and introduce unnecessary guilt. I believe that we each need to decide for ourselves the quantity and quality of male involvement in our child's life. We are fooling ourselves if we think we have real control over the kind and quality of interaction our children will have with men out in the world. What we can have some impact on, however, is what happens in the home environment and in the family setting.

> **“** I am more and more aware that I can't plan everything down **”** to the last detail. If men come into our life, fine. If they don't, that's fine too. I want my child to know some men, but I don't know exactly how I will make that happen and I don't believe it has to be the perfect interaction.

> **“** I am glad my daughter knows men. Her teacher is a man; we **”**

have a few men friends we spend time with, and there are boys of other lesbians in our circle.

## Considerations About Men in My Child's Life

In the following exercise, there are thought-provoking questions to help you clarify the quality and quantity of male involvement you imagine you would like in your child's life.

### INSTRUCTIONS

Answer the following questions as honestly as you can. Having up-to-date psychological information on this topic of men in children's lives may be essential to you, but the purpose of this exercise is to get a sense of your own thoughts and feelings, without the overlay of a "professional" viewpoint. It may be difficult to separate out how you think it *should* be and how you *want* it to be. Take time to get clear if you can. Your kids will get a richer experience if you are clear about what you want, and you in turn will be able to make clearer choices for yourself and for them through the years.

Answer these questions:

1. Do you think it is crucial to include men in children's lives?
2. If yes, list the reasons you feel it is important by completing the following sentence: I feel it is important to include men in children's lives because . . .
3. What do you see as reasons for not including men in children's lives? Complete this sentence: I feel it is not necessary to include men in children's lives because . . .
4. Now let's get specific. Describe how do you want to include men in your child's life. Be sure to include *who* the men would be (your brothers, grandfather(s), uncles, gay male friends, straight male friends, male teachers, donor(s), older boys raised in lesbian and/or lesbian feminist households, etc.). How much time would you want them to spend with your child? What kind of interaction would you hope they had? How would the amount of time change as your child gets older?

### THINGS TO CONSIDER

- There may be a specific quality and quantity of male involvement you can control. This would include how men spend time with your children, how much time, who they would be, what kinds of activities they would do together.

- There is also male involvement you cannot control. This includes male role models on TV, teachers in school, other children's parents (both male and female certainly), interactions with strangers, other children, and many more.

- Talk to others with whom you intend to parent. This topic generally brings up conflicting feelings for many lesbians, even those who feel reasonably resolved about their relationships with the men. You may find it difficult to discuss this topic calmly and clearly. Be gentle with each other.

- Some lesbians in the groups talk about not knowing many men and needing to find ways to meet men that they might then want to include in their lives and in the lives of their children. This may not be an easy task and may take a good deal of time and attention to find the kind of men you want.

**“** My son has found pleasure in spending regular time with certain gay men I know. His energy is always different, which is hard for me, but I feel it is part of his heritage and to deny him that exposure feels wrong to me. He needs to know how men act. I know he's going to get it somewhere; better that it be with men that I know and feel good about. **”**

**“** We didn't know any men! We would go to political events, talk with different men we met there, and try to figure out if we wanted to get to know them better. It was funny. How do you explain to them you are checking them out to see if you want them in your unborn child's life? **”**

Finally, keep in mind that you will need to be flexible on this issue. You will have plenty of opportunities to re-evaluate and reassess your thoughts on whether and how to include men if you choose to have children. Children test limits; as they begin to choose their own friends, some of them may be boys and men with whom you, too, will be expected to interact. Thinking about it, even superficially at this point in your decision-making process, can be helpful. Discussing it with others will give you more to think about and will force you to clarify your thinking and verbalize your thoughts. This isn't a subject to be treated lightly. There will be constant input from your friends, family, and people you know and don't know, regarding how *they* think you should be handling this aspect of parenting.

# BECOMING A NON-BIOLOGICAL MOTHER

Perhaps you do not want to bear a child but would like to raise a child with someone else. Or you get involved with a woman who already has children, and you are considering whether to parent these children (or child) with your partner. Or perhaps you are seeking to be a parent by adopting a child, or being a foster parent or a legal guardian. Whatever parenting situation you are considering, as the non-biological mother you will need to evaluate your choices just as carefully as you would with any other parenting option. The lesbian considering this option is called upon to weigh a number of intangible, yet very real, concerns.

Non-biological mothering is a complex and challenging parenting option. It is often laced with predictable and unpredictable surprises and dilemmas. Within this parenting choice, there is room for both expansiveness and creativity. Despite some of the problem areas, there is also enormous joy and reward to be found in being a non-biological mother.

I use the term "non-biological mother" to refer to the lesbian mother who has no biological link to the child but who identifies her role as one of mother/parent. How to label this particular role is a cause of some consternation among many women. You will hear "mother," "co-parent," "mama," "co-mom," "mommy," "mom," "non-biological mother" — all with slightly different meanings depending upon who is using the term, the community in which you live, and who is defining it. I use non-biological mother here to delineate the difference in biological relationship to the child, but at the same time acknowledge the potential for equality in the role of parenting.

Lesbians considering the option of non-biological motherhood need to read all sections of this book. This chapter contains an exercise to assist you in spelling out your expectations of yourself in the role of non-biological mother. An exploration of some of the more complex issues surrounding this option, such as bonding, power in relationships with childen, issues of possessiveness, and legal concerns, can be found in the "Co-parenting" chapter.

## Great Expectations

As you work on these questions, keep in mind that the parenting relationship is fluid — issues change and get reformulated as your child grows and as you (and your partner) learn more about your individual parenting styles. Because the nature of being a non-biological mother is largely undefined, there is a great deal of room to create and mold the role into one that best meets everyone's needs — yours, your partner's, your child's — and the way you want your family and your relationship to be. Be expansive. Paint the picture to look the way you want your life to be, realizing, of course, that the picture will be modified and reworked as time goes by. Roles and relationships will change. Nothing is ever static where children are concerned.

### INSTRUCTIONS

1. List your reasons for wanting to be a non-biological mother. These may include your general reasons for wanting to be a parent as well as specific reasons for wanting to be a non-biological mother.
2. What do you think will be difficult for you in the role of non-biological mother? Describe what you see as potential problems; be as explicit as possible. (These points will be important ones to talk over with others with whom you may be parenting.)
3. What do you think will be positive about this parenting option for you?
4. What are your expectations of yourself as a mother?
5. What are your expections of others (friends, family, co-workers, etc.) after you assume this role?

For lesbians who are not the legal adoptive mother of their children, the role of non-biological parent can seem ambiguous. Lacking models, role expectations are often unclear and usually different for each person, couple, or family. How do you explain your familial connection to your child in a society that puts so much weight on biological parenthood? If there are two lesbian parents, is the non-biological mother considered a father or a mother? Does she have equal status with the biological mother? These questions represent a not so subtle perspective that each lesbian family must examine and be prepared to face.

100

Unfortunately, non-biological mothers are even less visible, both legally and socially, than biological lesbian mothers. Often, their relationship to their child is discounted (are you the "real" mother?) and goes unacknowledged, even within the social context of the lesbian community.

The non-biological mother, whether a single mother (through adoption or foster parenting) or with a partner, may be repeatedly confronted by the painful reality of being unacknowledged as the "real" mother by family, friends, the community and society at large, as well as by the child. Because we are dealing with a culture-bound tradition — that a child only has one mother — it will take time and patience to educate ourselves and others to the validity of the non-biological mother role and to the shared and equal parenting potential of lesbians raising children together.

**"** I get tired of people always asking my partner about our kid. **"** It's almost like I'm not there.

**"** When I first got pregnant, I had to keep reminding everyone **"** that there were *two* of us having this baby. Everyone kept talking to me as though Leigh wasn't involved at all.

**"** Our friends have been great in seeing us as equal mothers. It's **"** actually not a problem for us.

**"** I wanted to adopt a child. I knew that was how I wanted to be **"** a mother. Parenting, not pregnancy, was important to me. If people don't want to recognize me as my child's real mother, that's their problem. I have what I want.

**"** I was raised by a woman who was not my mother. I don't have **"** some idea that you have to physically bear a child in order to be a mother.

The child's relationship to the non-biological mother may also be influenced by this general lack of recognition. Within our own friendship circles and support networks, where both parents are more likely to be seen and treated as equal parents of their child, the child is given positive reinforcement of the relationship with her/his mothers.

The outside world, however, presents a different perspective. Adults and other children often ask, "Who is your *real* mommy? Where is your daddy? How can you have two moms?" Questions like this can be confusing. Some lesbian mothers encourage their children to understand the difference between the two (or more) mothers. Others do not. And, some children must try to explain who this "other" mom is, often in terms that are not translatable to the nuclear family model.

**"** The idea of being pregnant never appealed to me but I wanted **"** to be a mother. I was so glad when I met Janice because she

wanted to be a mother and wanted to have a child with another woman.

   **“** When I wanted to have a child, ten years ago, I didn't know les- **”**
   bians could do it. Now that I am in my forties and my best
   friend is planning a pregnancy, I can have the child I can't bear
   myself.

In the "Co-parenting" chapter, both parents will have an opportunity to imagine how they will respond to some of the issues described
above. These kinds of issues will affect your relationship with your
parenting partner(s), your child, and your friends. How you respond to
them, share them with one another, and discuss them openly with your
friends can be very important as you build your lesbian family.

As a non-biological mother, you will be faced with many
dilemmas. If you are in a relationship with the biological mother, you
may have no legally binding relationship to your child. You may find
that the community and others fail to give you the recognition you deserve as a mother, and that you have emotions and feelings of intensity
and possessiveness for your child that others may criticize and question.
Through the loving tenderness of your co-parenting relationship, it is
hoped that some of these dilemmas can be openly talked about, shared,
and resolved.

   **“** The lesbian community needs to understand that when two **”**
   lesbians decide to have a child together, one has it biologically,
   but the child is *their* child. This is still a very difficult concept
   for people to grasp.

   **“** Who cares what I'm called! I am Jake's mom and he loves me **”**
   and knows I am his mother. He doesn't care about this biological or non-biological stuff. He doesn't even seem to know it's
   a problem. It's everyone else that keeps bringing it up.

Not all lesbians become non-biological mothers to a newborn
infant. A lesbian may get involved in a relationship with another lesbian
who already has a child(ren), and perhaps, after a period of time, finds
that she is parenting this child along with her partner. Or she may adopt
an older child. And certainly there are other situations that I have not
described here. Whatever your family situation, chances are you will be
faced with countless opportunities, unique challenges, and many questions in building a relationship with an older child, or a child you have
not known since her/his birth. You will want to talk with other non-
biological mothers who are doing this or who have done it. I encourage
you to do the exercises in the "Family of Origin" chapter, as well as those
in the chapter on children.

Frequently one of the most difficult and painful parts of being a non-biological mother surfaces when you try to explain your child to your family of origin. As I mentioned in the chapter "Getting the Support of Your Family," there is often a great deal of confusion about the kind of relationship a lesbian who is not the biological mother can have to her child. There may be little validation for the intensity of that bond and also limited, if any, acknowledgement of the commitment the non-biological mother has made, regardless of the biological ties. Some family members even refuse to recognize the child as a family member because she/he has no biological link to that family.

There are certainly any number of reasons for this behavior and these attitudes: denial that this is a real relationship; denial that a lesbian can parent a child that is not hers biologically; confusion about how to name, describe, or explain the relationship; refusal to give recognition because that may mean acknowledging their daughter's (sister's, niece's, grandaughter's) lesbianism and what they feel is a non-traditional and, possibly unacceptable, situation. These are just a few of the possibilities. Whatever the reasons, gaining recognition in her role as non-biological mother can be extremely difficult for the lesbian parent.

Completing the exercises in the "Family of Origin" chapter may help you to plan a strategy for talking with your family members about your parenting status. Remember that this is a process and that family members may need time to fully grasp the meaning of your relationship with your child. One non-biological mother explained to me that it wasn't until she took her child home for a visit one summer that her parents and siblings really understood the depth of the relationship and the commitment she had made to her child. It was only through actually observing the mother and child together that the family was able to comprehend a relationship that lacks any concrete definition in our culture.

Every woman's family will respond differently to this situation based on their own dynamics, attitudes, and experience. I remember being quite surprised by how readily and openly my family took Bridgette in as a family member, requiring little or no explanation in the beginning. There was a clear sense that they were willing and able to recognize my commitment to Bridgette, even though they did not fully understand it, or why I was being a parent. Their immediate acceptance meant a lot to me and allowed me to share more about my life than I might have otherwise.

# CO-PARENTING

Co-parents are generally two or more people assuming responsibility for parenting together. There are many possible co-parenting combinations, just like there are many lesbian family forms: lesbians parent with other lesbians, with heterosexual women, with gay men, and with straight men. Selecting the co-parenting situation that works best for you will probably take time, persistence, and more energy than you may anticipate. There will be a range of issues to be considered, many of which are discussed in this chapter. Co-parenting demands cooperation, mutual respect, and honesty. For most, it is a struggle — rewarding and frustrating — but well worth the effort.

Do the exercises in this chapter with your parenting partner(s). Discuss the issues raised, explore your feelings, share your concerns. Really focus on understanding where each person is starting from and why their responses might be similar or different from your own.

## *My Ideas of Being a Parent*

For this exercise, take time to think about and describe the kind of parenting relationship you want to have with a child. Here are a few questions to get you started. Be as thorough in your description as you can. You may want to add to this description if other ideas, thoughts, feelings, or changes come up for you.

1. How much time do you want to spend being a parent?
2. What kind of commitment do you want to make to a child? What kind of commitment do you feel you can make?

**3** Describe what you believe to be your strengths and weaknesses in your relationships with children.

Not all parenting relationships are 50-50 from the start, or ever. Some people actively choose to make an equal commitment to the relationship of parenting. Others may not want to commit to shared responsibility. We often confuse ourselves by thinking the balance in the parenting relationship has to be equal or it won't work at all. This is not necessarily true. What does appear to be true, however, is that being clear about how much you want to parent, how involved you want to be, and how involved you want your partner to be, will improve the parenting experience for everyone involved, especially your child.

**"** When I decided to have a second child, Jennifer was clear she **"** did not want to be a mother to another child. At first I was furious but it helped me to know what I could expect and that I would have to find support elsewhere.

**"** We shared parenting pretty equally right from the start. As **"** our lives have changed though, Louise is doing much more now than I am. She feels okay about this and we both hope to have an equal balance again some day.

**"** I never expected to be an equal parent with Chelsea. I figured **"** I'd help out now and then. Once Alexis was born I wanted to be as involved as I could. It was hard for both of us to adjust to my sudden change.

## Roles and Expectations

It isn't unusual for people who plan to parent with a partner(s) to have a wealth of expectations such as how that person will behave as a parent, what the experience will be like for each person, who will do what for the child at specific times, and how much time each person will commit to the child. (I am certain that there are other expectations that even I haven't yet imagined!) Usually, these kinds of expectations remain unspoken, and therefore unacknowledged. Unfortunately, these unspoken expectations can cause countless problems when people embark on the already difficult task of parenting together.

INSTRUCTIONS

In the following exercise, you will have a chance to express some of the expectations you may have of yourself and of your parenting partner(s). These are a hypothetical list of "shoulds" many of us have in our heads, but rarely discuss with others. Take this opportunity to elaborate on all the "shoulds" you can think of. Have fun with this exercise, and remember to be loving and gentle with yourself.

Begin by completing the following sentences, spending a few minutes on each one.

- To be a good parent, I should . . .
- If my lover and I parent together, she should. . .
- I expect that my parenting partner will . . .
- A good parent should . . .
- If my lover is going to have the baby, she should . . .
- If I am having our child, I should . . .
- As an adoptive parent, it is my responsibility to . . .
- The friends who help with parenting our child should . . .
- If I move in with my lover and her child(ren), I should . . .
- If I become a co-parent with my lover who already has children, I should . . .
- Any men who share in parenting our child should . . .

Compare your lists, with each person explaining the different "shoulds" that have been identified.

Talk about what you identified earlier as your strengths and weaknesses in being a parent. How do these match up with those of your parenting partner(s)? What would you like your partner to take more responsibility for? And what kinds of things do you imagine you would be willing to take more responsibility for?

Let's look at some of the unique issues associated with the co-parenting experience. Use the issues identified here as a starting point: others may come up for you depending upon your situation. We will be discussing the dynamics of asymmetrical power between a biological mother and a non-biological mother, bonding, possessiveness, and legal agreements. Co-parenting raises different issues for each of us: the exercises in this section will give you a format for discussing some of the other issues that are important to you but not covered here.

Families in which there is one biological mother and one (or possibly more) non-biological mothers will be faced with the challenging task of figuring out how people who may have biologically asymmetrical relationships to a child can successfully parent that child together. Having biologically asymmetrical relationships with one's child (where one person is biologically connected to the child and other(s) is not) is bound to affect the power balance between the biological and non-biological mothers. Many lesbian mothers describe an unspoken difference in the degree of responsibility felt by each parenting partner. Some biological mothers talk about the freedom they assume the non-biological parent has from the child because the intensity of the biological connection is absent. Some non-biological mothers, on the other hand, have explained they feel their commitment is questioned because of the lack of the biological relationship. Others express feelings of intense possessiveness of their child in an effort to establish and reinforce their relationship to the child.

If you are co-parenting, talk about the different kinds of power each of you feels in your parenting relationship. You do not necessarily have to do anything about it right away. Acknowledging these feelings of powerfulness and powerlessness can pave the way for better communication, mutual respect, and a richer gentleness with one another.

> **❝** It's true; there is a huge imbalance in our relationship to Maya **❞** because of the biological stuff. I try to remember that Liz is threatened by my tie to Maya, while she is sensitive to my fears that she can simply abandon me. I guess you could say we are aware of the imbalance and try to recognize it when it may be causing us trouble.

Bonding, possessiveness, and jealousy are each subtle aspects of this asymmetrical power issue. As one lesbian mother cautioned, "Be forewarned. You may be completely stunned by the emotions generated by the parenting experience – the exclusivity of it, the possessiveness you never imagined feeling, and the sheer intensity of bonding with your child." You may be surprised by the power of your emotional responses. Often, these kinds of feelings can't be anticipated or discussed beforehand. Realizing they may come up, however, can prepare you for the struggles with which you may be faced.

Bonding is one subject which creates a good deal of stress for many co-parents. They must come to terms with the undeniable biological bond that the biological mother has with the child and, at the same time, make room for the non-biological mother to develop a unique bond with the child herself. We often forget that the child does not know that one bond is more important than any other. Given the pressures of our culture, however, it is often difficult to keep that fact in mind.

So much of what you will find in most literature on bonding focuses on the bond between one mother and her child. We have been taught to believe that children only bond to their biological mother. But what kind of bonding happens when there are two mothers? Bonding is generally thought to occur very early in a child's development, usually during the first few months of life. Most "authorities" believe that bonding with the primary caregiver generally occurs through breastfeeding and constant support and contact with this nurturer. However, lesbian mothers are learning that bonding does not only occur through this physical connection. It grows out of consistency in relationships, trust, and intimacy. Children can develop bonds to others at various stages of their early development, and bonding happens in many different ways.

One of the biggest lessons a two-mother family can learn about promoting bonding between the non-biological mother and the child(ren) is the importance of each parent having equal alone time with the child. Whether that means the non-biological mother gets the kids off to school while the other mother is already at work, or each mother is gone one night a week or for an occassional weekend. There is nothing like quality time alone with a child to promote bonding.

As lesbians have and raise children together, and as those children bond to their mothers, we might begin to see some of the mystification around this bonding question change.

> **❝** When our daughter was three I began to notice how con- **❞** nected she was to me. It was then I realized we did have a special bond all our own.

> **❝** This has been our biggest problem; my making room for **❞** Eleanor to have a close relationship with our son. I was raised by my mother alone. She did everything, and I was completely attached to her. I have had to learn how to share this bonding experience. We keep working at it.

You will want to think about the kind of bonding you want to promote in your co-parenting relationship. Some biological mothers do not want their child to bond to another person, while some do and are happy to encourage that happening. Some non-biological mothers do not want to create a maternal bond with their child, while others definitely want this and work to create it. Decide what you want and what *you* will feel comfortable with. Sometimes, what we want is not always that which feels most comfortable. As the biological mother you may *want* to support your non-biological partner in bonding with your child, but when it comes right down to it, you may act in ways which makes that difficult or impossible. As the non-biological mother you may want to be given the room to bond with your child, but when the opportunity is offered you may feel ambivalent or even timid. As was mentioned earlier in the "Solving Problems" chapter, bonding is an issue which you will want to talk about at many times during your parenting decision and experience. Enabling bonding to happen may not be as easy as you would like it to be, and it may take more concerted effort and conscious attention than anyone initially anticipates.

Co-parents have suggested structuring activities in the early years of parenting a child to build the opportunity for bonding into the foundation of the family. If your child is an infant, you may want to be sure that each partner has the opportunity for feeding the child on a regular basis. The biological mother, if she is breast-feeding, can express milk for the non-biological mother's feeding time. You can trade off on the "night-shift," so that one of you is responsible for getting up and caring for the infant during the night. If your child is older, you may want to structure specific times in the week when you each have individual time with her/him. Or, each parent may be responsible for taking and picking the child up from childcare or school on a regularly scheduled basis. There are any number of ways to balance out parenting so that bonding to both (or all) parents can take place.

As mentioned in the chapter on "Being a Non-biological Mother," there is often a general lack of recognition of the non-biological mother. The question of who is the "real" mother comes up again and again, asked by both lesbians and heterosexuals. Lesbian co-parents will want to sort out their own feelings about this question and discuss how they want to respond. Talking about what comes up for you, what buttons get pushed, and what surprises you about your response to this question will be helpful in having an honest conversation.

For many lesbian parents, this "real" mother question raises feelings of anxiety, confusion, jealousy, and possessiveness. One non-biological mother confided, "I feel more possessive of our child than Alicia does and she is the biological mother. I have to continually re-establish my relationship with our son for myself, for him, and for others around us. I don't necessarily like feeling like this. But I do."

And what about when the child asks, "Who is my 'real' mommy?" How will you respond to *that* question? As an exercise with your co-parent(s), brainstorm how you want to answer your child if s/he were to ask that question. You may have to talk about this many times before you can settle on a response that feels comfortable for each person. Also, you will probably want to tell your child only as much as s/he can understand depending upon her/his age. You may want to give a more simple answer when s/he is younger and then elaborate on the answer as s/he is able to more fully understand a more complex explanation. Whatever you decide to say, be consistent over time. You will also want to tell friends who spend time with your child how you would like them to answer this question if and when they are asked. Finally, let one another know if your child has asked this question, what you said in response, and whether you feel it needs further discussion now.

> ❝ We were both surprised when Jenny said 'Sandra is not my real ❞
> mother.' She said that she wasn't born out of Sandra's belly,
> just out of Rachel's. So we asked her whether that meant that
> she wasn't Sandra's 'real' daughter. She didn't like that question
> at all and became very upset by the idea.

> ❝ We have tried to help Max understand that there are many ❞
> ways someone can be a 'real' mom. Now when his friends ask
> him who his 'real' mom is, he tells them, 'Liz carried me inside
> her body before I was born and Joanie carries me around now.'

Below is a checklist of things lesbians considering parenthood have identified as potential problem areas when planning to co-parent. Review the list and discuss the issues with your parenting partner(s) and others you know who are parenting together. Be sure to add any other potential problem areas that come to mind.

- ❏ styles of discipline
- ❏ needs for cleanliness
- ❏ how long to let your child cry
- ❏ freedom of your child to act as s/he wants
- ❏ language and tone of voice to use with your child
- ❏ how you express anger when you are angry at your child
- ❏ "perfect parent" syndrome — What does this mean to you? How does it come up?
- ❏ appropriate ways to express feelings?
- ❏ what to do if your child consistently shows more affection to one parent exclusively (if this is a problem for you)
- ❏ how to handle child's jealousy of co-parent or co-parent's jealousy of child
- ❏ arguing in front of your child
- ❏ the kinds of food your child can eat

Because parenting is an on-going process, you will want to check in with each other about these issues on a regular basis. Each of these may be problematic at different times and for different reasons each time. Talking them over consistently will make a difference in how disruptive they become to your parenting process. Remember, recognizing that you have problems in certain areas with your co-parent does not mean you cannot parent together. It may simply mean you have some issues to clear up in order to feel good about your parenting process. Don't be discouraged. Parenting, whether it be on your own or with others, is hard work.

## Legal Agreements

For lesbians parenting together, it is imperative that you draw up specific legal agreements to identify and protect the position of the non-biological mother. The relationship of the non-biological mother is not legally recognized; therefore we must take conscious steps to establish whatever legal bonds we can. The non-biological mother risks losing her child if the biological mother dies without a will designating a guardian for her child or if the relationship between the partners ends, and there is no clear plan delineating the continued parenting of the child.

Draw up a legal agreement or contract when you enter into a co-parenting relationship, prior to your child's birth or adoption, or as soon as possible after the child is born or adopted. You can include a clause stating when you will re-evaluate this agreement (after three to five years perhaps). You may also want a section detailing shared parenting privileges were your relationship to end. The non-biological mother should be included in the biological mother's will as the guardian of the child (the person who will be responsible for the child when the biological mother dies). Hopefully you will not need to use these kinds of agreements. Nevertheless, it is in the best interests of your child and yourselves that you make these agreements at the beginning of the process. They will serve your child well in making whatever transition is necessary if your parenting relationships change. Written statements of understanding may help you clarify the important issues, even though they may or may not help in arbitration or in the courts. In spite of this uncertainty, take the time to draw up an agreement. You do not need an attorney to do this. There are sample forms in Appendix E which will give you an idea of what to include. In addition, Donna Hitchens discusses these legal agreements in more detail in the "Legal Issues" chapter.

> **"** We didn't want to make everything legal; it seemed very pes- **"** simistic to both of us — like we were saying outloud we couldn't make it work. I'm glad we did though. We're still together, but we've had rocky moments. And, you know, having this agreement helps me feel secure that if we do split up, what happens to Melissa won't be part of it all.

> **"** We didn't have any agreements and we have managed to make **"** things work. We broke up very amicably. I can't say what it would have been like if we hadn't been able to talk this through together.

Despite the many obstacles and potential difficulties of co-parenting, many lesbians find this is the most fulfilling parenting style for them. Co-parenting takes many forms, there are no rules to follow or molds to fit into. Be creative and keep in mind that you want to nurture your loving for yourself, your partner, and your child(ren) in this process.

# SINGLE PARENTING

For many lesbians, single parenting is the only parenting option they will consider. For others it is definitely not a first choice and, in fact, may be a frightening possibility. You will find that taking time to weigh the pros and cons of this parenting choice will help you locate where *you* fall on this continuum.

This chapter contains the stories, thoughts, feelings, and experiences of many lesbians who are single parents. It will give you a general sense of the kinds of experiences you might have as a single parent and the issues with which single lesbian mothers struggle on a daily basis. As you read through this chapter, check in with yourself now and then, and notice your reactions to the different sections. Imagine how you would feel if you were a single parent in the situations being described and reflect on what about single parenthood appeals to you and what does not.

A single parent is that person who assumes total responsibility for the physical, emotional, psychic, and economic well-being of a child. There are many different ways in which lesbians arrive at single parenthood — some by choice, some by circumstance, others by default — and there are varying degrees of single parenting. Regardless of the family arrangement you have designed for yourself, it will be important to take this parenting option into careful consideration.

    **“** I wanted to be prepared to raise a child on my own, as a single **”** parent. I was open to having another adult involved, but I wasn't going to long for it or worry about not having that. Most important, I wasn't going to *wait* for it.

    **“** My ex-lover and I planned to raise a child together. Then, **”** when Rahima was six months old, Melanie decided she only wanted to help with occasional childcare. I was totally unprepared to be a single parent.

&& It's not that I wanted to be a *single* parent, I simply wanted to && be a parent and I was willing to do it alone.

&& Single parenting was my first choice. For me it was the only && possibility I would consider for a lot of reasons. Basically, I think I would be a better mother as a single parent than if I tried to parent with other people.

&& When it was clear to me that we were going to break up, my && biggest fear was — I won't be able to do this alone. But really, as it turned out, I was better off when Darlene was gone. We were fighting all the time, and that was a drain of the energy I needed to be raising Gregory.

If single parenting would not be your first choice, it is imperative that you recognize the ever-present possibility that at any moment you could be a single parent. Most life situations are out of our control, and anything can happen at any time to upset the most carefully made plans and dreams. As most women with children will tell you, every woman considering parenthood must be prepared to be a single parent.

## The Possibilities Revisited

Before going further, take a few minutes to review what does and does not appeal to you about this parenting option. In a few words, note what about single parenting makes it a good choice for you, and then what does not make it a good choice for you.

### INSTRUCTIONS

Use the following questions and sentences to help you establish a framework for thinking about this choice. You do not have to know all the answers or even be able to articulate what you feel. Keep these questions in mind as you read this chapter, and if you feel like it, come back to them later.

- What do you feel would be difficult for you as a single parent?
- What do you feel would be easy for you as a single parent?
- What elements of your own childhood will be valuable to you if you decide to be a single parent?
- What elements might make it difficult?

114

Complete the following sentences:
- ▶ As a single parent, I . . .
- ▶ As a single parent, I will want . . .
- ▶ As a single parent, I will need . . .
- ▶ My biggest fear about being a single parent is . . .
- ▶ I imagine my greatest joy will be . . .
- ▶ A single parent should be able to . . .
- ▶ I am choosing single parenthood because . . .

The sections that follow address some of the issues unique to single parenting and will give you a sense of the different components of this choice. Just reading about single parenting, however, may not be enough to help you sort through your feelings. Talk with single mothers — lesbian or heterosexual — to gain a richer understanding of their experiences.

## Work, Finances, and Single Parenting

As mentioned in an earlier chapter, work and money are probably the most frequent worries of anyone considering parenthood. For the lesbian who is choosing to be a single parent, however, these worries may be compounded by the reality that she is *the* one person responsible for the financial support of her family. It is difficult to balance the tasks of having a job and making enough money with those of being a single parent. Many single parents have said they were surprisingly unprepared for the kind of financial commitment single parenting demands. Be sure to do the exercises in the "Money" chapter to help you in thinking about where your money will come from and how much you will need. Above all, don't be discouraged. Even if your finances are not in great shape, managing as a single parent *is* possible.

In regard to finances and single parenthood, you will also want to think about:

- ▣ Whether you will live alone or with others.
- ▣ The kind of transportation you can afford — whether you will own a car, ride a bicycle, take the bus, etc.
- ▣ How much money you need to earn to pay for the amount and kind of childcare you will need.
- ▣ The hours you will need to work and the amount of flexibility you can have in a job, in case of child-related emergencies.

**❝** As a single parent, I can't be as flexible as an employer wants **❞** me to be, like a co-worker who doesn't have kids or another mother who has a co-parent. I can't come early or leave late.

115

Everything must be planned, and even then, I can't be sure those plans will ever happen until they are actually happening.

**❝** I became a nurse so that it would make life as a single parent **❞** more manageable, and it does. I work on-call and make arrangements for childcare as needed. When I work the ll p.m. to 7 a.m. shift, I have different friends spend the night at my house with my daughter. It works out great for all of us.

It is important to bear in mind that everything changes as your child gets older and as you get more skilled at juggling the various components of your life. Certainly the task of managing work and money to your satisfaction will depend to a large extent on your financial needs, and on your work skills and opportunities. Many single mothers choose to care for themselves and their children on very limited resources. Keep in mind that when it comes to work and money, it may take you more time to create things the way you want them than you might initially imagine.

**❝** I have a job I like. It's flexible and that's what I need as a single **❞** parent. I am sure I will want something different when Maya gets older.

**❝** I had about $2,000 saved before Joseph came to live with me. **❞** Then I lost my job and had a major health problem. We were on AFDC for almost two years before I got back on my feet.

Many single mothers have found support groups with other single mothers to be extremely helpful, especially discussing issues of work and money. The more suggestions and ideas you can gather for successful ways of managing financially (and in other ways) can make a tremendous difference in your experiences of single parenting.

## Time Commitment

Being a single parent is a time-consuming endeavor. For most, it is essentially a 24-hour-a-day job (even if you work an outside job as well) from which there is rarely any consistent break, especially during the first few years. Most single lesbian mothers agree that you can never be prepared for how much work it will be. This might be a good time to complete the Pie Exercise in the "Timetables and Life Planning" chapter if you haven't already done so.

**❝** As a single mother I never get to take time off. Sure, my friends **❞** help out by taking Joaquin for two or three hours at a time, some even take him overnight now and then. But when you think about it, that's a very short amount of time. I never manage to do anything special — oh, maybe I get a chance to do the laundry or talk on the telephone. Mostly I try to sleep.

**"** I never could have imagined how much time I would be devot- **"** ing to my parenting. Really, being a full-time mom to Jesse is a full-time job. I am on-call 24 hours a day.

Certainly the time commitment of single parenting changes as children get older, and the kind of attention you give your children takes different forms. When children are infants, you expend a good deal of energy attending to their immediate physical needs. When they are toddlers, you may be consumed with thinking about them — what they are doing, if they are are safe, where they are at any given moment. And through the school years and adolescence there is still that frequent thinking about them, this time with a sharper focus on how they are doing with friends, in school, and with the everyday routine of growing up. What is unique for the single parent is that she must manage this all on her own. At times this can feel like an overwhelming responsibility, one which demands your constant and focused attention when you might least expect it.

**"** It's hard to imagine at the time that this is forever. You are a **"** mother forever. I find the longevity of it to be very overwhelming. I am the sole provider for this human being and all her needs.

## My Child as Number One

With amazing consistency, many single lesbian mothers state that no one comes between the single mother and her child. Some explain that their child(ren) come first, before anyone else, sometimes even before themselves. Others say they don't always put their child first, they put *themselves* first, because for them, denying their own needs creates resentment towards their child(ren). As with other issues, there is clearly a spectrum, and you may be at one place along the spectrum at one time, and at another place at another time.

**"** I explain to anyone I get involved with that I am a packaged **"** deal. There will always be three of us, and if we break-up, it's the lover that will leave, not my child.

**"** My priorities have changed dramatically since I became a sin- **"** gle parent. Besides the fact that I just don't have any free time to go to meetings and hang out with friends spontaneously, I

really don't even want to do that anymore. I love the time I
have with Zola.

# Being a Single Parent in the Lesbian Community

The single parent family is just one of the many forms lesbian
families can take. Within the lesbian community, we are learning to
make room for all kinds of family configurations, recognizing each
woman's choices, including those which may differ from what we might
choose for ourselves. Because the attitudes and beliefs prevalent within
our communities help shape our lives and self-images, it is essential that
we recognize and acknowledge the choices lesbian mothers are making.

Within many lesbian communities, as in the heterosexual culture
at large, there are often both subtle and not so subtle pressures to be part
of a couple. In addition, there is the usually unconscious expectation that
a lesbian family should be made up of two, or even three, parents. These
attitudes convey judgments about the way a lesbian family "ought" to be.

> **❝** I am a single parent. I mean, I identify as a single parent even **❞**
> though my lover and I live together. You see, she has not made
> a commitment to Kim, so I don't count on her for anything.
> A lot of people think we are a family, and treat me as if I can
> get support when I need it. Sometimes I wish people wouldn't
> always go by how things appear.

This couple mentality lends itself to the expectation that lesbians
will recreate nuclear families and leaves little room for support of single
parent families by other lesbians. This subtle bias is conveyed in many
ways — assuming the single lesbian mother is a straight woman, telling
the single lesbian mother it is not the responsibility of other lesbians to
assist in the care of a child she chooses to have, or assuming that if a lesbian is choosing to be a parent, she must be doing it with her partner,
because no one would choose to do this alone. Because of these frequently unexplored attitudes, it is often difficult for single lesbian
mothers to find the support and recognition they deserve. Although this
is not true for all mothers in all communities, it is true often enough that
we must recognize the impact it may have on single lesbians choosing to
be parents and on the children of these lesbians.

> **❝** I don't think people mean to be hurtful, but when they imply **❞**
> that it is my fault I have this child on my own and I should be
> able to manage without their having to go out of their way, I
> feel angry. If I had a partner, their attitudes would probably be
> the same, but my partner and I would have each other to figure
> out what to do.

118

**"** In the world it is hard to be a lesbian, a mother, and single. **"** When you are a single lesbian mother you realize how much you need the support of the lesbian community.

Most lesbians who are single parents find that many people — both gay and straight — assume they are heterosexual. This phenomenon of "passing" tests one's level of internalized homophobia and has some single lesbian mothers ambivalent about whether to come out as a lesbian parent or let people think what they choose.

**"** If there are two women parenting together, I think most peo- **"** ple around here figure they are lesbians. But when there is just one mother, everyone thinks she is straight. Even other lesbians think I am straight. I don't want to wear a sign that says 'I'm one too.'

**"** When I enter a new situation, I consciously decide if I am **"** going to explain that I am a *lesbian* parent. People usually think I am divorced or got pregnant and had a kid on my own. I like having the choice. I do 'pass' when I think I need to be guarded about my sexuality.

**"** I'm right out there that I am a dyke. I am not interested in hid- **"** ing behind heterosexual priviledge. I think it is too confusing for my daughter. There are times, especially at work, when I am more low-key. But for the most part, I don't let the assumption that I am straight go by without clearing up the mistake.

In the heterosexual world most people expect you to have two parents — one male and one female. In the lesbian community, many think children have two parents as well, only this time, they are two women. Typical explanations are that two moms are just as good as a mom and a dad, or that what makes lesbian families "special" is that a child of lesbian parents has two moms instead of one. This doesn't leave much room for the child(ren) with a single lesbian parent to feel good about her/his family. In fact, to most single lesbian mothers, these explanations are oppressive. Our children need to know that their families are "special" no matter how many moms a child has. We need to learn that our children can get the kind of love, support, nurturing, and tenderness they need from us, whether we are parenting alone or with others.

## *Your Support Network and What You Can Expect*

Building a support network of family and friends can be crucial in making single parenthood a manageable life. You will want to find people who can make a commitment to you and your child, and who are willing to be there for you when they least expect to be asked. You may find you need to be flexible in your expectations of others – people's lives change, their commitments change, they move away. Have plenty of back-up plans because you may find that the offers you get may never match what you really want.

As a single parent, you have the opportunity to build a support network that works best for you and your child. This will probably take at least a year or two to create initially, and will inevitably change as your child gets older and your needs for support change. These unpredictable fluctuations can be frustrating for all parents. For the single lesbian parent this is especially troublesome, because when her network is not in operation, she is the only one who is available to care for her child. No matter what your situation, this can be a strain.

> **“** After three nights of hearing my daughter cry the whole night **”** I wanted to put her in the car, just get her out of the house. I was afraid of how I felt. I took her over to my best friend's house at one in the morning and shoved her into Harriet's arms. I said, 'Here, you take her tonight, I need to sleep.' She was great, she took her, didn't ask any questions, she was just there. I'll never forget that.

> **“** Things change with friends. Their work hours may fluctuate; **”** they get involved in other activities. For one reason or another, they can't follow through on their commitment to you and your child. I find that having such intense childcare needs puts a big strain on my friendships.

> **“** Maybe if I had been more conscientious in developing a sup- **”** port network I wouldn't be so overwhelmed now. If I had incorporated more friends from the beginning it might be different. I don't like my friends any less if they can't help me out. I do understand. It's just exhausting to have to ask people to help me out all the time.

> **“** My family is my support network. I call on my friends once **”** in a while, but most of them just don't have the kind of commitment to my child that makes them choose to help. One day I called around for help and one friend explained she couldn't take Sam because she had to do the laundry. I thought, I do the laundry with the baby on my hip all the time.

Many single parents find that their family or friends genuinely want to be actively involved in their children's lives, but not all of them follow through. This is one of the most difficult realities about single parenting. Some single mothers feel so strongly about this that they will tell you that you can't count on *anything*.

**&&** I do childcare exchanges with other single mothers. So, for **&&**
every night of childcare that someone gives me, I end up having to take another child in return. It's hard because I feel that
I don't have that much time alone with Corrinne as it is.

**&&** We have pulled together this parent group of lesbian and **&&**
straight women and even one straight couple. We each have
two nights a month when the kids can stay at our house, we
rotate. Some nights I have four kids and sometimes only one.
It works for everyone, but it took five months to get it all together.

**&&** I am actually happy with how things have worked out for me. **&&**
I have two friends who are committed to spending time with
Zena each month. That feels good for now. I might need more
or less in the future.

For the single parent, perhaps the most exhausting aspect of
building a support network has to do with what many describe as
"hustling" — constantly having to make arrangements for childcare and
soliciting help from others. It can be extremely exhausting to be asking
others to help you out on a regular basis. Some single mothers find they
get to a point where they simply stop asking, hoping their friends will
offer when they want to spend time with their children. And others
directly tell their friends what they need and when, so that friends will
say either "yes" or "no."

## Getting the Support You Need

In the "Friends and Support Networks" chapter, you will find an
exercise which helps you explore what you want, need, and expect to get.
I encourage you to do this exercise as you begin to build your support
network. In addition, you may want to do the exercise below, which will
give you some practice in asking for what you need.

INSTRUCTIONS

1. Make a list of things that you would like but don't ask for
   because you assume you wouldn't get them (from
   friends, lovers, children, employers, family members,
   etc.).
2. What are some of your reasons for not asking for what
   you want and need (can't ask unless I'm desperate, won't
   ask unless I'm sure I'll get it, what I want is silly, inap-
   propriate, etc.)?

121

3. Select something you would like to ask for from your friends. This can be something small for starters, asking them to invite you for a meal once a week, or help you out with a house or garden task. Then you can slowly build up to bigger requests like lending you money to buy something you've been wanting or taking care of your cats so you can go away for the weekend. Choose two or three friends and practice.

4. Notice how it feels to ask for what you want and/or need. What happens when you don't get it? What happens when you do get it?

5. This may help you make a list of "hints for getting what I want" that you can refer to later while parenting and when your network is or is not working the way you might like it to be.

## Decisions – Doing It On Your Own

Most single parents are struck by the paradox of their sole decision-making power – it is one of the things they like best about being a single parent, and at the same time one of the things they like the least.

As any parent will tell you, numerous large and small decisions are made many times everyday concerning a child – what s/he should wear to school, what s/he should eat, if s/he can eat sugar, how to handle a discipline situation, what to say when a child asks a particularly difficult question, and on and on. The single parent usually makes these decisions on her own. Some women find this to be "just the way they wanted it"; others find it overwhelming and immobilizing. And, of course, most fall somewhere in between, depending upon the decision to be made, the time of the day, the day of the week, and all the other influences on one's decision-making capabilities.

**❝** It is definitely a big responsiblity being the only parent and **❞** making most of the decisions alone. It is difficult at times, but it certainly seems easier than having to work out each decision with someone else. I do whatever it is I want to do, whatever I think is best.

**❝** I usually talk things over with a few friends who are also par- **❞** ents. I listen to what they have to say and then make up my own mind. I don't ever have to do what someone else thinks I ought to do. I am not worried about offending someone else's values.

**❝** It continues to be important to me that I do not have to **❞** struggle with someone about the major decisions in my child's life, things like education, health care, and religion. My parents fought about those things all my life. I just didn't want my child to be faced with that kind of constant conflict.

This may be a good time to recall what you learned about your decision-making style in the chapter "Getting Acquainted With Whats to Come." Remember, making decisions you feel good about takes practice. Review those early decision-making exercises to help you focus on your particular style and what works best for you.


# The Single Lesbian Parent and Her Lover(s)

You might be wondering, "How will I fit a lover into this life of single parenting?" For many lesbians, this is a surprisingly complex and difficult question to answer. To help you in thinking about single parenting and relationships (to whatever degree that is possible at this point), I have compiled a list of questions to think about and to discuss with others — mothers and non-mothers, lovers and friends, lesbians and straight women. Get as much input as you can. Different perspectives on these questions can be quite helpful in expanding your impressions of what is possible.

This may be another situation in which you will be unable to predict how you will feel until you actually have a child in your life. Nonetheless, do the best you can to identify how you are feeling about this issue right now.

1. Are you hoping you will find another adult who will be your lover *and* a parent to your child?

    If so, what qualities will this person have to possess in order to be the "right" person?

    If not, how will you make your expectations and limitations clear to women with whom you become involved?

2. Do you expect your lover(s) to share in parenting your child?

    If so, how much responsibility do you want her to take? What do you imagine she would do in contrast to what you do?

If not, what problems do you anticipate as a result of being a single parent with a lover who does not share in the parenting?

3. How will you explain to your child the relationship s/he has to your lover? How will your child explain the relationship to others?

4. Do you feel you have to "protect" your child from other adults abandoning her/him if an intimate relationship ends?

If so, how do you think you want to handle that kind of situation?

5. How will you decide who comes first in any given situation, your child or your lover?

6. How will you handle a situation in which you and your lover disagree about discipline, or other potentially charged issues?

Whether you choose to have an intimate relationship at any given time during your parenting years will depend upon many factors — how available you feel to being intimately involved with someone else besides your child, how much time you have, your child's age, what needs are being met in other places, how open you feel to sharing your life and child with someone else, and so on.

Single mothers choose to have lover relationships for many different reasons — some because they simply want a lover, some because they hope to find another woman who wants to share in the parenting of her child, and others because they want a companion with whom to share their time but not necessarily their parenting responsibilities. Still others find that even though they miss the emotional, physical, and sexual intimacy of another adult, they are not yet "ready" to be in a relationship.

> 66 I haven't had a relationship since just after Lindy was born, 99 more from choice, oh, and maybe because I just don't have much energy right now. It's been three years and I am just now feeling like I'd like to meet someone. I got pretty isolated just being with my child, but I haven't fought it, so I guess it's probably what I needed.

> 66 The truth is there is not a lot of time for romantic walks in the 99 moonlight, but we manage to find time together. It's different than if I didn't have a child. Our time together is focused around chores — cooking dinner, doing the laundry, picking up around the house.

As mentioned earlier, most single mothers want to make it perfectly clear to a lover (or friends) that her child will come first if she is put in a position in which she has to choose one over the other. Sometimes this is not a problem, and at other times it creates a great deal of conflict. It is important to be clear about your limits, expectations, and loyalties right from the start. Many single mothers have said this kind of good communication has helped to make their intimate relationships easier.

Single mothers seeking to get involved in intimate relationships are not always looking for other women to parent their children. In fact, some can't imagine how anyone else could be parents to their children. Many single mothers are comfortable being the only parent and feel that having another parenting partner would not work for them. Still others feel their children only know the single parent model and might not be as secure in a two-parent arrangement. Even if a lover takes on parental responsibilities or tasks, it does not necessarily mean she will have the label of "parent." These are the kinds of issues that will require good communication, frequent attention, and careful handling as single mothers create intimate relationships with lovers.

    **❝** Privacy is our biggest problem. With a six-year-old you can't **❞** assume they will leave you alone. Somehow they just 'know' when you want privacy and find all kinds of reasons to demand attention. I have had to be very clear with my child about my limits, my needs for private time, and my rules about when we have time together and when we don't. When it's our time, I am there 100%. That way, my child knows there will be time with just me alone.

    **❝** I met a woman who wanted to be a co-parent. Even though **❞** that hadn't been something I was looking for it's been really great. We've been together just over two years now, I met Frances when Benjy was three. She considers herself a parent to Benjy, but we are clear that I am the primary person and she does what she wants because she wants to, not for me.

There are many struggles for the lesbian choosing single parenting, just as there are with any of the parenting choices. When you choose a particular family form, you are essentially choosing your struggles concerning work, change, and growth. Single parenting is not an impossible task. In fact, most women are being single parents all the time, whatever their parenting arrangement. What may seem difficult about single parenting to some women may be exactly what makes it an enormously positive choice for others. And, the paradox of single parenting seems to be that all the elements that make it sound difficult and frightening are the very same ones that make it seem appealing and rewarding.

    **❝** I don't regret single parenting. Even if I had known how hard **❞** it would be, I would still do it. I love being a mother.

**"** For me it is easier being a single parent. I don't know that I **"** could be constantly working things out with someone else. It just wasn't what appealed to me about being a mom. I wanted to be totally focused on a kid, and believe me, as a single parent, I am!

**"** I never knew it would be this great, and I never knew it would **"** be this hard. I had no idea I would feel crazy one minute and sane the next! I compromise myself more than I thought I would. I never imagined I would let my daughter watch cartoons so I could get things done around the house. I don't feel great about that, but I've stopped worrying about it. All in all, the whole experience has really changed my life.

# FOR DISABLED LESBIANS
# CONSIDERING PARENTHOOD

For the disabled lesbian, there are often a number of additional concerns which may require further exploration in the process of considering parenthood. There are some differences in the issues to be considered — the most obvious being that the choice of parenthood may be complicated by the reality of a particular disability. In this section you will find some of these issues and differences identified. Certainly for each disabled lesbian the questions or concerns will be slightly different depending upon her disability and the extent to which that disability affects any aspect of her functioning. This subject, like many others in this book, undoubtedly demands a book of its own. In these few pages, I have tried to include information which will be useful as a starting point for disabled lesbians considering parenthood. I hope the general information and personal stories included here will guide your thinking in the areas which are most relevant for your life and life choices. Also, check the bibliography for other books which may be useful to you.

"Disability" refers to all physical and developmental disabilities. I have a very broad view of the range of disabilities. Some lesbians may be visually and/or hearing impaired, physically different or physically limited by their disability, or developmentally disabled. Others may have hidden disabilities such as Crones Disease, diabetes, chronic pain, colitis, or environmental illness. Disability can take many forms, some more severe and limiting than others. A disability may be *any* condition which limits you, your movement, and your options.

    **❝** None of us are considered very sexual, so the idea of our hav- **❞**
    ing children seems totally absurd to most people.

    **❝** I am constantly having to deal with this message from the **❞**
    whole world that I couldn't possibly be a good parent because

of my disabilities. It's funny, no one seems to be worried that I am a lesbian; they are completely fixated on my being disabled.

From very early on, most disabled women have probably been bombarded with negative messages about themselves as sexual beings and potential parents. It is not unusual for a disabled woman, regardless of her disability, to be told that she will be unable to bear a child, and that if she were to have a child, she would not be able to parent that child competently because of the limitations of her disability. Much could be written about the abuse disabled women everywhere have had to endure regarding their reproductive choices. Many have been sterilized without their consent; others have been told horror stories — often untrue — of what would happen to them were they to become pregnant, and others have simply been told that due to their disability, they will not be capable of bearing children.

**❝** You know, I was always told I couldn't be a good mother **❞** because of my disability. In fact, one doctor told me it would be cruel to have a child because I might die young! Well, I'm 37 now and I am the mother of a four year old. It has taken me many years to realize all those stories were untrue. Sure, being a parent is hard work, but I don't think it is any harder for me than for any other woman.

Simply because you are disabled does not mean you cannot become a parent or be a competent parent. As one disabled lesbian mother explained, "There are lots of different ways to parent, many adaptive things a woman can do. Just because a lesbian is disabled doesn't mean she can't be a parent, too. Able-bodied women don't have a corner on the market of being qualified for parenthood. We should not let our disabilities get in the way of seeing this as an option in our lives, too."

## Disability and Parenting

Below you will find a series of questions and issues which have been suggested by other disabled lesbian mothers. These are things you may want to think about while considering parenthood. Be sure to jot down other thoughts that come to mind as you read along. You do not have to have all the answers to these questions. In fact, you may not be able to answer many of them on your own, and you may want to get help from other disabled women or supportive health care practitioners. Some of your questions may go unanswered. Part of making the decision to parent demands a philosophical "leap of faith" — which means you may have to decide if you will go ahead with parenthood even if all your concerns cannot be adequately addressed and answered.

- ▶ Will pregnancy make my disability worse? If so, in what ways? How do I feel about the possibility of my disability changing and getting worse?
- ▶ If I become pregnant and bear a child, will I pass my disability on? Is there an inherited genetic risk of my disability? What *are* the chances I will pass on my disability to my child?
- ▶ Will I be able to become pregnant given my particular disability?
- ▶ Can I adopt a child? What will I have to do to convince a social service agency that I can be a competent parent in spite of my disability? Do I want to adopt a disabled or non-disabled child?
- ▶ Will I be able to manage on my own as a parent? Do I need to consider parenting with others? How much outside involvement will I want/need to have?
- ▶ What kind of support network do I have now? How committed and reliable are the people whom I will depend upon once I have a child?
- ▶ If I parent with another person, how will we divide the parenting responsibilities? Will I be given enough room to do the things I can? How will we balance our different skills and still parent effectively together?
- ▶ How will my disability affect my mobility as a parent of an infant, a toddler, a preschool child, a school age child, and a teenager?
- ▶ How can I prepare myself to deal with my child's feelings about my disability? What are my fears concerning this?
- ▶ What will I do if my disability gets worse and I become unable to care for my child?
- ▶ How much time can I take off from work in the event that my disability requires me to spend time in bed before the birth or if I need an extended period of time for post-partum recovery?
- ▶ Will I need a Caesarian section, or can I deliver my baby vaginally? How much medical intervention will I need during the birth of my child?

All the disabled lesbian mothers I spoke with stressed the importance of seeing a geneticist prior to becoming pregnant. Each one felt it was an important step in the process of considering parenthood, even though it may mean confronting some issues of denial. Unfortunately, genetic counseling can sometimes be unsatisfying because you may not get enough information to enable you to make an informed decision.

You might be given an estimated percentage of your chance of having a disabled child. However, for some disabled women, genetic counseling can prove to be very useful. A good deal depends on your disability, your knowledge of it, and your feelings about passing on that disability to your child.

> **❝** I talked with at least three doctors about my disability before **❞** trying to get pregnant. They all told me my disability was not hereditary. Then, *after* I was pregnant, I went to a geneticist who told me that my condition *is* hereditary.

> **❝** Going to a genetic counselor was frightening for me. I thought **❞** for sure she would discourage me from getting pregnant just because I am disabled. But the worst part was that by going to see her I was admitting to someone that I think there is a hereditary component to my disability. I never really allowed myself to think about that before.

Many disabled mothers talked about the assumption that disabled women want to *birth* disabled children. For some that may be true, but it is not necessarily true for *all* disabled women. In fact, most disabled women, like able-bodied women, want able-bodied children. As one disabled lesbian mother explained it to me, "Perhaps people think that we are better equipped to deal with a disabled child and have better skills in dealing with disability. That may be true, but it doesn't mean we want to create a disabled child. What does seem to be true, however, at least for the disabled women I know, is that we have less denial around whether our child will be disabled; somehow the experience and reality of it are not as foreign or frightening to us."

If you are a disabled woman who is considering adoption, however, you *might* want to adopt a disabled child. You may feel that you could provide a supportive environment for that child. For the disabled woman, choosing to adopt a child with a disability is different than wishing to birth a disabled child.

> **❝** I had to ask myself if I wanted a disabled child. It took a lot of **❞** soul-searching. I felt guilty at first when I realized I didn't want my kid to be disabled.

> **❝** My family keeps asking me what right I think I have to bring **❞** a child into the world. Can you imagine? And then they go on to say, 'What if it is born with a disability, what would you do then?' I am shocked by their insensitivity.

If you have an interest in being a parent, take time to explore the possibilities available to you. If you are planning to become pregnant, find a sympathetic practitioner with whom to discuss your concerns.

What you may have been told about your disability and how it affects your reproductive abilities may not be true.

Unfortunately, as you may already know, finding a practitioner who is supportive may not be an easy task. Use whatever networks and resources are available to you in your community to find a practitioner with whom you can feel comfortable. This should be someone who will continue to encourage you to keep trying to get pregnant, even if you are having trouble becoming pregnant. It should be someone who will treat you with respect and as an adult, and someone who will answer your questions about pregnancy and childbirth as they relate to your disability.

Some disabled women prefer to continue seeing their regular physician with whom they have an on-going relationship, in order to avoid telling their medical history to someone new. Others may prefer to work with a new practitioner. Whatever you decide, be sure your practitioner is working *for* you and *with* you in your efforts to become pregnant. Many disabled women find they have to educate their practitioners about disability and pregnancy. If that is the case, be sure your practitioner is willing to learn from you and will not be intimidated by the knowledge you have about yourself.

> **“** Pregnancy was more difficult for me than I had initially antici- **”** pated. I had severe back, hip, and leg problems from early on. That endless discomfort was a big surprise and made the experience of being pregnant hard in a lot of ways.

Because pregnancy may be more physically limiting than one might first imagine, you may find you need a great deal of help immediately before and after the birth. Having a fully developed, reliable, and committed support network, prior to giving birth or adopting a child, will be important. You may want to do the exercises in the “Friends and Support Networks” chapter. This will help you get some idea of what kind of support you want and what you think you will need. If you give birth, it may take you more time than you expect to recuperate. This will be especially true for disabled women who have Caesarian delivery.

> **“** I don’t have the greatest back in the world, and then with the **”** C-section on top of that, I could barely carry Yashuki from one room to the next during those first two weeks. I needed a lot of help. I can’t imagine how I would have done my own shopping, laundry, or cooking. Also, I needed lots of rest just to recuperate from the C-section.

> **“** I was lucky to have my family close by when I had my baby. **”** They have been very supportive and were an enormous help when my child was first born. I needed 24-hour a day help

those first few weeks. I think my friends would have pulled through to help me out, but with my family I had no doubts.

If you are planning a pregnancy, chances are you may be faced with the possibility of more medical intervention than you anticipated — more tests, frequent visits to your practitioner, the possibility of a Caesarian section. Think about the kind of medical intervention that may be necessary. Read anything you can find that will tell you what you might need and the implications of that measure. Talk with other disabled women who have been pregnant and have given birth. You will learn a lot from their experiences. Be sure that your practitioner and the people in your support network know and understand what you want and do not want, well before the time of the birth. This may help you to avoid complications and problems at an already stressful time.

Some disabled women, with certain physical disabilities, assume a Caesarian section is necessary and is the only birthing choice available to them. It is possible that having a Caesarian section *is* the right choice for you given your particular disability. Be sure to discuss this thoroughly with your health care practitioner. Accepting that a Caesarian section may be the best option for you is not always easy for everyone. Again, I encourage you to talk with other disabled women for support and additional information.

Disabled lesbians seeking to adopt may be frustrated by the negative and often condescending attitudes of agency personnel. Their assumptions abound: you couldn't possibly manage with a child; you probably *only* want a child who is disabled like you; you want a child who will take care of you. Those disabled lesbians who have adopted children say the road is long and often rough, but not impossible. You will find yourself in a position in which you are scrutinized, analyzed, and essentially viewed as an object — "the disabled woman" — not necessarily as a whole and multi-dimensional person. Find yourself an advocate. This might be a friend or someone within the adoption agency. This person should be someone who will attest to your skills and competency and who will support you through the process of finding a child for adoption. If you want to adopt a child, don't give up. Your disability does not have to be a barrier. Often, disabled women considering parenthood wonder about how their disabilities will affect their children and how their children will feel about their disabilities. Many are concerned because of the general public's attitudes and assumptions about disabilities and disabled women with children. Other people often think it will be a difficult adjustment for a child to have a disabled mother. Children of disabled mothers, however, don't really have to *adjust* to their mother's disability, because they are raised with it and this is what they know. But they may find it difficult to deal with people always asking them to explain "What happened to your mom?" or "What's 'wrong' with your mother?" In addition, it is not unusual for the child of a disabled woman

132

to be approached by others concerning her/his mother's wants and needs. Often, people simply assume that the disabled woman has a child so that there is someone to care for her. Behaviors and attitudes such as these are troublesome. They contribute to the oppression of disabled women.

**“** People think I brought this child into the world to take care of **”** me. Many have *actually* asked me if I had a child so that there would be someone to take care of me when I got older.

**“** If we are in a store or a restaurant, my son gets asked by others **”** what I want; he is spoken to instead of me. It is a very interesting role reversal.

**“** Many people think we want to have babies to prove we are **”** women or some nonsense like that. Well, certainly for some that may be the case. But frankly, the disabled women I know who are mothers didn't make this decision lightly. We understand the difficulties our children may face, but the potential joys of parenting far outweigh the fears.

Finally, I want to end this section with excerpts from stories that disabled lesbian mothers shared with me as I was writing this portion of the book. These brief quotations begin to give a broader dimension to the richness of this experience and the many aspects which are unique to the lesbian who is also a disabled woman.

**“** Since I have had a baby, a lot of internal stuff has come up for **”** me about my disability. More people ask about my disability now. As a woman with a child I am suddenly more visible in the world. Other parents are interested in me. At first it's almost as if they want to grab their kids away because they see I am a crip, but then they see I have a baby. I can literally see them trying to figure it all out in their heads.

**“** We put our child in a community childcare center not far from **”** our home. My lover picks him up a few days a week, and I get him the other days. We go to parent meetings together. At the first few meetings, the other parents assumed he was Jennifer's son. It took some explaining to help everyone understand. After the other parents got used to me, then they wanted to tell me everything that went through their minds about me before and the process they went through to get used to me.

**“** Being a mother I am forced to confront my disability more **”** than I had before. Frankly, I am forced to deal more directly with people's curiosity about my disability because as a parent I have become alarmingly more visible in the world. I find myself in a lot more situations with other children who want to know what is 'wrong' with me.

# CHOOSING NOT TO PARENT

Although lesbians are now realizing they *can* become parents, this does not mean you have to choose parenthood. There is no implicit imperative that lesbians must have children.

Perhaps you have done all the exercises in this book, reviewed all the alternatives, and carefully thought through your considerations. You may have talked with friends about your thoughts, feelings, and decisions and considered this choice for what feels like a long time. And after all this, you chose not to be a parent. Or, perhaps you just picked up this book and turned to this chapter, because you have already decided not to parent. Or, you think this is where you want to start in your considering parenthood process. You may want to explore the possibilities available if you chose not to parent before you seriously consider *parenthood* as an option.

Considering parenthood means giving yourself room to make a choice. As you may have experienced throughout this book, there is not just one choice — whether or not to parent — but a multitude of choices to be made on a variety of issues, many of them ambiguous. Thinking about not parenting is yet another aspect of this option. For some lesbians, it is the last choice they consider; for others, it is what they want to think about first. And there are others for whom this option is on their minds all the time.

This chapter explores the challenging questions raised by choosing not to parent. I will talk about the often difficult and painful feelings that come up for some women making this decision. And I will discuss what some women in my groups have identified as the positive and negative aspects of choosing not to have children. Finally, there is an exercise to help you imagine and design how, if you wish, you can include children in your life in other ways.

135

Many feelings come up when considering choosing not to parent, but primary among them are feelings of loss, relief, and fear. The sense of loss — of missing out on the experience of having a child and the things associated with having children in your life — may have to do with the intense indoctrination most of us received while growing up that told us that women must have children. Even if you are choosing not to have a child, the subtle longing instilled by our socialization may remain. The loss may also be a physical one — of missing the experience of physically having a child and experiencing the growth, birth, and bonding involved in that process.

There may be times when it is difficult to accept that you are choosing not to have children. You may wonder if you made (or are making) the right decision, even though you know that it is the right decision for you now. You may even wish for a child at different times throughout your life, knowing full well you really don't want to be responsible for raising one. This is all perfectly common. There is a tremendous amount of ambivalence associated with this part of the decision, just as there is ambivalence associated with deciding to parent. You may always have questions about your choice — healthy questions which are simply a part of life and of all the choices we make.

There is often a feeling of relief in deciding not to parent — relief at having gone through the process of considering and then coming to a decision which feels right, even though it may not be the one you thought you would make.

Choosing not to parent is not necessarily a rejection of motherhood or of others who choose to be mothers. It is a choice you make about your life, for yourself. It does not have to be a reflection of your politics or your support of lesbians who are choosing to have children. It is a decision, however, that you will want to be able to live with for a long time.

There may come a time in your life when you want to rethink this decision or even change your mind. Depending upon a variety of factors (your age, lifestyle, financial resources, etc.), you may still be able to reconsider your decision at another time. You may be choosing not to parent at this particular time for very specific reasons related to where you are in your life and what you are doing now. Any and all of this could change and you could once again want to reconsider parenthood.

&& I have a few children in my life already. I did think about having or adopting one of my own, but I realized that I can be as involved as I want with the children I know now, so it's not necessary for me to have my *own* child. &&

&& I realized I don't want to be a parent. It took me a while to get to this, but it feels right. I feel sad right now, and maybe I'll change my mind, but I doubt it. &&

136

**❝** I have never wanted to be a mother – it's simply not been a **❞** question in my life. I might have children in my life and I might not. Somehow it's not just an issue for me.

For many years after parenting Bridgette and experiencing my own limitations as a parent, I was certain I did not want to parent another child. There came a time, however, when I once again started thinking I wanted to have a baby. I experienced a death close to me and I felt the desire to bring another life into the world. I spent a number of weeks living with the idea that I was going to get pregnant. I thought about how I would tell my family, talked about it to friends, and concretely visualized what it might be like for me to have a child. I imagined how my life would change, itemized the things I still wanted for myself, and discussed these plans with close friends. Through this process, I remembered why I had originally chosen not to parent; going through the process again reaffirmed my reasons for choosing not to parent. What does it mean to you to choose not to be a parent? What does it say to you about yourself? How does it fit with your self-image? All too often, lesbians making the decision not to be parents are hard on themselves. I frequently hear, "I am too selfish to be a parent," or "I am too independent; a child would never fit into my life." These statements are made as if there is something wrong with taking care of yourself, recognizing your own limitations and a lifestyle with which you are comfortable. For so long, most lesbians didn't know they could be mothers. Now that we realize that it is possible for lesbians to have children, choosing not to parent is more emotionally and politically charged. You may be challenged about your reasons; you may feel isolated and separate from those lesbians having children; you may feel your friendship circle will change as your close friends become mothers and/or become friends with other lesbians who are mothers.

Another fear that arises comes with knowing what you are *not* choosing, while not yet having a clear idea of what you *are* choosing. When you decide not to be a parent, you make room for other choices to come into your life. This may seem simplistic to you, but when you have put so much time and energy into thinking about something, it takes time to redirect your thoughts and energies into other avenues you will pursue. This may be a good time to do (or repeat) the Lifeline Exercise.

It is interesting that lesbians who choose not to be mothers are rarely, if ever, subjected to the kind of social pressure their heterosexual counterparts experience when making the same decision. So often, it is simply assumed that lesbians don't like kids and therefore don't want to be parents. There is certainly a continuum of the degree to which lesbians want and seek to have children in their lives.

**❝** The women at my job are always talking about their biologi- **❞** cal clocks running out. Since they all know I am a lesbian, they assume I'm not worried about this. What they don't realize is that I had to think long and hard about this decision.

**❝** Everyone always said I would make a wonderful mother. **❞** Frankly, I never wanted to have children. I like them and like having them as friends. I don't need to be a mother.

Choosing not to parent does not necessarily mean you don't want or can't have children in your life. In fact, many lesbians who choose not to parent do so knowing they can be actively involved in the lives of children of friends, without the attendant responsibilities associated with parenting. Being a friend to a child, spending time with a child on a regular basis, or simply being involved in a child's life without any formal set-up are only a few of the ways lesbians have found for having children in their lives.

## *Having Children in My Life*

The following exercise asks you to formulate your thoughts on how you want to have children in your life and how you will go about achieving that if you do want to be involved with children in some way. If that is not true for you, skip this exercise.

1. Describe the way(s) you want to have children in your life. Include how you see yourself relating to children — how often you will see them, what kinds of activities you will do together, for how long at a time, etc.
2. How would you hope to bring a child into your life?
3. How would you describe the role you want to play in a child's life?
4. What kind of role would you like children to play in your life?
5. What appeals to you most about this particular choice you've described for yourself?
6. What appeals to you least about this choice?
7. If you know another person who has chosen this option for having children in her life, talk with her about what she likes and does not like about it. Understand what is difficult for her. Does she think about having a child of her own? What does she see as the limitations and drawbacks, as well as the joys and challenges?

**❝** I take care of Benjy every Tuesday. I've been doing it for years. **❞** I pick him up from school, he stays over at my house and then

138

I take him to school on Wednesday. It's just a part of my week — I wouldn't give it up for anything.

**&#x201C;** My time with Caitlin is very precious to me. We hang out, sing **&#x201D;** songs, color, go to the beach — any number of things. Sometimes we just go out for an ice cream cone. Being with her is a very special part of my life.

People may ask you why you decided *not* to parent, just as they will ask another lesbian why she decided *to* parent. I strongly urge you to write down your reasons. Look back at the earlier section in this book where you listed your reasons for having and not having children. As with that exercise, writing down your reasons is not so much to answer others who ask, but to remind yourself how you arrived at this decision and choice.

Over the years, women choosing not to parent have identified specific positive and negative aspects of this choice. I have listed a few of these below. Add any others that are relevant for you. Looking at these aspects, one becomes aware of the assumptions and expectations we all have of what it means to have children in our lives and how having children changes one's life.

## PRO'S OF CHOOSING NOT TO PARENT

- More freedom and flexibility in time, lifestyle, activities.
- Not tied down to child and family unit.
- More time to develop relationship with self, friends, lover(s).
- More time to pursue interests, develop new skills, explore new parts of self.
- Increased mobility for travel, work, etc.
- Financial responsibity for self only.
- Children in your life by choice when you want them.
- A commitment to children without feeling responsible for them.
- More time and energy for political activism.

## CON'S TO CHOOSING NOT TO PARENT

- Lack of a cohesive family in traditional sense (one that includes children).
- Loss of the intimate connection of bearing a child and being a parent.
- Missing out on the birthing experience.
- Having no one to take care of you when you are older.

- ▣ Missing out on the experience of having children intimately in your life.
- ▣ Missing out on parenting experience and the way that can affect your life.
- ▣ Not having intimate relationships with people who are at different points in the life cycle than you are.
- ▣ Lacking the dimension that children bring to life.
- ▣ Necessary to seek out others with whom to create family.
- ▣ Missing the challenge of living out your ideals and values in raising a child and learning the meaning of compromise.

I want to address one issue that comes up repeatedly in my work with lesbian couples considering parenthood. It sometimes happens that one woman decides she wants to be a parent and her lover chooses not to parent. There is no one way to handle this often perplexing and difficult situation. Working it out can take a good deal of time and energy. Imagining, discussing, and then negotiating all the possible alternatives is a good place to start. While many couples separate over this issue, it is not inevitable if both women feel committed to the relationship and to finding a middle ground on which to work out their different decisions.

> **❝** I didn't know if it would work for us. We had been together **❞** three years and Jane didn't want me to have a baby. But I was firm about my choice. She has come around; she helps out but doesn't see herself as a parent. I'm glad I made my choice, I know I would have resented her horribly if she had fought my decision.

> **❝** Noelle wanted to be a mother since she was a kid. She told me **❞** that the first week we knew each other. I have two nephews and didn't want a child of my own. We have gone back and forth about it a lot. Since we haven't been able to figure out how we would keep our relationship together if she had a kid we have decided to wait a little longer.

The first step is for each woman in the couple to define what she wants from the relationship. This way, each woman can honestly assess if this is the best relationship for her at this time in her life. Pay attention to the fact that this kind of disagreement is a warning that there are things to be worked out individually and together before choosing either option. This might be a good time to do the first exercise in the "Building and Maintaining Intimacy" chapter.

In discussing various alternatives, you may strike upon one that works for both of you. You will still have to continue negotiating in order to avoid the resentment that can come with compromise if both people are not honest and clear with one another. There is no getting around this dilemma. It is probably one of the most difficult situations you will find yourselves faced with in the consideration process. Some couples have made it in spite of this disagreement; others have not. The struggle is difficult and the end results unpredictable.

> **"** Janet gave me a lot of room to be a mother even though she **"** didn't want a child. She was clear from the start, she supports my choice, but is not thrilled when I spend hours focused on Matthew. We work hard at communicating our discontent. Seeing a counselor has helped us make things work.

> **"** What can I say? It couldn't work. I didn't want a kid and she **"** did. We have stayed good friends, and that helps. It was hard to give up that relationship, but I knew if we both tried to compromise without really wanting to change, things would go bad eventually. This way we still have a good friendship.

Often, the reasons lesbians choose *not* to parent get misinterpreted as meaning, "I am not going to be a mother because I don't want to be oppressed like you," when that is not the meaning intended at all. We live in a time in which motherhood is "respected" and "expected," but not sufficiently supported. It is not necessary that all women choose to raise children. What is needed, especially within the lesbian community, is that each woman feel supported for the choice she makes. For lesbian mothers, that may be support from others for what is needed to raise children. For those choosing not to parent, it may be support for that choice without judgment of the life they are choosing to live.

# CONSIDERING ANOTHER CHILD

**❝** What do you mean she's pregnant again? I thought lesbians **❞** were only supposed to have *one* child?

To the surprise of many, some lesbians *do* have more than one child. Some decide to birth another child, others choose to adopt, and still others become foster parents. In some lesbian families, one partner may birth a child, while the other one adopts. Or both partners may birth children at carefully planned intervals. There are any number of possibilities. If you think you are alone in wanting more than one child, let me reassure you that some lesbians do choose to have two children, others three, and others still more.

**❝** I never imagined I would want another child. But when Ali- **❞** son was about three I started thinking I wanted another baby. I did get pregnant again.

**❝** Our donor was leaving the country, probably never to return. **❞** I knew I wanted another child someday and I wanted my children to have the same father. But my son was only a year. We decided to have our donor's semen frozen so I could inseminate at a later date.

**❝** We wanted another child so we planned to adopt when **❞** Patrick was four. He was quite excited about the idea of having a baby brother or sister. We adopted a three year old boy within about six months. They have been a handful, but we're glad we did it this way.

**❝** When Sue and I split up we agreed that we wanted to each care **❞** for Lonnie half-time. Now I am in a new relationship and my lover wants us to have a child together too. In my mind, there are a lot of things to consider.

If you are considering a second (third, fourth, or more) child, there are particular exercises in this book you may want to do. I recommend the Lifeline Exercise and Pie Exercise — Children, all the exercises having to do with money and finances, those in the "Building A Family" chapter, and the Childhood Memories exercise in "Getting Acquainted With What's To Come." There are probably others you will want to do depending on your life and the concerns which are most pressing for you at this time. I suggest you go through the list of exercises at the end of this book, look at the ones that seem most relevant to you now, and complete them at your own pace.

As with many subjects in this book, this topic needs a book of its own. Since you won't find the subject covered in as much depth as you might like here, I encourage you to talk with others who are making or have made this decision, *and* to those who are not even considering it. Respect your own decision-making style and be sure to identify the things you need in order to sort through your thoughts, feelings, and ideas about this possibility.

The three exercises in this chapter are designed to help you focus on the possibility of having more than one child. You may want to come back to these exercises a few times if you find your thoughts and feelings changing as your child(ren) grows up.

## *"You Are Here" — Revisited*

Once again I encourage you to find a spot which marks that "You Are Here" as you begin this next part of your considering parenthood journey. In order to help you do this, I have included a list of questions as well as some additional issues to think about when it comes to considering another child.

1. Describe what is appealing to you about having another child. Be elaborate. Include all your fantasies, plans, hopes and dreams. Give yourself permission to imagine this possibility without having to consider issues such as time, finances, or energy just yet.
2. Make a list of all your reasons for wanting another child at this time.
3. Make a list of all your reasons for not wanting another child at this time.
4. If you decide to bring another child into your life, what do you imagine will change?
5. What do you imagine will stay the same?
6. How would you like to bring another child into your life? Make a list of the pros and cons for each of the possi-

ble ways of bringing a child into your life if you haven't done so already. Evaluate what you think about those options now.

As you work on these questions and lists, be aware of how you feel. Remember that your gut reactions are just as important as what you *think* about these concerns. Listen to those gut reactions, and try to put those feelings into words as well.

## "Things to Consider" – Revisited

As you try to locate where you are in beginning to make this particular decision, it may be helpful to identify the different issues that are influencing your thinking. Below, you will find a list of issues other lesbians making this decision have identified as critical. As you review this list, note the issues which are of concern to you. Then, be sure to add any other issues which are not on this list but are important to you. You can come back to this list and add to it at any time.

❏ Time
  • What is my time like now?
  • Do I have time to raise another child?
  • Will I still have the kind of time I want for myself, my lover(s), my friends, my other child(ren)?
❏ Money
  • How much money do I need/want to have if I have another child?
  • What resources for money do I have?
  • How is my sense of the importance of money and financial stability different now than it was when I chose to be a parent the first time?
  • How will I bring money into my life if I have another child?
❏ Work
  • What plans do I have about working if I have another child?
  • How much time can I take off work?
  • When will I have to go back to work?
  • Will I have to change my job?
  • Could I manage my present job if I were to have another child?
  • If not, what would I do about work?
❏ Energy
  • How much energy do I have for another child?

- How much more energy do I think it will take to raise another child?
- Realistically, what can I expect of myself? Of my partner(s)? Of the child(ren) I already have in sharing the responsibilities of parenting?

❑ Relationships
- How will having another child affect my relationships with my friends?
- In what ways will this affect my relationship(s) with my lover(s)?
- How do I imagine these relationships will have to change in order to accommodate another child?

❑ Support Network
- Will I parent this child alone, with one other person, or with more than one person?
- What kind of support network do I need in order to feel secure in making the decision to have another child?
- What is essential for me in a support network?
- What is desireable, but not necessarily essential?
- What do I expect of myself, my friends, my family, my other child, my parenting partner(s)?

❑ Family Ties
- Who will parent this new child?
- Will s/he have the same parent(s) as the other child(ren)?
- How will I explain the different parenting relationships to my children?
- How do I feel about one child having an involved donor or co-parent while I am raising the other child on my own?
- How will this be for the children?

These are tough questions to answer, so give yourself lots of time to think them over, talk about them with friends and family, and read whatever you think would be helpful to you as you sort through your concerns.

**❝** I had my first child on my own. It has been hard being a single **❞** parent. I want to be sure I have another adult committed to parenting with me before I have another child.

**❝** Brad has me, his dad, and my lover as parents. I want another **❞** child and neither my lover nor Brad's dad want to make a commitment to another child. This is a real problem for me. How do I explain to a new child that Brad has this whole family scene but s/he does not?

**66** My ideas about money have really changed. I can't believe I **99** decided to parent my first child on so little income. If I do have another child, I want to be sure I am financially stable. It's one thing to have one child on a low income, it's a whole different story to have two children that way.

## *Do Children Need Siblings?*

One question that many people with children ask themselves is whether or not it would be best for their child to be an only child or to have siblings. You will hear arguments on both sides of this question, and some will be more convincing that others. It is important for you to have an idea of where you stand on this question, how your life experience has influenced your thinking and how you feel about it now. The following exercise asks you to look at your own family/sibling experiences, reflect on the myths in this culture about being an only child, and finally, imagine ways in which to bring other children into your child's life to create sibling ties. If you are parenting with others, I encourage you to do this exercise separately and then review your answers together.

1. Were you an only child? What did you like or not like about that when you were younger? What do you like or not like about it now?
2. Did you have brothers and/or sisters? What did you like or not like about that when you were younger? What do you like or not like about it now?
3. If it could have been different in your family around being an only child or having siblings, how would you have wanted it to be? Explain why you would want it like that.
4. Make a list of what you have heard and what you believe to be the pros and cons of being an only child.
5. Now, make a list of what you have heard and what you believe to be the pros and cons of having siblings. (For questions 4 and 5, you may want to talk with friends who are only children or those who grew up with other siblings.)
6. What do you imagine would be best for *your* child — being an only child or having siblings? List your reasons for your choice.
7. In what ways do you imagine you could help your child create sibling relationships with other children in her/his life if you decide not to have another child? Make a list of these ideas and discuss them with others. Find out how other mothers have answered this dilemma for themselves.

**❝** I had two other sisters but we are all seven years apart, so I feel **❞** as if I was an only child. I really didn't feel as though I had siblings until I was an adult.

**❝** I grew up in a big family and I learned that you can't always **❞** have all the attention all the time. I think that was a valuable lesson to me. I also learned about sharing and caring from my sisters and brother. I want my children to have that kind of experience.

**❝** Part of what was great about being an only child was that my **❞** parents always had enough time for me and themselves. I mean, they weren't having to divide themselves between so many children and I think I ended up getting more quality attention because of it.

Just as the initial decision to parent is not always a simple and straightforward one, neither is the decision to parent another child. In fact, many lesbians who are considering another child have said that they felt this was a completely different decision. Often the decision to have another child is unrelated to earlier decisions.

**❝** Let's see if I can explain this. Ricki and I had Elena together. **❞** We broke up and Elena lives with me half of the time. I'm going to adopt another child by myself. I guess I need to figure out how much energy I have, what my commitment to Elena will be, and how much my relationship with Elena will change if I bring another child into our lives.

**❝** Holly wants to have another baby and I think it's a big mis- **❞** take. Jenna is just now three, and our relationship barely survived those early years. It makes me wonder if she wants children more than she wants a relationship.

**❝** We thought this over for a long time. We have worked hard to **❞** make our family work and stay together. But we knew that was how it would be. Now we are having our second child. Sure we know there will be hard times, but now we know we can make it. We're very excited.

Again, be gentle with yourself as you begin this part of your parenting journey. Do as many exercises as you need to in order to maximize your consciousness about yourself and your desires. Don't feel that you have to rush into this decision. You have plenty of time. Above all, remind yourself that you were able to make a decision about parenting before, and even though you may not make the same choice again, you *are* capable of making this kind of decision in your life.

# Becoming a Parent

# EXPLORING THE OPTIONS

There are a number of ways in which lesbians can become parents. That may seem obvious, but I have talked with many lesbians who think that there is only *one* way to do it. Interestingly, that one way usually varies from person to person.

In this section we explore the variety of ways to become a parent, with the focus on paying attention to your gut-level response to each of them. Later, we look at each choice in detail. The first exercise will help you begin thinking about the possible ways of becoming a lesbian parent, and how you feel about these methods.

## *Identifying the Options*

Below is a list of the many ways in which a lesbian can become a parent. If you know of other ways, or variations of the options stated, please add them to this list. For each choice, state (a) what you think about this particular choice; and (b) what your gut-level reaction is to this choice:

- ❏ Alternative fertilization with known or unknown donor (also known as artificial insemination, involves introducing semen into the vaginal canal or cervix for the purpose of fertilizing an egg and achieving pregnancy).
- ❏ Sexual intercourse with a man (known partner).
- ❏ Sexual intercourse with a man (unknown partner – that is, someone you don't know at all except for the purpose of sexual contact).

❑ Adoption (public, private, open, inter-country).
❑ Foster parenting.
❑ Non-biological parenting (with a friend or lover, in nuclear family model, or collective parenting model).
❑ Legal guardianship.

You may not know everything you want to know about each choice, but go with what you do know. In some cases, that may simply mean going with your intuitive response. After you gather additional information and think through the choices further, you can repeat this exercise.

Each choice carries with it a whole set of pros and cons. All the options require extensive planning, logistical arrangements, and, in some cases, financial investments to carry out. Often lesbians find themselves choosing one way of becoming a parent over another, not because it is their first choice, but because it is more simple logistically or it is what they can afford financially. It is especially important to explore all these possibilities and your responses to each in case your first choice does not work for you.

Remember, you are not making any decisions yet; you are simply looking at the possible ways of becoming a parent and taking time to experience how you feel about these alternatives. Many lesbians find they don't know why they would choose one option over another, but they *do* have a preference. This will happen often throughout this decision-making process. The reasons for one choice instead of another do not always have to be clear to you in order to proceed with considering parenthood.

## QUESTIONS TO ASK YOURSELF

❑ With which method do I feel most comfortable, given who I am, my lifestyle, and my values?
❑ How will I tell my child how s/he was conceived/brought into my life?
❑ What method will I feel most comfortable with having chosen ten years from now?
❑ Which method can I comfortably afford given my financial resources?

How you feel about your parenting choice will undoubtedly be communicated to your child. If you feel it was a good choice for you, then your child will probably feel good about how s/he was brought into your life. After you read the following sections, you may want to come back to these questions and answer them again. As you gather more information about the various options, your thoughts and feelings about them as possibilities in your life may change.

The chapters that follow are not an exhaustive study or the definitive statement of the options available to the lesbian considering parenthood. While a good deal of information is included here, there is more available from other sources as well. (See the bibliography.) Read as much as you can on the topic, talk to other lesbians who are considering parenthood, talk with lesbians you know who are parents, and check with attorneys in your state regarding the laws concerning artificial insemination, adoption, foster care, and legal guardianship as they may affect you as a lesbian.

I include here general areas to explore and consider, raising questions, and presenting different aspects of each choice. Use this information as a stepping-off point to help you formulate your best choice and further your decision-making process.

# ADOPTION

So often we think that the only way to have children is by becoming pregnant ourselves. Adoption and foster parenting are often considered as "last resorts" . The reality for many is that these alternatives are not only appealing but may, in fact, be a first choice.

Lesbians have adopted children in a variety of ways. Some have gone through state and local public adoption agencies or private adoption agencies. Others have found a child with the help of an attorney or through contacts with physicians, nurses, midwives, and hospitals. Other women have made agreements for private, independent, or cooperative adoptions. And some women have had success with inter-country/foreign adoptions. Whatever way you go about adopting your child, you must be approved by a social worker from your state Department of Social Services (sometimes called Department of Human Services) and finally by the state courts.

This section contains some general information on public, private, independent, open, and foreign adoptions. Although there are a variety of well-researched adoption guides on the book market, none of them addresses concerns specific to lesbians and gay men. However, the Lesbian Rights Project in San Francisco is currently working on an adoption pamphlet for lesbians and gay men.

To research adoption in your state, contact your county adoption agency. They will be able to give you a general idea of how someone can adopt a child through the county system. They will also know of private agencies and of agencies facilitating foreign adoptions.

Keep in mind that all adoption procedures are designed for the heterosexual married couple to be the adoptive parents. Only in some states is single-parent adoption common, and in all cases it must be perceived by the state to be in the best interests of the child. In no state can two unrelated people adopt the same child. If you are planning to adopt a child with someone else, therefore, you need to decide which of you will be the "adoptive" parent in the eyes of the adoption agency. In San Francisco, for example, gay men and lesbians have adopted children, and have been regarded as a family unit during the home study. However, only one person in the couple is given legal custody. Since adoption practices are constantly changing, be sure and talk about successful adoptions with whomever you can, both heterosexual and homosexual people who have gone through the process.

The process of adopting a child can take up to five years from the time you start until you sign the final adoption papers. The length of time it takes depends on many things, particularly on the availability of adoptive children and the time needed to go through the necessary legal steps. In some instances, however, the process can move quite swiftly, and you may have a child sooner than you expected.

> 66 We filed for adoption in June. They told us it would take at 99 least two years before we could adopt a baby. They did the home study during the summer. One day in November they called us and said they had a baby and could we come in by the end of the week to bring her home.

> 66 We were relieved it wouldn't take us long to find a child to 99 adopt. Since there were several Hispanic children available for adoption at the time we were looking, we were told we would be able to have a child within three months.

> 66 It was really nerve-wracking not having any control over the 99 whole process, never knowing when things were going to happen. It's just not a nine month wait. Everyday I wondered whether *this* would be the day they called me.

Talk to everyone you know who could be helpful in assisting you in finding a child to adopt. Talk to health care workers, especially those who work in maternity and delivery settings. You might also want to draft a letter describing yourself (and your partner if you plan to adopt with someone else). Send this letter to as many people as possible letting them know you are looking for a child to adopt. If you prefer to be more active, then get out there and do whatever you can. Many women call local obstetricians, asking to be notified if they have any patients seeking to relinquish an unborn child for adoption. Though all these methods are good ideas, as lesbians we are in something of a bind. Most physicians and attorneys who deal with adoption usually have hundreds, and I do mean hundreds, of heterosexual couples seeking to adopt children. In order to get a child as a lesbian, or as a lesbian couple, you will have to be very persistent and use your personal contacts wherever you can.

The question of whether or not to come out to your adoption worker is a tricky one, and one for which there is no simple answer. You must weigh the possible risks and benefits, taking into account the attitudes in your particular area. In the San Francisco area there seems to be a slightly more liberal attitude about who would make a suitable adoptive parent; in the past few years "out" gay men and lesbians have been able to adopt through the state adoption agency in a few counties. This may be true in other areas, but in general it is *not* the norm. The adoption process takes time and patience. Throughout, it may involve reminding the adoption personnel in a variety of direct and indirect ways that you (and your partner) would be good parent material, regardless of your sexual preference.

Lesbians who have gone through the process of adoption have varying opinions on how to handle the question of whether to come out. One adoptive mother explained, "Don't volunteer the information. But, if you are asked directly, don't be dishonest about it." Another lesbian mother added, "There are definite advantages to coming out to your worker. It reduces your anxiety that s/he will 'find out' you are a lesbian and suddenly eliminate you from being considered for any number of obscure reasons. You may get support from a sympathetic worker, and, in the long run, coming out creates a more realistic foundation for a long-term process." You will have to use your intuition, knowledge of attitudes and sentiment towards homosexuals in your community, and finally, your best judgment to determine how, when, and if to come out.

The time it takes for the adoption to happen can be very difficult. You will be confronted with many feelings and complex issues to explore. There will be unpredictable build ups and letdowns. There will be dashed hopes and lost dreams. Get support from friends and others who are intimately involved in your quest to adopt a child. The rewards will certainly be worth the time you have invested once you find and adopt a child.

## Public Adoption

Public adoption is adoption through your county adoption agency. Each state has this service, which can be located through your state or local Department of Social Services (this may be called something slightly different in your state). Generally speaking, this is the least expensive way to adopt a child.

You may want to begin by making some calls to your county agency for information. When you call, you will probably speak with a social worker or intake worker who screens calls regarding adoption. Many of the children available for adoption are at least two or three years old, from various ethnic backgrounds, and sometimes with emotional or medical problems. It is possible to find a newborn infant to adopt; however, this is generally easier for women of color than for Caucasian women. In California, the state has mandated that children be placed in a home that most closely resembles their ethnic background. In other words, at the present time, the Department of Social Services is only placing Black, Asian, Hispanic, or other ethnic group children in homes in which at least one parent is representative of the child's ethnic background. Because of this, adoption for women of color may be easier than for Caucasian women, at least in some states.

## QUESTIONS TO CONSIDER

Below are some questions you might want to ask when you make your initial phone call. Remember, you do not need to identify yourself; you are simply gathering information.

- What children are available for adoption (ages, ethnic background, cultural, or religious background, etc.)?
- Do you place children with single women seeking to adopt?
- What criteria do you take into consideration when determining if someone is qualified to adopt a child? (Specifically, financial resources, job stability, marital status, etc.)
- How is it determined if a child is best suited for a single-parent or a two-parent household?
- How long does the adoption process take?

Most public adoption agencies have an orientation meeting for people interested in adopting. Go to this meeting and gather as much information as you can to help in figuring out how to best approach adoption in your county.

At the meeting, if you are interested in pursuing this route, you will be asked to complete a rather long and detailed application form, and you will be assigned to a worker. Once you have a worker, you will then participate in what is sometimes called the "home study" . The home study is a series of visits to your home that can take from one to five months to complete. In the meantime, you will be asked to provide further information about yourself including employment verification, medical examination, fingerprinting, an autobiography, and possibly other tests or information.

In some states, there is a direct link between the adoption agency and the foster care agency. If this is the case, you should check into the possibility of a new program called Fost-Adopt. This is explained more fully in the section on foster care, but briefly, this program allows for people who qualify to be adoptive parents to be licensed as foster parents; that way, they can care as foster parents for a child who may be free for adoption at a later date.

You will hear mention of a "list" on which you will be put to wait for a child to adopt. This is not a list at which you start at the bottom and gradually move your way to the top. Instead, the list is used to match the needs of children who need placement with the families and individuals who are seeking to adopt. All qualified applicants on the list will be reviewed to see which one(s) would make the best placement for a particular child. It certainly helps to have a caseworker who likes you and with whom you have developed a good rapport, since such a worker will promote you as a potentially good adoptive parent.

## Private Adoption

In each state, licensed private agencies provide services similar to the county adoption agency. These agencies have a comparable system for initiating an adoption but may have access to a different population of children. Check your phone directory for the private adoption agencies in your state and speak with them about their adoption procedures. The basic difference between a private and a public agency is that it usually costs more money to adopt through a private agency. However, you may find there is less red tape and possibly a shorter waiting time. Some private agencies may place children with special needs or children of specific ethnic or religious backgrounds (Jewish, Baptist, Mormon, etc.). Check with personnel at your state public adoption agency. They will have these resources for you.

## Independent Adoption

Through independent adoption, the birth parent(s) selects the family for the child and places the child directly with the selected family. This type of adoption is generally facilitated by an attorney or private agency specializing in independent adoption. The birth parents review files of potential adoptive parents, have the opportunity to meet these parents, and make the final decision regarding placement.

In most states, the designated family must be approved by the State Department of Social Services. This means a caseworker will make home visits and determine whether the adoptive parent's home is suitable for this child. The caseworker is the one who recommends that the court approve the selected individual or couple as the adoptive parent(s).

When a birth parent makes an independent adoption placement, s/he signs a "consent" agreeing to adoption by the specific couple or individual with whom the child is to be placed. Birth parents relinquishing their children for independent adoption may request return of the child at any time before the court formalizes the adoption placement.

Many attorneys and physicians in metropolitan areas now specialize in adoptions. Adoption has become a lucrative business. In the past ten to 15 years, the number of children available for adoption has diminished dramatically. Desperate to find children to adopt, people are willing to pay a hefty sum to locate an adoptive child. In an independent adoption, you contact an attorney or agency, go through the screening process, and wait to be selected by the birth parent(s). If you decide to go this route, be wary. Be sure you know the attorney and his/her reputation. Ask for references and for information regarding the sources of children.

Most attorneys or agency personnel working in the field of independent adoption think that all interested adoptive parents are heterosexual. Because of pervasive homophobia towards lesbians raising children, some lesbians have chosen to pass as a heterosexual in order to locate and eventually adopt a child. A lot depends on who you are working with, what the situation is in your state, and the risks you may be taking as an "out" lesbian seeking to adopt a child. Deciding when to come out in this particular adoption process may be more complicated since the birth parents will be the ones making the final decision. You may want to consider telling the attorney or agency right up front, waiting to meet the parents and then telling them yourself, or not talking about your lesbianism at all. It is up to you.

## Cooperative Adoptions

Cooperative, or open, adoption also allows birth parents to place their children with adoptive parents they have selected. In this type of adoption, however, the birth parents negotiate a contract with the adoptive parents, detailing the contact they can have with the child. People establish many different kinds of contact — letters and pictures on a regular basis, a visit on specific holidays, monthly visits, participation in parenting — the range of alternatives is vast.

Open adoption means acknowledging the birth mother and her relationship to her child. Birth mothers are not awful people about whom children should not be told or to whom children should be denied access. Many lesbians in our communities who were adopted or who gave children up for adoption have explained that it is more than likely that someday in the future the adopted child will search for her/his birth mother and that the birth mother may also search for that child. For many, cooperative adoption provides all involved with a way of having and maintaining an on-going, acknowledged relationship.

Too frequently in the adoption process, the birth mother is treated as though she does not exist. Some adoptive parents would prefer to ignore the reality of her connection to her child altogether. They avoid any contact with her for fear she may want some kind of relationship with her child, now or in the future. It is thought that most birth parents do not want their children or are unable to care for them adequately. They are often ignored as the "real" parents and must live in a society which colludes with adoptive parents, at least during a child's early years, in denying them acknowledgment as the child's birth parents.

In considering cooperative adoption, you will need to be very honest with yourself concerning how able and willing you would be to have an on-going relationship with the birth mother or parents. Be sure to review the questions at the end of this chapter, answering the ones that apply to you and your adoption choices.

## *Foreign/Inter-country Adoptions*

Within the last ten years, more and more children from foreign countries have become available for adoption. Each country has its own laws about foreigners adopting their children and procedures for adopting also vary from country to country. In addition, states have their own laws about inter-country adoptions. Check with the public adoption agency or an attorney regarding laws governing foreign adoptions in your state. You will find a few private adoption agencies and some attorneys specializing in foreign adoptions. Again, be cautious. Be sure you are working with an agency or person who has an established reputation and is willing to let you talk with people for whom they have previously located children.

Lesbians I have spoken with have adopted children from India, Korea, Mexico, Columbia, and Bangladesh. Each experience was different, took a good deal of time (at least two years), and cost from $1,000 to $5,000. Sometimes the woman herself was required to go to the country and stay for a period of time. Others simply had to pay the child's air fare and other travel expenses from their country of origin.

You will be told that foreign children are voluntarily given up by families who cannot care for them and want them to have good homes. I cannot say whether or not this is true. The political implications of inter-country adoption are far reaching. Birth parents may be forced to give up a child because of the economic, political, social, or cultural changes occurring in that country. Foreign intervention in many countries has left countless numbers of children homeless. Although many in the U.S. seek to provide "good homes" for foreign children, we must not forget the situations through which many of them become available for adoption. In so many instances, what makes inter-country adoption an option are the workings of a system based on divisions by class and race. Therefore, I encourage you to be conscious of the implications which we often choose to ignore.

In some instances, you will be able to meet the families, especially if the country requires you to live with the family for a period of time. Some lesbians have stayed in touch with the child's family of origin as a way of maintaining biological and cultural ties. Others have chosen not to, or simply have been unable to do so.

As with public adoptions, only one person in an unmarried couple can legally adopt the child. You will want to check with the agency facilitating the foreign adoption to see what qualifications they are looking for. That way you can decide which person in a couple might be more likely to be approved for the adoption. Single women have been able to find children for adoption through inter-country programs somewhat more easily than through the public and private local adoption route.

## QUESTIONS TO CONSIDER

The decision to adopt demands that you consider a variety of ethical and socially relevant questions. Here are some areas you might want to explore while initiating the adoption procedure:

- Passing as a single heterosexual woman: Will I need to do this? Am I willing to do it? What would it mean to me? Is it an important factor in the whole scheme of things?
- Adopting a child from a dramatically different ethnic background: What problems might this cause in my family or community? What racist attitudes in myself will I need to confront and change? How might I/we maintain the child's ethnic ties?
- Who will be the "legal" parent (if you adopt with a parenting partner) and how each of you will share custody of this child: Who gets the child if the parenting relationship ends? What kind of agreements need to be made right from the start regarding custody and visitation questions?
- Adopting a child with severe medical and/or emotional problems: Realistically, what are your capacities? Your limits? Your expectations?
- Having an on-going and consistent relationship with the birth mother or birth parents? Providing your child with an opportunity to know her/his birth parent(s). How open are you to this kind of arrangement? What type of problems do you anticipate experiencing? What would make this an attractive arrangement to you?
- What do you plan to tell your child about her/his birth parents? Will you assist your child in finding her/his birth parents when s/he chooses to do so?

These are only some of the areas which need to be taken into consideration as you proceed with the adoption process. Read whatever you can find that will help you in your search to find a child. (Check the bibliography.) Remember the road may be long, but the rewards of finding a child will be well worth the journey.

# FOSTER CARE

Foster care is another way of bringing a child into your life. Foster care placements are generally temporary, lasting anywhere from one day to one year or longer, depending upon the situation. Regardless of the length of the placement, the important point is that it is temporary. Foster parenting provides you with the experience of being a parent without the long-term commitment and responsibility. For some, it offers a chance to see how you enjoy parenting, either alone or with your parenting partner-to-be. Some states have programs giving foster parents the option to adopt their foster child when, and if, that child becomes free for adoption. Check with your county adoption agency about such a program. In some states this is called Fost-Adopt.

A child becomes "free" for adoption because a mother feels she is unable to care for this child, because she is found to be unable to adequately care for the child by the court, or possibly because she is a lesbian. Do not underestimate the significant role our economy, Reaganomics, sexism (putting women in low paying jobs, last hired, first fired), being deserted with no job skills, and racism play in creating these scenarios.

It may not be easy being a foster parent. The children may be suffering from severe emotional trauma, and may need and want a good deal of your time and energy. In addition, you may develop a strong bond to your foster child only to have her/him removed from your home and returned to the natural parents. This can be emotionally wrenching for all concerned.

As with adoption, the children available for foster care are rarely infants. Although infants are sometimes available, the children are usually between three and 18 years of age, and may have a range of medical, psychological, or physical problems. Some may have come from homes in which they were physically, psychologically, or sexually abused. Others may have been removed from their homes because their parent(s) lacked the resources to care for them. Be sure you know the limits of your emotional capabilities. The worker who licenses you as a foster parent will probably discuss these issues with you in detail, but take time to think through your feelings and attitudes on your own. You want to be able to handle difficult situations that could come up, both for yourself and the child.

To be a foster parent, you must become licensed by the state. As with adoption, you will be asked to fill out an application and participate in a series of home visits by the county social worker. You will also be fingerprinted and asked to disclose any criminal record. Each state handles their home study part of the licensing process differently. Check with the county office to determine what they are looking for in a home setting and what guidelines they have established to determine if a home is suitable for licensing. If you call to get information, you will usually be invited to attend an orientation meeting. Go with your questions in hand. This is usually a good place to get information about the attitudes of the department, the workers, and the system. It will also give you some idea of what you can expect from them and how you might be treated.

Once you are licensed, you will have ongoing home visits and monitoring by the social service agency's foster care department. The visits may be infrequent and may not bother you at all. Some lesbians, however, experienced so many visits that they decided to stop participating in the program. There are subtle and not so subtle forms of harassment to be aware of. One lesbian couple mentioned to me that despite being licensed for over a year, their worker insisted there simply were no appropriate children for their home setting.

Check with your county foster care agency to see the kind and quality of support they offer to their licensed foster parents. See if they provide you with training as well as a contact person to call on when things are difficult at home or if you simply need someone to talk to about your foster care situation.

On the issue of whether to come out to the foster care licensing people, again you must use your best judgment. In all likelihood, the homophobic bias is quite strong. I know of one situation in which the natural parent was asked to sign a form stating she knew her child was being placed with an identified lesbian, releasing the social service department from any responsibility.

Each situation is different and demands your careful assessment. Lesbians trying to adopt or to become foster parents are making in-roads for other women in alternative families seeking to provide homes for children. It is through our relationships with people such as adoption and foster care personnel that we broaden prevailing attitudes about lesbians and demonstrate the reality that lesbians are women geniunely interested in raising children, and can provide them with loving, caring, and supportive homes.

# LEGAL GUARDIANSHIP

Legal guardianship of a child falls somewhere between adoption and foster care (and may be called Conservatorship in some states). It is not as final as adoption, but is more permanent than foster care. Like adoption however, only one adult may be the guardian of a child at a time. This means that a biological mother must give up some of her parental rights in order for another person to assume legal guardianship of her child. The legal guardian agrees to take care of the personal and financial needs of the child. In many states, these two areas of responsibility may be split into guardianship of the child (personal care) and guardianship of the estate (the child's financial assets). In some states, both these areas of responsibility must be assumed by one person.

Lesbians have become legal guardians of children of all ages. You may want to become the guardian of a child you know during a time when her/his parent is not able to care for her/him. Or you may want to be named as the legal guardian of your lover's biological child in order to have some legal connection to that child. Although this *is* possible, remember that the biological mother must agree to give up some of her parental rights in order for that to happen. Instead, you may want to consider naming the non-biological mother as the legal guardian of her child in the biological mother's will (in the event of the biological mother's death). Perhaps you are caring for the child of a friend in a situation which you anticipate will be long-term. If you find yourself in a situation in which you are assuming parenting responsibility for a child, you may want to take steps necessary to become the legal guardian.

**❝** Helen knew she couldn't care for Bert but didn't want to put **❞** him into foster care. She asked me to take him and offered to let me become the legal guardian. We have agreed she can terminate this guardianship when she's ready.

**❝** I've known Nance since she was six. When her mother decided **❞** to move to Nebraska and Nance didn't want to go, I said I

165

would be her legal guardian. We went to an attorney who took care of the logistics.

**❝** When Hank was born, we tried to figure out how Carolyn **❞** could be a legal parent too. We thought this guardianship thing would work but then we discovered I would lose my rights as a mom. So now she's in my will as the legal guardian. We think my folks will be fine with it.

If you are seeking to become the legal guardian of a child and are not a blood relative of the child you will probably have to go through a social service evaluation, similar to the adoption evaluation procedure, or be licensed as a foster parent. In addition, once appointed as guardian, your home may have to be periodically inspected, including a home visit by social service personnel each time you move. Guardianships are subject to review by the court or state authorities; guardianships of the (financial) estate require periodic reports by the guardian to the court regarding how the child's money is being managed.

As a legal guardian, you may be eligible for financial assistance such as foster care payments and Medicaid. This assistance is usually not tied to your income. Lesbians who are legal guardians have said that this financial assistance system is not as difficult or unpleasant to deal with as the welfare system. A guardian has the right to consent to and choose health care for the child, as well as to make all decisions concerning schooling, religion and other aspects of the child's life.

Legal guardianship can be granted if the biological parent(s) of a child voluntarily consent to the placement, or if a court decides it is in the best interests of the child to end the parent's rights and place the child with a guardian over the parent's objections. Children over the age of 14 can usually have a say in whom their guardian is going to be.

A guardianship may be permanent, when there is no plan for the child to return to her/his biological parent(s), or temporary when the parent(s) are only temporarily unable to care for the child. Even if the guardianship is intended to be permanent, it may be ended upon the request of the biological parent(s) or others, if the court believes this would be best for the child. Unlike foster care, in which a child's placement is periodically reviewed and the state has custody of the child, a guardianship is not reviewed automatically, and the guardian has full custody of the child. A guardianship is established or terminated at a court hearing. If a guardianship is being terminated by the court, the guardian may argue against the requested change.

The legal fees for establishing legal guardianship will vary from case to case and from state to state. The usual fee can range from $300 to $1,500. If your income is low, your local Legal Aid Society may be able to do the guardianship for no charge.

You will want to check with an attorney about the guidelines for assuming legal guardianship in your state. Talk with others you know who are parenting in this way to get a sharper picture of the potential benefits and risks of this parenting option.

# ALTERNATIVE FERTILIZATION

I use the term "alternative fertilization" rather than "artificial insemination" to describe the many ways a woman can choose to become pregnant outside of the traditional method of having sexual intercourse with a man. This term, as pointed out in *Lesbian Health Matters!*, more closely describes a process of woman-controlled conception than does that of "artificial insemination" which refers primarily to a medical procedure.

An estimated 300,000 babies have been born through alternative fertilization since World War II. With increasing regularity, women outside the traditional nuclear family are choosing this method for conception. Both unmarried heterosexual women and lesbians are utilizing the range of insemination services previously thought to be available only to married women. Contrary to what the medical establishment might like us to think, alternative fertilization is really very simple. A woman obtains semen from a private physician, sperm bank, or donor. Within a few hours, she places the semen into her vagina by using an eyedropper, diaphragm cup, turkey baster, or plastic syringe without a needle. Lesbians around the world have used this method to become pregnant.

In the United States, state laws vary concerning insemination services. In some states, it is a felony for an insemination to be performed without a physician. In others, doctors are directed to inseminate married women only. Often, no provision is made regarding the insemination of unmarried women, regardless of their sexual orientation. In order to use this method, you need to know your menstrual cycle and be able to predict when you ovulate. The following section briefly covers the basic anatomy and physiology of a woman's reproductive organs, the menstrual cycle, the logistics of determining when you ovulate using fertility awareness techniques, and the how to's of alternative fertilization. There are a few other fine booklets and articles on this topic (see the bibliography). I suggest you read at least one other source, since there is no definitive work on the subject for the lay person to date. Each article or booklet offers a slightly different perspective on the process of alternative fertilization or artificial insemination. For some lesbians, considering different aspects may be helpful in understanding the process and deciding if this is the option for them; for others, considering these different perspectives may simply be confusing. Recall your decision-making style and use the process that has worked best for you in the past.

## *Anatomy and Physiology*

Though many women know and understand the process of ovulation (when the ovary releases the egg) and the menstrual cycle, I have found that everyone is usually unclear about some aspect or other. A thorough explanation can help to demystify the whole sequence. My health education background reminds me that people must have the correct information in order to make informed choices. I encourage you to take the time to review this information, here or in one of the recommended readings, even if you think you already know it.

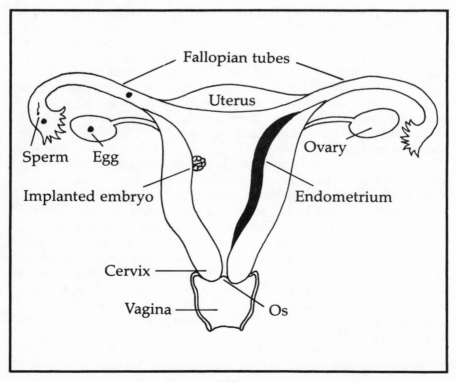

During her reproductive years, each woman has a menstrual cycle that can last from 21 to 35 days (from the beginning of one menstrual period to the beginning of the next menstrual period). Ovulation usually occurs between six and fourteen days before the start of the next menstrual period. At the time of ovulation, hormone levels peak and the uterine lining thickens in preparation for the possibility of a fertilized egg. In most women, each month one of the ovaries releases an egg. For conception to occur, the egg must be fertilized.

Fertilization occurs when a viable sperm penetrates a viable egg. The timing factors are somewhat complex. It is thought that sperm can live from three to five days in the fertile mucus. Over the course of these few days, sperm then make their way to the fallopian tubes. The egg, however, is only available for fertilization during a 24 hour period. This means you could inseminate on a Monday, ovulate on a Wednesday, and fertilization could still take place because viable sperm may still be in the fallopian tubes. The problem is, you never know for certain if you inseminate on Monday that you will ovulate on Wednesday.

If the egg is not fertilized, it simply dissolves. Hormonal changes then signal the uterine lining to slough off, causing what is commonly known as a woman's menstrual period. The first day of a woman's menstrual period marks the beginning of her cycle. During the next few weeks, the lining of the uterus begins to build once again in preparation for a possible pregnancy. The horomonal levels peak in preparation for ovulation and the time for fertilization occurs again.

## Charting Your Menstrual Cycle

The following information includes some basic guidelines for charting your menstrual cycles, along with tips and suggestions for making your charting more complete and perhaps easier to do. The purpose of charting is to determine as accurately as possible when ovulation occurs. This is a sometimes tedious and anxiety-inducing process. I have included suggestions that may help make charting a bit easier. Be alert for any other things that may make charting easier for you. The point of learning about your cycle from any of the following methods is to increase you ability to *predict* ovulation more accurately. On a given month you will not know for certain when you are going to ovulate or even exactly when you are ovulating. You can learn when it is near, likely, or over. This is a real problem because so much of the literature suggests if you chart your cycle correctly, you will know exactly when to inseminate. I encourage you to drop this expectation as soon as possible.

For a more detailed discussion of these different charting techniques, check the bibliography for one of the books that discusses fertility awareness. You can also check with a family planning center or women's clinic in your area. Most of these clinics offer courses in fertility awareness, more commonly called Natural Family Planning. These classes are usually designed for heterosexual women trying to *avoid* pregnancy without having to use contraceptives. Some clinics in larger metropolitan areas are offering courses for lesbians. You may want to organize your own class to learn how to use charting to *achieve* a pregnancy. Perhaps you could get a group of friends together and invite a speaker from one of these clinics to make a presentation to your group. You may find it helpful to consult with someone who knows about the subtle nuances of charting and who can explain how to read the graphs you will be keeping.

Charting your menstrual cycle can be divided into four separate processes:

- taking your basal body temperature
- checking your cervical mucus
- checking for changes in the os (the opening of the cervix)
- keeping a running account of your emotions, daily stresses, and lifestyle habits

You will achieve the greatest accuracy possible if you record each of these on a daily basis. It has been my experience that a combination of all of these "measurements" increases your chances of determining with greater accuracy the time of ovulation. Whether you use any or all of these methods or you decide to use tarot card readings, an inner psychic sense, or any other method you have heard to be useful, will depend on your decision-making style. You may find that each month you use another method as you learn from experience the limitations of one or more of the other methods. Don't expect to be deliberate about how you choose which method to use or how effectively you use these different methods at first. Over time you will find the method(s) that suits you.

I suggest you plan to chart your menstrual cycle for at least six months before beginning to try to become pregnant. "Why six months?" you may be wondering increduously. The point of charting is to have more information about your body before you begin inseminating. You want to eliminate as many factors as possible that would make the process of becoming pregnant more difficult. A six-month block of time gives you a broad picture of your menstrual cycle and ovulation pattern, enabling you to predict the time of ovulation with more accuracy. For some women, three months may be long enough to see the pattern. Use your own judgment in deciding how long you plan to chart your cycles before you begin trying to become pregnant. Once you begin inseminating, you will want to continue charting your cycles until you achieve pregnancy.

As you prepare to chart your fertility, it is not unusual for unsettling feelings to come up. You may wonder, "Will recording my menstrual cycle be easy? Will it be possible? Are my cycles so irregular I won't be able to ever know when I ovulate?" It can be a very traumatic time for some women. It is also the time that doubts and questions about one's fertility arise. This, too, although common, produces a good deal of anxiety nonetheless. Women who have had past pregnancies or previous abortions will be reminded of those experiences and may find those memories bring up a range of emotions they had not anticipated. If this happens for you, take time to acknowledge those feelings and memories. You may want to talk with a close friend or with someone with whom you feel safe to share these emotions. Whatever you choose to do, take good care of yourself around these memories. Pamper yourself and give yourself room to feel the emotions that come up for you.

> **"** I was worried that I ovulated so infrequently I would never be **"**
> able to get pregnant. Once I started charting my periods I saw
> there was a pattern to my ovulation and it wasn't as irregular
> as I imagined.

> **"** I had an abortion six years ago. There are moments now when **"**
> I think that if I had kept that baby I would already be a
> mother. Usually, I remember I was totally unprepared to have
> a child at that time in my life.

> **"** I got pregnant on my first try before. I know I expect that to **"**
> happen now, too. It's hard to wait for pregnancy to happen
> when all you want is to be pregnant.

## HOW TO TAKE YOUR BASAL BODY TEMPERATURE

1. First, purchase a basal body thermometer. They are available for $8-$12 at most drug stores and pharmacies. This thermometer marks the degrees more accurately than a regular thermometer. Included with the thermometer is a small graph for your charting. I have also included a chart (in Appendix D) which you can copy for your monthly graphs. (Some women get quite creative, using crayons and coloring pens.)

2. Take your temperature in the morning before moving around in bed. For some women that means minimal movement, before getting up to use the bathroom, feed the cat, or even rolling over to kiss your girlfriend. For other women, movement doesn't seem to matter. You will have to test this out for yourself. If you are someone who sleeps a regular schedule, take your temperature at the same time every morning and then go back to sleep. You can read the thermometer later.

Keep the thermometer right next to the bed, within easy reach. You may want to find ways to remind yourself to take your temperature but after the first few times, chances are it will become an integral part of your morning routine. With some couples, the woman not taking her temperature is responsible for shaking down the thermometer, charting the temperature, and even giving the thermometer to her lover so that the woman taking her temperature doesn't have to move. Although it may seem silly to be so deliberate, this is a way of involving both partners in the process right from the start.

Once you remove the thermometer from your mouth, the temperature will stay registered, so you don't have to read and chart it immediately. Be sure to shake down the thermometer after charting and place it back next to the bed. Take your temperature at approximately the same time every day. If you work irregular shifts and wake up at different times on different days, be sure to make a note of that on your chart.

How can you tell ovulation has occurred according to your chart? You will find that for the first few days of your cycle your temperature will follow a somewhat up-and-down pattern. Around the time of ovulation, your temperature may drop lower than before and will then rise to a new higher level. There is often some confusion as to exactly when ovulation occurs -- whether it is before, during, or after the drop in temperature. There is general agreement, however, that when your temperature has *risen*, ovulation has occurred. This slightly more pronounced drop and then rise in temperature generally occurs within the span of two days. Following ovulation, your temperature pattern will continue to show some up-and-down variation until your period begins.

As a final note on this method of charting, you may want to have an extra thermometer in case you don't spend the night at home or in case you break the thermometer you have. I have heard countless stories from women who were sure they ovulated on a particular day but didn't have their thermometer with them. Or times when the person who was shaking down the thermometer accidentally knocked it against something and it broke. Having an extra thermometer in a pinch can relieve a great deal of unnecessary worry or anxiety.

> **"** I got so into this it was all I could think about. I would take my **"** temperature regularly and then get all excited when I realized I ovulated.

> **"** My lover's cycle was very irregular at first. But after a few **"** months of taking her temperature, we saw a pattern of regularity. That was exciting.

> **"** You just can't call someone up and say, 'Wow, I ovulated **"** today!' But I sure wanted to do that.

172

## MITTLESCHMERTZ

I believe that our bodies know what is going on inside, but it may not always be easy to get that information to our consciousness. Mittleschmertz is one of those messages; it refers to a cramp-like pain some women experience right at the time of ovulation. This is also called midcycle pain. You may feel it on the right or left side; sometimes it is associated with the ovary that is releasing the egg. Note on your chart when this pain occurs. Then when you get your period, check to see if this Mittleschmertz occurred on or around the time that your other charting methods suggested ovulation might be occurring. Some women also have slight spotting or bleeding at this time. This is perfectly normal, as long as the bleeding does not last more than one or two days.

Pay close attention to this Mittleschmertz. For some women this is a better predictor of when ovulation occurs than any other method.

## CHECKING YOUR CERVICAL MUCUS

The consistency of the cervical mucus can be a critical factor in determining ovulation for some women. For others, it may not help at all. The difference depends on your vaginal discharge and the amount of cervical mucus you have throughout your menstrual cycle. Your cervical mucus will assist you in knowing beforehand that ovulation will occur, whereas taking your basal body temperature indicates ovulation after the fact. They are both good methods to use as back-up for one another.

Check the consistency and color of your vaginal mucus daily. You can do this by inserting one or two fingers into your vagina to get a sample of the mucus or you may prefer to collect it on toilet paper. Simply do it in whatever manner you are most comfortable. It is best to put two fingers in your vagina and squeeze a little mucus out of your cervix and onto your finger. Or you can run your finger along the inner lips of your vagina, another place some women find this mucus collecting. When you look at the mucus, note its color and consistency. Is it slippery, stretchy, clear, cloudy, thick, thin? At the beginning of your cycle you may have little or no mucus. As your cycle progresses, the mucus may increase until ovulation, at which time many women have mucus which becomes sticky and stretchy in consistency, and appears either slightly cloudy or clear. This type of mucus is called "spin." If you press the mucus between two fingers and then gently draw the fingers apart, you will see the mucus spin and stretch, like egg whites. It is this type of cervical mucus that carries the sperm up into the cervix, enabling them to then swim into the uterus and the fallopian tubes. This stretchy, wet stringy mucus guides the sperm, nourishes it, and makes its access to the egg easier. This stretchy spin mucus may last one to four days. Learn your pattern. You may find the stretch gets clearer and wetter as ovulation approaches. If you have spin for several days and inseminate when it first appears, you may be inseminating too early. Watch your pattern over the period of a few months.

Not everyone has this clearly distinctive mucus. However, you will find that keeping track of the mucus you do have may assist you in calculating when ovulation occurs. You may simply get a sensation of additional wetness and the mucus may be no different than mucus from previous days. Note the feeling of wetness, and as you continue charting, notice if it concurs with the time that your temperature shifts to suggest ovulation.

Check your cervical mucus each day, at the same time each day if possible. Some women like to check their mucus three times a day, because it can change dramatically around the time of ovulation even within a 24 hour time period. One lesbian mother has suggested that a good time to check your mucus is after a bowel movement. Check your wiping tissue. Remember it may be hard to find any first thing in the morning because no gravity has been pulling it down. Note on your chart what the mucus looks and feels like.

> **❝** Once I figured out my fertile mucus, I felt more relaxed. My **❞**
> lover and I couldn't figure out whether the mucus was sticky
> enough. There were some funny moments, but all in all, it's
> been frustrating.

## FERNING

There is a test that involves looking at cervical mucus under a microscope to see when it forms a fern-like pattern. This can be useful if you have access to a microscope. You can buy a kid's toy microscope for $8-$20, put a little mucus on the slide — the stretchiest you can find on a given day — heat the slide with a candle, then look for the fern-like pattern. As you observe your cervical mucus throughout your cycle, you will see the changing patterns. You want to be able to identify what the ferning pattern looks like just prior to ovulation and when ovulation might be occurring. Learn how many days you are likely to have ferns. You may find you have several days with ferns and that the mucus gets wetter and more slippery as you approach ovulation.

> **❝** Some friends bought me a toy microscope when I told them I **❞**
> was starting to do this whole thing. It took me a few months
> to finally see ferning, but when I did I was so excited I called
> my friends and we celebrated.

## CHECKING FOR CHANGES IN THE OS

Throughout your cycle changes in your cervix and the os (the opening to the cervix) are good indicators for predicting when ovulation may occur. The position of the cervix changes during the menstrual cycle, going from low to high (near the time of ovulation) and then to low again. The os opens around the time of ovulation and becomes softer and fuller. You may want to use a speculum to check for these changes, or you can feel for the changes in your os with a finger. If you use this method, you will need to check for changes on a daily basis.

> **❝** I went to the women's health clinic and learned how to do a **❞** self-exam. I bought a plastic speculum and started looking at my cervix. I was timid at first, but once I got over that, I liked watching the changes in my os.

## EMOTIONS, STRESSES AND LIFESTYLE HABITS

Emotions, daily stresses, and lifestyle habits have an enormous impact on our bodily functions. Any dramatic change in your usual routine or pattern could change your time of ovulation. Keep a daily record on your graph, making note of illnesses (something as slight as a cold, the flu, allergies), stress at work, stress at home, travel (from one time zone to another and frequent airplane travel), going to bed later than usual or waking up at a time that is not usual for you, bad moods, good moods, significant changes in your diet (i.e., increase/decrease in use of alcohol, salt, sugar, or in general caloric consumption).

All these factors contribute to how our bodies work. When something is changed, the body may adjust its functioning in such a way as to alter the time of ovulation.

> **❝** None of these methods worked for me. I just couldn't figure **❞** out my ovulation with them. I saw a hypnotist who specializes in women's fertility. She taught me how to hypnotize myself and feel what was happening in my own body. That's what finally worked for me.

> **❝** I am a very emotional person, so keeping a journal of my emo- **❞** tions was impractical. I would write down if I had a big fight with my lover, or something like that.

> **❝** I had so many emotions once I started taking my temperature **❞** and waiting for ovulation to occur I felt crazier than ever. I decided to just keep a record of my day-to-day life changes, because my emotions were unchartable!

Beginning to chart your menstrual cycle is a challenging, exciting, and sometimes overwhelming part of this process of planning for parenthood. You may make mistakes in the beginning, but keep at it. In the long run, I can guarantee you will be glad you did. Check with friends who are also charting or who have charted their cycles in the past. Talk with them about the ups and downs. Surprising as it may seem, charting can be a difficult task to stay with because the long range rewards seem so far away. Do your charting in whatever way seems right to you in a given month. See this as part of your process. As the months go by you may notice you are getting more involved with predicting ovulation or less involved. Take time to think about what that means for you. Remember you can always take a break from charting for a month or more and come back to it.

# *How To's of Alternative Fertilization*

Contrary to what we have been led to believe, the mechanics of alternative fertilization are relatively easy. It's the logistics and emotional realities of making it all happen that pose the biggest obstacles to the process. This section is divided into three parts:

- Instructions for donors
- Instructions for the woman who is inseminating
- Things to remember while trying to become pregnant.

I have also included suggestions that women from my groups found helpful to them. (Other sources in the bibliography will have information not included here which you may want to read.)

Most of this information will be useful whether you obtain the semen directly from a donor, from a sperm bank, or through a private physician. Women who choose to have sexual intercourse with a man may also find some of this information helpful.

## INSTRUCTIONS FOR DONORS

Here is a list of instructions you can share with your donor prior to his providing you with sperm. If you have a go-between, that person should go over this information with your donor. Though there is no guarantee that your donor will follow all these instructions, it can't hurt to make sure he is informed.

1. Have a V.D. test just prior to giving your semen for an insemination if you have been sexually active with a new partner or with more than one partner.

2. Avoid masturbation or sexual activity involving ejaculation for one to two days prior to donating sperm. Also avoid wearing tight pants. Avoiding both of these will increase your sperm count and the woman's chances for achieving pregnancy.

3. Don't take a hot shower prior to donating sperm. This can decrease the number of sperm.
4. Ejaculate into a clean glass jar. Something with a wide mouth is best (like baby food or artichoke heart jars).
5. Keep the semen at body temperature. Do not refrigerate it.
6. Ejaculate as close to the time when semen is to be used as possible. The sperm are most viable when used within one hour of ejaculation.
7. Avoid using drugs or alcohol prior to donating semen.

## INSTRUCTIONS FOR THE WOMAN WHO IS INSEMINATING

As you begin the process of insemination, you may want some basic information about semen. It is important to know that semen has a strong and sometimes unpleasant odor and it is rather stringy and/or lumpy in texture. The amount of semen in a single ejaculation is approximately one tablespoon. This amount of semen contains millions of tiny sperm cells. Don't be alarmed if you find that dealing with semen is more difficult than you imagined. This is not uncommon, expecially if this is your first exposure to it.

1. Use fresh sperm within one to two hours of ejaculation. Make arrangements to get the semen as close to the time of ejaculation as possible.
2. Keep the semen warm — at body temperature is best. If it is to be transported, place the jar in a sock or towel and keep it close to your body.
3. When inseminating, lie on your back. Put a pillow under your hips to elevate your pelvis slightly. This will encourage the sperm to swim towards your uterus.
4. You can inseminate using any of the methods discussed later in this section. Women have used various techniques for actually inserting the semen into the vagina. I don't know that one way works better than any other. It is best to choose the method that most appeals to you, remembering that if you don't get pregnant the first time you can try a different way another time.
5. After inserting the semen into the vagina, stay in a reclining position with your hips elevated for approximately 20 minutes. Some women place their feet high on a wall. This may help the sperm travel to your uterus.

Women have used glass eyedroppers, a diaphragm cup or cervical cap, a plastic syringe without the needle, and even a turkey baster for inserting semen. The diaphragm and cervical cap are made of rubber and allow you to place the semen in your vagina very close to the cervix. You need to be fitted for a diaphragm by a health practitioner, and cervical caps are not available in all parts of the country. Getting either of these two devices into the vagina usually takes some practice.

If you are using a diaphragm, put the semen in just before you are going to insert the diaphragm into your vagina. Get as much semen into the diaphragm cup as you can. Once in place, the diaphragm rests against the os, the opening of the cervix, and holds the semen close to the cervix. Some people think that the sperm may stick to the inside of the diaphragm and never make it into the fallopian tubes. Others have used the diaphragm and become pregnant.

A plastic syringe without the needle is also a good choice. You can get one from your health care provider or any friend who works in a hospital or clinic. It is easy to use and not quite as messy as other methods — the semen is less likely to spill out. You draw the semen into the syringe by pulling back slowly on the plunger. Then, insert the syringe far back inside your vagina, but not into the cervix itself as this can be extremely dangerous, and sometimes fatal. Press gently on the plunger.

Children conceived through alternative fertilization are most often identified in conjunction with the turkey baster. This has been an unfortunate association and has been the source of a great deal of anger in the lesbian community among mothers, their friends, and support networks.

The difficulty most people describe with the turkey baster has to do with its overly large opening. You might want to practice taking fluid in and squeezing it out. Use something fairly thick like salad dressing to practice. Remember, technique is important here! After you draw up the semen, you need to place your finger over the bottom opening, then place it up to the vagina, removing the finger at the last moment as you insert it into the vagina.

As one lesbian mother explained to me, some women have especially loved using the turkey baster as a means of redefining a female cooking tool, changing it from a tool of "keep her in the kitchen and pregnant," to one of woman-controlled conception. She then went on to exclaim, "As Mao said, 'Everything becomes its opposite.' Isn't it fun!"

There are undoubtedly other methods for achieving pregnancy through alternative fertilization. Ask women you know who might be willing to discuss with you how they achieved pregnancy. Not everyone will be willing to talk with you about this. Be sensitive when approaching lesbians who have become pregnant through alternative fertilization, especially if you are asking for detailed, specific information.

If you are planning this pregnancy and parenthood with others, find ways to include them in the insemination process. You can use your imagination here. One couple told me how they set up a very romantic afternoon, making the whole insemination experience memorable, even if a pregnancy wasn't achieved that time. Another woman described in great detail how each of the important people in her life were involved in helping to make the insemination happen. Some lesbians want this to be a "team" effort or an effort of the primary people involved; others are very clear they want to keep it as simple and private as possible. How you do the insemination will probably change from one time to the next. Be open and flexible. Do what feels right for this time.

> ** We practiced with the diaphragm a few times before doing the **
> actual insemination. It was a good thing; we were so nervous
> and laughed so much that if we had used semen the first time
> it would have been on the floor!

> ** My best friend helped me inseminate. She got the stuff from **
> my donor, rushed it to my house and then waited while I
> inseminated. We read poetry about babies and children and
> did a fertility meditation.

> ** This whole process took much more coordination than I **
> expected. You know, predicting my ovulation, then getting
> my donor to deliver the semen on the designated day, putting
> it in the turkey baster and finally getting it into my vagina.
> Surprisingly enough, I got pregnant the first time.

## Sex Preference

It is inevitable that some women will have a preference for having a boy or having a girl. You don't have to talk yourself out of having a preference. However, the question of what you will do if you don't get your preference needs to be explored. Although there are a few theories that offer techniques to help you increase your chances of having one sex over another, there are no guarantees. You need to be very clear, before you start trying to become pregnant, that what you want is a child. Be sure to read the "Considering the Children" chapter in which you have an opportunity to explore your feelings about having boys versus having girls and your thoughts about how you imagine it will be to raise a child of one sex or another.

When it comes to the subject of sex selection, lesbians are often accused of wanting only girls. There is frequently outright hostility from those who make this assumption. It is not unusual for a potential lesbian mother to be asked, "What will you do if you get a boy?" It is quite striking to me that when a heterosexual woman conveys a preference for a child of one sex or the other, no one seems to think twice about it. Were a lesbian to state she wanted only a girl or to be clear about her preference for boy children, there would be a great deal of concern, criticism, and questions as to *why* she prefers one sex to another.

## TIMING THE INSEMINATION

Timing of insemination is what appears to be the critical factor in determining the sex of your child. That is because sex preference techniques are based on the different characteristics of the sperm that produce one sex or another. The female-producing sperm swim more slowly, live longer, and are thought to do better in an acid environment. The male-producing sperm swim faster, live for a shorter period of time, and prefer an alkaline environment. (Some literature states that having an orgasm at the time of insemination creates an alkaline environment in the vagina, thereby increasing the chance of having a boy. There is no definitive documentation on this.) In addition, there are a variety of ways of creating a more acid or alkaline environment in the vagina with a vinegar or baking soda douche. (These are described in greater detail in *Lesbian Health Matters!*)

It is thought that the closer to the time of ovulation that you inseminate, the greater are your chances for having a boy. If you inseminate a few days prior to ovulation, you increase your chances of having a girl. It is thought that the female-producing sperm are hardier and can live longer in the fallopian tubes, and will be there waiting to fertilize the egg even two to three days after insemination. Some people also feel the placement of sperm in the vagina can assist in sex selection. Placing the sperm near the cervix gives the faster males the advantage of a shorter course to run. Placing the sperm near the outside opening of the vagina (after using a vinegar douche) puts the male producing sperm in longer contact with an unfriendly (acid) environment, thereby giving advantage to the female producers.

It is always possible that by inseminating earlier than you expect to ovulate or by using douches which can reduce the amount of cervical mucus, you may make it harder to become pregnant at all. You may want to weigh becoming pregnant during a particular cycle against getting your sex preference.

Whatever method you use, be sure to think through what it will be like for you to have a child of either sex. None of these methods is foolproof; there are no promises that you will get the sex preference you desire.

**❝** I tried inseminating two or three days before ovulation the **❞** first few months. When I didn't get pregnant, I had to really think about whether I was willing to have a boy.

**❝** It took me four months to get pregnant. The first two times I **❞** inseminated right at the time I was supposed to be ovulating.

180

The next two, I did it a few days before. Now I'm expecting in three months and frankly, I don't care what I have, I am just glad I am pregnant.

**“** We decided to inseminate just before I ovulated *and* right **”** when I ovulated. This way we figured we really had a fifty-fifty chance and we might get pregnant.

## *Logisitics and Feelings*

The mere logistics of coordinating a single insemination can be complex at best. Be prepared for possible frustration, mistakes, foul-ups, and mishaps. If you are working with a go-between and a donor, you will have a variety of schedules to coordinate around a given "predicted" ovulation date. Everyone has her part to do. Sometimes the whole process might seem hilariously comical; other times you will want to scream with frustration. Being prepared for the unexpected helps a lot.

Once you begin trying to become pregnant, let your friends know that you will tell them *when* you become pregnant. Persistent questioning from well-meaning friends may make you feel increasingly discouraged if you do not become pregnant on the first few tries. Letting people know you will tell them as soon as you know may make it easier while you are going through the process of trying to become pregnant. Remember that on the average, it takes heterosexual couples six months to get pregnant, and they can try all the time.

Don't underestimate the strain that inseminating and trying to become pregnant may have on you, your partner, and your relationships. You may be more sensitive, pick a fight more quickly, or feel down more often. Keep in mind that trying to become pregnant is hard work. It takes time, energy, and a certain amount of determination, more than you may have originally thought. You may find you will need to reorganize you life slightly to make a space for the insemination process. Be as gentle with yourself as you can. Encourage your friends and loved ones to do the same.

**“** I felt like I was on an emotional roller coaster all the time. I **”** would wonder, am I ovulating? Yes, no, yes? Am I pregnant? I might be pregnant, is it too soon to tell? If I am, will it stick?

**“** I started to realize that whether I got pregnant or not made an **”** enormous difference in my life. I spent the first part of every month waiting to inseminate, and the rest of the month hoping my period wouldn't come.

It is not unusual for the partner or partners of the woman trying to become pregnant to experience feelings of frustration and discouragement during this insemination process as well. If there are other children in your family, they too may experience some of these feelings. Whether they are consciously aware of what is going on or not, children will pick up on the energy and feelings of the people around them. During this time, everyone involved may find they need support, understanding, and plenty of room to experience all the emotions that may surface. Mobilize whatever support networks you have to help you through this time.

Finally, I want to add a note of caution. Despite the fact that we have a good deal of scientific data and knowledge of the how to's of alternative fertilization, there is still a certain degree of unpredictability that surrounds this process. This unpredictability has to do with when and how we get pregnant, who gets pregnant and who doesn't, who carries a pregnancy to term and who does not. Keep in mind that these kinds of unknowns cannot always be dealt with by improving our knowledge or insemination technique. They are simply factors that are out there in the universe and may always be out of our control.

# SPERM – THE ESSENTIAL INGREDIENT

For many lesbians, the most complicated part of planning for a pregnancy is finding the sperm (or semen). I have chosen to speak of "sperm" in this somewhat depersonalized manner because, for many lesbians, the sperm is the essential ingredient in becoming pregnant, not necessarily the man supplying it. I also don't want to confuse the issue of sperm donor with that of father (a man who may or may not provide the sperm, but who is actively involved in the parenting and care of a child). Later in this section we will talk about finding a donor, and another chapter in this book addresses the issue of men in children's lives.

In this chapter, we will discuss where you can get sperm, the advantages and disadvantages of fresh versus frozen sperm, and the implications of Acquired Immune Deficiency Syndrome (also known as AIDS) for lesbians becoming pregnant via alternative fertilization. Also included is a discussion of some suggested medical tests for your donor and tips on how to find a donor.

## *Where to Get It*

There are a number of commonly known ways of obtaining sperm. Each source presents a unique legal, social, emotional, and ethical dilemma. Thus the task is not simply a matter of finding the sperm. One must also sort out the various questions associated with each source. Discussions with other lesbians about the issues involved in obtaining sperm will provide you with a range of perspectives.

Potential sperm sources include sperm from a known donor, sperm from an unknown donor, sperm from a reputable sperm bank, or sperm from a reputable private physician. "Reputable" means that you or someone you trust has determined that the provider has conducted routine testing of donors. These include a sperm count, tests for allergies, gonorrhea culture and syphillis testing, and a complete medical history. You should also determine that the source has utilized proper semen storage techniques and has had some success with performing alternative fertilization.

## INSTRUCTIONS

The exercise below is designed to encourage you to identify what you consider to be the strengths and weaknesses of each of the possible sources of semen. Along with your concrete concerns associated with these choices, be sure you include your feelings. While lesbians are choosing to do things differently from the way they have been done in the past in regard to parenting and pregnancy, we continue to be products of our times, struggling with the changes. As times change, our attitudes may change along with them. Often, however, the feelings remain, causing us to question our choices until we feel resolved enough to act on them.

For each of the categories identified below, make a list of what you consider to be the strengths and weaknesses of each sperm source for you.

▣ Sperm from a known donor:
▣ Sperm from an unknown donor:
▣ Sperm from a reputable sperm bank:
▣ Sperm from a reputable private physician:

After you have gone through each choice, mark which would be your first, second, third, and fourth choice and briefly explain why. In the chapter on "Legal Issues in Donor Insemination," attorney Donna Hitchens elaborates on the pros and cons of each choice. After reviewing that section, come back to this exercise and check to see if you would change your first choice and if there are other strengths and weaknesses you want to be sure you are considering.

## QUESTIONS TO ASK YOURSELF

▣ What are my reasons for wanting a known sperm donor?
▣ What are the issues that worry me about having a known sperm donor?
▣ What are my reasons for wanting an unknown sperm donor?
▣ What are the issues that worry me about having an unknown sperm donor?

Whatever source you choose for obtaining sperm, try to get as much information as you want about the donor prior to insemination, including his medical and sexual health history. Be sure this information is written down and filed somewhere, so you can have easy access to it at a later date if necessary. Read over the sample health history form in Appendix D. Are there other items you want or need to know about your donor given your own family health history? If you have other health history forms available to you, take the parts from each that you like and make up your own form. Gather as much information as you feel is necessary to have. All too often, we fall into the trap of trying to find the "perfect" donor to then have the "perfect" baby. Too much testing may medicalize the process for some women. Do only what you feel comfortable with given the other choices you are making for yourself.

I strongly urge you to be sure your donor takes any necessary tests early on in your plans to inseminate. Most important is a semen analysis and a V.D. test. You will also want to consider a CMV titer, Hepatitis B test, and Chlamydia culture (these are all explained in greater detail in the "Test for Donors" chapter). Test for what *you* want to know. If the tests raise a medical reason for not using that donor, you will need time to find another. One couple I know had made all the preliminary arrangements to use a certain donor. They had completed legal agreements, talked at length about parenting arrangements, and felt comfortable with each other. Their donor did not complete medical testing, however, until the month they were planning to inseminate. Because the results of his tests were worrisome, they decided not to use him as their donor. Frustrated and discouraged, they had to begin the entire process all over again. You might want to be sure you have a semen analysis performed on your donor's semen either before beginning to negotiate any legal agreements or at least as the same time. Waiting until the time of insemination may prove disappointing and problematic.

If you get sperm from a private physician or sperm bank, be sure the donor has had a complete medical work-up. Ask to see the results of these tests and have them thoroughly explained. Get as much medical health history and sexual health history information as you possibly can about your donor. Ask for a copy for your own files. Be persistent if necessary. None of this may seem critical right now, but in a few years, should your child develop any health problem, having a copy of this health history might be important. Be sure to have a health history of your own as well, so you can look critically at any potential risks to your unborn child. Ask the physician, nurse practitioner, or midwife you are working with to review these for you. S/he may find something you missed.

## Fresh Versus Frozen Sperm

There is no definitive data indicating that either fresh or frozen semen is significantly better. In the lists below you will find some identified advantages and disadvantages of using each type of semen, compiled with help from the women at The Sperm Bank of Northern California. Add anything else that you are aware of.

## ADVANTAGES OF FRESH SEMEN

- There are more motile sperm in fresh donation ("motile" refers to the ability of the sperm to move).
- Many studies show higher pregnancy rates using fresh semen.
- Sperm are maintained in what some feel is more "natural" state.
- The number of sperm in a fresh donation may be higher than the number in a frozen donation. This is due to the fact that with a fresh donation you receive the entire ejaculate, whereas with frozen sperm, you receive a portion (usually one-half to one-fourth) of the ejaculate.
- There may be no cost if fresh semen is obtained from a private donor (known or unknown).

## DISADVANTAGES OF FRESH SEMEN

- The availability of the donor at time you wish to inseminate is uncertain.
- It requires elaborate coordination and scheduling to secure a timely donation.
- Although gonorrhea testing can be performed on semen, it usually takes a full 48 hours to get the results. Therefore, you would be using the semen sample without knowing whether or not the sample contained gonorrhea.
- Semen must be used within a short period of time to ensure that sperm are viable.
- It can cost between $90 and $150 per specimen if obtained from a private physician or sperm bank.

## ADVANTAGES OF FROZEN SEMEN

- If a woman has an irregular cycle and is unable to predict ovulation, it may be easier to use frozen sperm since she can contact the sperm bank or physician the day of ovulation.
- It is ideal for a woman who lives in an outlying community and has fresh sperm donor close by.
- Gonorrhea culture results are known before specimens are released and used. Frozen semen would not be

released to you if it were shown to contain gonorrhea. This is an important health aspect of using frozen semen.

- The birth defect rate is lower with frozen semen. In theory, it may be that the "weaker" sperm cannot survive the freezing process.
- Multiple specimens are available, therefore a woman has the opportunity to inseminate with semen of her donor on consecutive days (without risking the lowered sperm count that can result if her donor ejaculates more than once in a 48-hour period).
- You can easily and safely store frozen specimens in your home providing you have an adequate supply of dry ice.

## DISADVANTAGES OF FROZEN SEMEN

- There are lower pregnancy rates with frozen semen.
- There are fewer motile sperm than with fresh semen.
- Sperm have been subjected to a process that alters their natural environment.
- You must let the specimen thaw prior to use.
- It can cost between $50 and $100 per specimen.

One commonly asked question about frozen semen is whether the freezing process will affect the child's genetic make-up in any way. Barbara Raboy, director of the Oakland Feminist Women's Health Center Sperm Bank of Northern California, explained that the freezing process does not alter the genetic material.

Women sometimes wonder whether the choice of fresh or frozen semen will increase chances for having a child of one sex or another. Many practitioners say that it is not so much whether you use fresh or frozen semen, but, as discussed earlier, rather it's the *timing* of the insemination that influences whether you will have a boy or a girl. Inseminating close to the time of ovulation may increase your chances for having a boy, while inseminating slightly before ovulation may increase your chances of having a girl. If women using frozen sperm have male children, it is usually because they tend to inseminate closer to ovulation. It is also thought that the freezing process may in fact select out some of the female sperm, thus leaving a larger number of male sperm in the specimen.

Finally, another question that has aroused a good deal of discussion is whether or not to mix semen from a few different donors so that *you* do not know who the donor really is. There is some concern that certain semen might cancel out the sperm in other semen because of the acid/base balance in the different specimens. You may want to discuss this with your health care practitioner or sperm bank if you plan to use the semen in this way.

# SEXUAL INTERCOURSE WITH A MAN

If you are choosing to become pregnant through sexual intercourse with a man, follow the instructions in the previous section on charting, as it will be important for you to determine when you are ovulating. If you know the man, gather any relevant medical and health information you can. If at all possible, be sure he has a gonorrhea and syphilis test prior to your having sexual intercourse with him. If he is someone you know, you may want him to follow the suggestions in the chapter "Instructions for Donors." Read the section on the how-to's of insemination; some of these suggestions will be helpful to you in achieving a pregnancy.

Lesbians choosing to become pregnant in this manner do so for a variety of reasons. For some women there are no alternative methods available to them. For others, it is the most comfortable of all the alternatives. And for still others, becoming pregnant through sexual intercourse is how they imagined becoming pregnant and they are not interested in alternative technologies.

> **“** I got pregnant the old-fashioned way. I slept with this man I **”** knew. It was how I wanted to do this.

> **“** For me artificial insemination just didn't feel like the way to **”** go. I have bad attitudes about medical technology. It wasn't easy for me to get it on with some guy, but somehow in my mind it was the lesser of two evils.

> **“** Where I live we hadn't heard about alternative fertilization **”** techniques. So I slept with this man I met and got pregnant. It wasn't easy by any means. I wish I had known how to do it another way.

Using this particular method for becoming pregnant can be problematic for some lesbians. This is especially true for women in couples. Many complex and difficult issues can come up if the woman choosing to become pregnant decides to have sex with a man. The woman's partner may feel jealous, resentful, and/or angry, and she may fear that her lover will prefer being with this man, or any man. Issues around sexual intimacy are frequently complicated and intense. Many of us have strong reactions when we feel threatened, abandoned, or in the least bit insecure about our intimate relationships. It may be hard to predict how each woman in a couple will feel if this is the method used to become pregnant. If these issues come up for you, talk about them, confront them, and take whatever steps you can to work them out in the interests of preserving your relationship(s).

In addition to the issues that may come up concerning being sexually intimate with a man, many couples have said they fear this man might want more involvement with their child than both women would like. This could be especially troublesome if the donor is known. You will want to clarify your expectations and his beforehand. You may want to have a legal contract or some kind of written agreement (see Appendix E for sample legal forms) which clearly delineates the boundaries of his relationship with any potential child.

There has always been some hostility in the lesbian community towards women who choose to become pregnant in this way. This has become a controversial method for becoming pregnant. There is often an underlying distrust of lesbians who choose to become pregnant through sex with a man, the assumption being that this method represents a betrayal of one's lesbian identity. Some lesbians feel that having sex with a man, instead of relying on methods of women-controlled conception to become pregnant, contributes to the oppression of all lesbians.

“ Most of my friends would be surprised to learn this is an ” option for me. I'd like to discuss it with others and be able to say *why* I'd do it this way. It is controversial, and not at all the expected way a lesbian would do it.

Each woman must feel free to choose the method which seems best to her, for any number of complicated and intensely personal reasons. Lesbians selecting this method want and need support in discussing this choice openly. In many ways, how we choose to conceive our children is totally irrelevant. We must learn not to judge ourselves or our children by their method of conception, remembering no method is in any way superior to any other.

# FINDING (AND KEEPING) A DONOR

There are many factors to take into consideration when you begin looking for a donor. The search is usually more involved than you may initially imagine. Some fundamental questions may continue to come up as you look for a suitable sperm donor. Will you use a known or unknown donor? Do you want your child to be able to know the donor and be able to contact him in years to come? Do you want the donor involved in the parenting process? Should you have more than one donor so that you can mix sperm or increase the chance of the biological father being unknown? Even if you do not have all your questions answered before you begin your search, begin anyway. Some of your questions will get answered in the process of looking for a donor and talking with potential donors. Keep noticing how you feel as the search unfolds.

The search for a donor — known or unknown — can take you in a number of surprising directions. Lesbians in my groups who decided to become pregnant have a wide variety of stories about how they found their donors. One of my recent groups put together the following list of "how to's" for finding a donor.

## *Tips for Finding a Donor*

• Get the word out to as many people as you feel comfortable telling. Describe the kind of donor you are looking for, being as specific as possible. (See the exercise below on "Donor Profile".) Take your own preferences for a donor seriously, even if it seems that you are looking for what others might call the "perfect" donor. You *can* find the kind of donor you want, though it might take you longer than you had hoped at the start.
• Give yourself a timetable for finding a donor. It is also a good idea to have an alternative plan in mind for getting pregnant. You can look for

a donor for many months and be frustrated because you are ready to inseminate. After you have searched for a donor for a specific length of time, you may want to consider a sperm bank or private physician, if those resources are available to you.

• Some women find a go-between to help locate a donor (both for known or unknown) and to assist with picking up and dropping off the semen if anonymity is desired. Some lesbians have used two go-betweens. One go-between knows the lesbian or lesbian couple seeking to become pregnant; the other knows the donor and the first go-between, but not the woman seeking to inseminate (or her partner). Lesbians who have used this method of finding a donor have indicated that while it is a bit more complicated, they felt more secure in their anonymity.

• To many lesbians, using their lover's brother as the donor seems like the ideal way for both women to be biologically connected to the child. In spite of what appears to be a potentially good idea, I generally do not encourage using brothers as donors. If the brother is a straight man and at some point chooses to file for custody of the child, the lesbian couple runs the risk of losing custody of their child. Most people say, "That would never happen to us; he's her brother." It can happen. You avoid complicated legal situations by not selecting next-of-kin as donors. As it is, even having a known donor may be somewhat risky for some lesbians. Having a donor who is the brother of one of the women may create a difficult situation for the couple, and ultimately for the child. If the couple were to separate, the donor or the parents of the donor may choose to sue for joint custody, causing the child to then become a battleground for these competing interests. Some lesbians do choose to struggle with brothers in making this choice, taking great pains to draw up legal agreements and clarify the details of custody were the situation to change.

Be sure to talk with male friends whom you would consider as donors or who might know other men interested in donating their sperm. Many lesbians have been successful in locating a donor in this way. But be forewarned, men suddenly become very possessive of their sperm, so to speak, when approached by lesbians planning pregnancy.

Lesbians seeking a known donor to be actively involved in the parenting of their child have found both gay and straight men interested in this kind of arrangement. In a few large cities, gay men seeking to become fathers with lesbians have formed groups and advertise in local gay, lesbian and women's newspapers. Be sure to check these out; go to the meetings if possible, or attend one of their social events to meet the men who are interested in becoming parents.

## Race of the Donor/Race of Your Child

All lesbians, regardless of their racial or ethnic background, have a choice regarding the race of their donor, and consequently a choice as to whether to have a bi-racial or racially mixed child. Because more and more lesbians are choosing to adopt children of other races or to have bi-racial and racially mixed children, these exercises have been included to make the various elements of this choice conscious. In addition, this section may be especially useful to interracial couples and groups, as well as any single lesbian actively seeking to birth or adopt a bi-racial or racially mixed child.

> **❝** There are so many white children in our community. I expect **❞** every lesbian to consider having a bi-racial child. Why not? It may be more difficult for a bi-racial child in some ways, but that is not reason enough to keep someone from making that choice.

> **❝** We don't talk about it much as a community, but a lot of chil- **❞** dren of lesbian mothers *are* bi-racial. Our children are much less segregated than we are.

No matter what decision you make concerning the race/ethnic background of your donor, and ultimately your child, there are profound issues of racism and societal oppression to be considered. It is altogether possible that *whatever* choice you make, others may criticize you of racism.

> **❝** The racism inherent in all of this is not necessarily in the **❞** choice, but in the practice of raising the child.

> **❝** Just because we think our children would suffer oppression is **❞** no reason not to do something. If we believed that, many of us wouldn't be lesbians.

The exercises that follow offer you a framework in which to consider some of the questions posed by these choices. They are designed to assist you in recognizing your attitudes, identifying your options, and clarifying your feelings about those options. As you do these exercises, try to avoid judging yourself or your answers. Use these to gather more information about where you stand on this issue.

## WHAT MADE ME FEEL DIFFERENT

1. What do you recall about your childhood that made you feel different or similar to other children and adults? Did any part of these feelings have to do with your race/ethnic background? If so, describe how your race/ethnic background affected how you felt around your peers and other adults.

2. Were there other things that made you feel "different?" Was being different okay? Who or what supported you in being different?

3. What do you value about your background and heritage? What do you feel will be important for you to pass on to your child from your background? From a different heritage than your own?

4. How do you want to share the different aspects of your background or another background with a child (through family, religion, cultural activities, social activities, literature, experience, etc.)?

## RACE OF MY CHILD – SOME CONSIDERATIONS

1. Make a list of reasons you *would* choose to have a bi-racial or racially-mixed child. How would your list be different if you were considering adopting a child who is bi-racial or racially-mixed?

2. Make a list of reasons you would *not* choose to have a bi-racial or racially-mixed child. Again, how would your list be different if you were listing reasons for choosing not to adopt a bi-racial or racially mixed child?

3. If you have or adopt a child whose race/ethnic background is in some way different from your own, do you plan to teach your child about her/his cultural background? If yes, how will you go about doing this at different times in your child's life? If not, what are your reasons for not exposing your child to information about her/his cultural background?

You may find that the questions regarding your reasons for choosing or not choosing to have or adopt a bi-racial or racially-mixed child can be very difficult to answer. As one lesbian mother explained, "For every reason you may think of, you may hear an interior voice criticizing you for having that reason." These are questions you may want to discuss with others and then come back to again. And, at some point, it may simply be easier to get in touch with what *you want* – plain and simple – without dwelling on the reasons for wanting it.

## CONSIDERATIONS FOR COUPLES

The following questions are meant to be answered by lesbians who are part of an interracial couple or group:

1. Each person should think about the race/ethnic background from which she hopes the donor will be. Make a list of your reasons for this choice.

2. Compare your list with that of your partner(s). How are your reasons similar and/or different?
3. How will you decide together the race/ethnic background of your donor?
4. How will you decide on the race/ethnic background of your child?
5. How will each parent be able to share aspects of her ethnic background and cultural heritage with the child?
6. If your relationship ends, will your child's race/ethnic background be a factor in deciding with whom the child will live? If so, how will you make this decision, and what factors will you have to take into consideration?
7. How do you think it will be for a bi-racial or racially mixed child to be raised by lesbian parents? In what ways do you imagine it would be any different for a child with a similar race/ethnic background to the lesbian parents?

As you try to answer these questions, other concerns will undoubtedly come up. This issue poses a challenging choice and usually generates many politically and emotionally charged discussions. Those who have taken on this decision have remarked that there are many tears, fears, and arguments; it is the kind of choice which demands a high degree of struggle as well as focused energy and attention.

    **“** It is interesting how people get all upset when you talk about **”** *having* a bi-racial child. But if you are thinking of adopting a child of another race than your own, they seem to find it easier to accept.

    **“** I didn't think the race of my child would be an issue for any- **”** one. But many of my friends were shocked when my son was born and he was not 100 per cent Caucasian. It never crossed anyone's mind that I would want to have a bi-racial child.

    **“** If LaVerne left me, I don't think I would feel right about raising **”** Amanda alone. She is bi-racial, but she looks black and I am white. It just doesn't feel right to me. I'm not afraid of it; I just don't think it would be good for her.


## *Donor Profile Exercise*

Make a checklist of characteristics for your "ideal" donor. I have included some broad categories to guide you, but they are simply suggestions. Fashion this checklist to best reflect your specifications for a donor.

## PHYSICAL CHARACTERISTICS

- [ ] hair color
- [ ] eye color
- [ ] physical build
- [ ] height and weight
- [ ] specific health factors to be aware of

## BACKGROUND AND LIFE CHOICES

- [ ] cultural background
- [ ] ethnic background
- [ ] religion
- [ ] sexual orientation
- [ ] sexual history
- [ ] drug history
- [ ] alcohol history

## MISCELLANEOUS INFORMATION

- [ ] known donor
- [ ] want child to be able to contact donor
- [ ] want donor involved in parenting
- [ ] amount of involvement desired
- [ ] kind of involvement desired
- [ ] financial support desired
- [ ] unknown donor

Once you find a donor, then begins the process of negotiating a legal agreement, gathering necessary medical information, and having a variety of medical tests performed (see the "Sperm" chapter). How much of this gets done before you begin to inseminate is up to you. You may want to read the "Tests for Donors" and "Legal Issues" chapters as you are thinking about when to go ahead. Some lesbians spend months talking with their donor about the different issues that could come up, seeking to clarify everything before beginning to inseminate. Others simply choose to go ahead with the insemination and figure out more of the "details" later. You may be at one end of the spectrum or the other, or you may fall somewhere in between.

> **"** We found a donor through a friend and inseminated even **"**
> before knowing anything about his medical history. Our child
> is fine and healthy, but I'm not sure I would do it that way
> again.

> **"** My donor plans to be involved in parenting our child. I have **"**
> known him for a few years. My lover and I feel good about the

196

set-up we've created. It took us almost a year to agree on how we wanted it and I'm sure this is not the end of it.

**❝** I got semen from a sperm bank. I specified the qualities and **❞** characteristics I wanted and they came pretty close to giving me that. Most importantly, they did a complete physical on the guy, and he agreed to stay in touch with them yearly.

Keeping your donor is yet another concern. Lesbians have expressed frustration about trying to keep their donors once they begin the insemination process. If the woman inseminating does not get pregnant during the first few months, some donors may decide that they no longer want to donate sperm. Other donors begin to have "second thoughts" and may choose to stop donating sperm. One way lesbians have chosen to deal with this problem is to have their donor store his sperm with a sperm bank or private physician. That way, he does not have to donate each month, and you have fewer people to coordinate each time you want to inseminate. In some states, the sperm bank or private physician is licensed to perform inseminations with semen you obtain from an identified donor and will store the semen for you until you need it. Many women choose to do it this way, thereby insuring additional legal protection. (Some lesbians consciously do not choose to use a sperm bank or private physician because of prohibitive financial costs, attitudes of staff to lesbians choosing to be parents, and quantity and type of questions asked.)

# TESTS FOR DONORS *

Below you will find a list of some of the factors you will want to include in your donor screening. You may need to gather further information on each of these tests, as new tests are currently being developed for certain conditions and costs vary depending upon where you have the tests done. For further information, you can contact a sperm bank, an infertility clinic, a family planning nurse practitioner or certified nurse midwife, a gynecologist, the family planning program of your local public health department, or your local women's health clinic.

## SEMEN EVALUATION

This test can give you a great deal of information about the fertility potential of your donor. Commonly referred to as a semen analysis, this test will give you accurate information about your donor's sperm count as well as the motility and morphology (shape) of the sperm. If you choose to freeze the sperm for future use (cryopreservation), "post-thaw" motility can also be evaluated.

## PERSONAL AND FAMILY HEALTH HISTORY

As stated earlier, it is absolutely essential that you gather as much information about your donor's personal and family health history as you possibly can. See Appendix D for a sample history form which you

---

*Some of the information included here was furnished by The Sperm Bank of Northern California, located in Oakland, CA.

can give to your donor to complete. If you go to a private physician or sperm bank, check its history form to be sure it includes everything you want to know. You may want to look for a history of pharmaceutical and/or recreational drug use, history of alcohol use, repeated exposure to toxic chemicals or radiation, frequent sexual contact with multiple partners, personal history of infertility, family history of miscarriage, health status of family members going back two or three generations, and so on.

## PHYSICAL EXAMINATION

Once you have gathered a personal and family health history, you may want your donor to have a thorough physical examination, including the laboratory tests discussed below. This may cost you from $90-$150. Some lesbians feel strongly about having this done, others are not as adamant. If you choose the exam, be sure the donor will agree to the release of any results.

## LABORATORY TESTS

There are a series of bacteriological tests you may want your donor to have, all of which can be done as part of a physical exam. These test for specific bacteria in the urethra (male urinary tract). You can check with a urologist concerning the types of tests available and their cost.

One laboratory test I strongly recommend is a Chlamydia (cla-mid-ia) culture. Chlamydia is rapidly becoming the most prevalent of all sexually transmitted diseases (along with gonorrhea, herpes, and syphilis). It is a bacterial infection which has been known to contribute to pelvic inflammatory disease, tubal or ectopic pregnancies, and miscarriages, and may increase the risks of premature delivery or stillbirth. The mother can transmit the disease to the child in the form of conjunctivitis (an inflammation of the eye) or as pneumonia. The symptoms may be masked or may appear to be similar to those associated with gonorrhea or a urinary tract infection. A new diagnostic test has recently been developed to screen for chlamydia.

If possible, be sure your donor is tested for gonorrhea and syphilis as close to the time of insemination as possible. This can be done routinely at a men's clinic or at the local public health department, usually at no cost.

## HEPATITIS B

It is especially important to have this test done if you are using a gay donor. Hepatitis B is a highly infectious and serious disease which can cause major health problems. It can be done in conjunction with other blood tests such as those for blood type, Rh factor, and a complete blood count (CBC).

# TEST FOR CYTO-MEGALO VIRUS

Cyto-megalo virus, commonly known as C.M.V., has been found to be one of the most common causes of miscarriage and birth defects. It can be detected in semen and cervical mucus. Testing is performed on the semen for the actual virus, whereas blood testing can reveal levels of C.M.V. antibodies indicating past infection. This testing should be done if there is special concern about birth defects or if you are using a gay donor. Even though C.M.V. is frequently found in the general population, its incidence is higher among gay men.

These tests will give you a better indication of your donor's current state of health and of the health of the semen you will be using for insemination.

# SOME REPRODUCTIVE
# HEALTH CONCERNS

It no longer surprises me that when we do introductions in my groups, most women immediately follow their name with their age. Most women are concerned about their reproductive health as they grow older, and for those over 35, the question of fertility is especially pressing and pertinent.

This section is a potpourri of reproductive health information. It contains information about fertility and infertility, prenatal screening DES (a hormone given to women from 1940 to 1971 to prevent miscarriage), a few of the newer medical procedures available to pregnant women, and miscarriage and stillbirth. Check the annotated bibliography for further readings on the subjects that are of interest to you.

## *Fertility Concerns*

Many women struggle with the nebulous concept of the biological time clock. "How long do I have to become pregnant?" is a commonly asked question. There is no absolute answer. More and more women are having babies in their late thirties and early forties. Much depends on your health, your fitness, and your menstrual cycle. It is best to assume you *can* become pregnant until you discover you cannot. If you have reasons to believe you may not be able to conceive (i.e., you have had Pelvic Inflammatory Disease, or you have been sexually active with men without using birth control but have never gotten pregnant), you may want to talk over your concerns with a fertility specialist.

There are both psychological and physical factors influencing whether a woman becomes pregnant. Things such as stress and ambivalence about pregnancy may play a part, as may physical problems and health problems of the sperm donor. If you have been trying to become pregnant for eight months or more with no success, there are two simple steps to try first: 1) have a sperm count done on your donor's sperm, and 2) make sure you are inseminating at the correct time. If neither of these seems to be the cause of the problem, talk with a person who specializes in infertility problems. Take a month or two off from inseminating; a short break can sometimes make all the difference. And, remember, getting pregnant is not always as easy as we would like it to be. You may just be someone for whom it is going to take a little longer. You may also want to do some reading on infertility testing, including the kinds of tests that are done and what to expect. In Appendix B you will find a description of a typical preliminary evaluation for infertility.

It is easy to get panicky about one's fertility if you have been unable to get pregnant after a few months of trying. It is best to stay as calm as possible in order to reduce any anxiety that could add strain to your body. There are ways to deal with infertility or suspected infertility. Find a fertility specialist you like and trust. Since you may encounter a homophobic or anti-lesbian bias in dealing with some health care practitioners, you may want to contact a women's health clinic for the names of practitioners known to be supportive of lesbians trying to become pregnant. In addition, you will want to get some emotional support for yourself and those close to you.

> **❝** I tried to get pregnant for over eight months. I was severely **❞** depressed. I thought I would never have a baby. Then I went to see a nurse practitioner who does fertility work. We talked about a lot of things. She did a regular pelvic exam and told me everything seemed fine and that I should just keep trying. I felt better, I felt like it was still possible for me. Sure enough, I got pregnant three months later.

Finally, if you are unable to conceive or carry a pregnancy to term, you can still bring a child into your life through one of the other parenting options discussed earlier. You may have to rethink your plans and parenting choice, but there may still be a way for you to have a child.

> **❝** I went through the whole series of tests. The doctor wanted to **❞** start me on Clomid (a fertility drug). He didn't have much information about it, but I read what I could find. It didn't sound like something I wanted to take. Then a friend told me about a baby who was going to be up for independent adoption. I decided to go that route instead.

> **❝** After one year of my trying to become pregnant, my doctor **❞** suggested I try Clomid. I did and was able to get pregnant after three months. I have a healthy one-year old now. I don't know what the long-term effects of this drug are, but I read everything that I can get my hands on. I just hope it's not another DES-type drug.

**ct** It was scary not to be able to get pregnant. We tried for **>>**
months. Our donor's sperm count was high, I ovulated on a
regular basis, but we simply couldn't get it to happen. I was
having trouble finding work, and our relationship was going
through some changes I wasn't willing to look at. We split up.
I think now it's best that I didn't get pregnant. I really wasn't
ready then.

## Prenatal Screening

Amniocentesis, Alpha-feto Protein screening, Ultrasound, and
Chorionic Villi Sampling (CVS) are procedures commonly referred to as
prenatal screening techniques. They are used for a variety of reasons,
including detection of particular diseases (such as Down's Syndrome and
Spina Bifida) or any chromosomal abnormalities in the developing fetus,
determination of the position of the fetus in utero, and for providing
information regarding the developing fetus to the expectant parent(s)
and medical practitioners.

Women who are 35 and over, are often "encouraged" by the medical community to avail themselves of prenatal screening procedures.
However, none of these are required. You can *choose* to have amniocentesis, for example, if you wish to learn whether your developing fetus has
Down's Syndrome or if you want to know the sex of your child. In fact,
some states offer this test free to women 35 and over.

I firmly believe in every woman's right to choose what she
believes is best for herself, her child, and her life. But, I must state my
bias, which for some may seem contradictory to other health and medical information I have given in this book. I question the motives behind
prenatal screening and the necessity of such screening tests.

There appear to be some basic assumptions underlying the need
for prenatal screening: that disability is a tragedy, that disability must be
avoided, and that disability cannot be managed. It is important to
remember that disability is *not* a health problem. It is a social problem
and civil rights issue. As one disabled woman told me, "Most of my problems are not caused by my disability."

These screening procedures encourage us to *think* we have control over something we don't — the future of our children's health. They
also contribute to the myth that disability is preventable, ignoring the
possibility that anyone can become disabled at any time in her/his life.
Such procedures overlook the need for an accessible environment and for
regulation of exposure to toxins in the workplace and in the environment. They serve to perpetuate stereotypes of the disabled as living a life
of suffering. They contribute directly to the profound discrimination experienced by disabled people. The negative stereotypes about disability,

205

which are so pervasive in our culture, make an informed choice concerning prenatal screening a difficult one.

We must ask ourselves what are the implications (social, psychological, cultural, medical) of aborting a *wanted* pregnancy. We must recognize that we live in a society in which procedures such as amniocentesis are socially sanctioned. There is often an implicit assumption that if your child (fetus) is in some way "damaged," you will abort it. A woman only rarely uses amniocentesis as a way of learning more about the health of her child so that she can be prepared to care for that child were it to be born disabled. Instead, she is reminded of the hardships that child will face and of the difficulties she (and her partner) will have to endure. She is often told she can have a "normal" or "healthy" child next time. We must look carefully at these attitudes and the messages they convey about disability, disabled people, what is "normal," and what constitutes a "healthy" pregnancy.

I support every woman's right to abortion at any point in her pregnancy. I believe she should have the choice to bear a child if and when she so chooses, and she should have the right to bear a child she feels capable of caring for. However, I think we must be aware of what it means to the future of our culture, to the status of the human race, and to our control over our own bodies, if we are subtly and not so subtly encouraged to abort children who are in some way "abnormal" or allegedly "defective."

Prenatal screening procedures can not tell you how serious any disability will be, or what kind of person your child will be. They can only tell you *if* some condition is present. As Ruth Hubbard so eloquently concludes in her essay "Personal Courage is Not Enough: Some Hazards of Childbearing in the 1980's" in *Test-Tube Women*, "Our decision to have [children] will continue to need to be based on that peculiar mix of unpredictability and planning that makes childbearing and childrearing often joyful, often painful, and always chancy."

If you are over thirty-five and considering prenatal screening, I encourage you to gather as much up-to-date information as you want in order to make an informed decision. You can contact women's health organizations for any educational materials they have on prenatal screening techniques. I also direct you to the essays in *Test-Tube Women* which address the medical, political, social and psychological aspects of these procedures. Finally, you may want to talk with other women you know who have had these procedures.

It is a good idea to have some idea of how you plan to proceed if you learn you are carrying a disabled fetus. For most women, this is not a simple or straightforward decision. It can be complicated, confusing, ethically and morally challenging, and anxiety-producing. Below you will find a few questions which may be helpful in guiding your thinking. I also encourage you to get professional counseling if you or you and your partner(s) feel unable to make a decision alone.

1. What do I want to learn from having these procedures?
2. What will I do if I learn my child has Down's Syndrome? Another disability?
3. What kind of support (emotional, financial, medical, childcare) will I need to raise a child with a disability?
4. How will I decide what I am going to do if I learn my child is in some way disabled?
5. How would it be different if my child was to have one kind of disability instead of another? Do I feel capable of managing some disabilities? If so, which ones?
6. What strengths do I bring to the situation of raising a child with special needs?
7. What would be difficult for me about raising a child with special needs?
8. What are my limits? How comfortable am I with acknowledging those limits and living with the choices I decide to make?

The questions raised by prenatal screening procedures are not easy ones to answer. They present each of us with profound ethical dilemmas as well as practical concerns. We are still learning about these procedures, the benefits we will reap from them, their long-term effects on us and on our children, and who they really serve.

# DES Daughters

If you are a DES daughter you need to be aware that your exposure to this prenatal hormone may increase your risks for miscarriage and premature labor. A DES daughter who becomes pregnant should receive high-risk prenatal care as soon as she thinks she might be pregnant. For more information on DES daughters and pregnancy, be sure to contact DES Action (see the "Bibliography" for the address).

# New Medical Procedures and Pregnancy

If you choose to become pregnant, a number of current medical practices might be suggested to you during the course of your pregnancy, even if everything seems to be going well. These procedures during pregnancy include amniocentesis (a procedure that can detect about one hundred fetal chromosomal abnormalities, the most well-known of which is Down's Syndrome) and ultrasound (the use of sound waves to produce moving pictures of the fetus in the womb). Fetal monitoring, drugs during prenatal care, labor, and delivery, caesarian section, and other medical technologies performed during labor and delivery may also be suggested. Be an informed consumer. Take time to read informational materials, explore your feelings about the use of such procedures and talk candidly with your health care practitioner about her/his thoughts on these technologies and their application to you and your pregnancy. Finally, contact women's health organizations, which can provide you with up-to-date information on the risks and benefits of these procedures. Many of these technological procedures raise pressing ethical questions. I encourage you to take the time to explore those questions, on your own and with friends, to increase your chances of making responsible choices.

## *Miscarriage and Stillbirth*

Miscarriage and stillbirth are two aspects of pregnancy that receive little attention unless they happen to you or someone you know. Most of us would like to ignore the shocking reality of losing a pregnancy in these ways. Miscarriage is most likely to occur within the first trimester (the first three months) of pregnancy, although it has been known to occur later and sometimes occurs following an amniocentesis procedure. (The risk of miscarriage following amniocentesis is close to 0.5 percent.) Stillbirth can occur very close to, or at, term. Stillbirth usually results from loss of oxygen supply to the baby in the uterus.

Many of us find it difficult to believe that we could lose a baby after having had to try so hard to even *get* pregnant. Unfortunately it does happen. Women who inseminate experience about the same miscarriage rate as other pregnant women. About 15% of all pregnancies end in miscarriage. Approximately 75% of these occur in the first trimester and are frequently unavoidable. Although much is still unknown about the specific causes of miscarriage, there are some documented reasons why miscarriage can happen.

### SOME POSSIBLE REASONS FOR MISCARRIAGE

- genetic causes: a genetic abnormality in the fetus
- malformations of the uterus: Most commonly this involves an extra wall in the uterus that partially divides it into two cavities. (A DES daughter is also more likely to have a small or constricted (T-shaped) uterus.)
- hormonal deficiencies
- anatomical problems of the cervix
- blighted ovum: The fertilized egg never develops properly. This is cited as the most common reason for miscarriage in the first trimester.

**"I went into this horrible depression right after I miscarried."** My midwife explained I felt that way because of all the hormonal changes my body was going through, as well as the overwhelming feelings of loss I was experiencing.

**"I knew my mom had miscarried once or twice. When I was"** able to tell my mother what happened, she was wonderful. She seemed to forget that I was this lesbian trying to have a kid and saw me as a woman who was like her and had lost a child. It has brought us closer together.

As hard as it is for some women to believe, it is important to remember that miscarriage and stillbirth are not a punishment. They can, and do, happen to anyone. You will want to begin prenatal care early in your pregnancy (preferably during the first three months), eat well, exercise regularly, and take good care of yourself. These are measures that might help prevent miscarriage.

Whether you are a biological or non-biological mother, don't underestimate the emotional impact of a miscarriage or stillbirth on your life. One of the reasons miscarriage is so frightening is that the woman and/or her partner are rarely prepared for it and often do not understand the physiological details of the event. These problems are then compounded by the intense emotions that accompany the loss of a pregnancy. Women experiencing such a loss need to take time to heal emotionally as well as physically. It can be a deeply traumatic and emotionally stressful time. Seek out other women, lesbian or straight, who have shared this experience. You will find a great deal of support among these women. Above all, take time to grieve.

**"I didn't want to tell anyone in my family I had a stillbirth. I"** was frightened they would be relieved that I wasn't going to have a baby.

**"Did we do something wrong? Had we not taken good enough"** care while Jennifer was pregnant? Were we being punished because we are lesbians? These are the kinds of questions that continue to haunt me.

**"I feel sad all the time. My friends have been wonderful, but I"** get the feeling they wish I would get over this loss and just start trying again. No one is being hurtful or intentionally thoughtless. I think they just don't understand how long it will take me to accept this loss.

Each person experiences grief in her own way and at her own pace. Don't let yourself be rushed through your grieving process. Move at what feels to you like the best pace. Many women have found that feelings of grief can come up again at significant anniversaries. Be sensitive to those times and be gentle with yourself as those times approach. Remember, you can try to become pregnant again. Check with your health care provider and only begin the process again when you feel ready.

# LESBIANS, AIDS, AND ALTERNATIVE FERTILIZATION*

For many years, lesbians choosing to become parents by means of alternative fertilization have preferred to use gay men as sperm donors. One reason for this choice is strictly legal. It is often thought that were a lesbian to be challenged by a heterosexual man over the custody of a child, she would be faced with losing her children. However, if a gay man were to file for child custody, the two biological parents would most probably be at an equal disadvantage.

Another reason lesbians choose gay men as donors is political. Many gay men support the idea of lesbians having children and choose to demonstrate this support by donating their sperm for inseminations. Some gay men may want to be parents as well. Donating sperm becomes an avenue by which they, too, can become parents, depending upon the agreement reached with the woman (and her partner).

Finally, many lesbians enjoy the feeling of "gay pride" that having a gay donor brings. They would rather be dependent upon a gay man for sperm, and would rather tell the child that his/her donor is gay. Making this choice has become increasingly more difficult, however. During the past few years, we have had to acknowledge that the presence of AIDS (Acquired Immune Deficiency Syndrome) and its prevalence in the gay male community is having a significant effect on lesbians' choice of donors.

This chapter provides basic information about AIDS, the AIDS antibody test, and the question of using gay men as donors. Also included

---

*Significant sections of this text were taken from pamphlets entitled "Women and AIDS" and "Lesbians and AIDS" written by the Women's AIDS Network, 333 Valencia Street, 4th floor, San Francisco, CA 94103 and from *Lesbian Passion: Loving Ourselves and Each Other*, JoAnn Loulan, Spinsters/Aunt Lute, 1987.

211

are specific suggestions for donor screening techniques which may reduce a woman's risk of exposure to the AIDS virus through alternative fertilization. In discussing the topic of AIDS, it is essential that we be aware of our own homophobia, and of the assumptions and stereotypes that this disease raises and potentially reinforces.

The AIDS epidemic, with its accompanying worldwide attention, has brought about an all-too-careful scrutiny and subsequent condemnation of the sexual habits of gay men. Once again, we see the media presenting gay men solely as sexual beings with no other dimensions or interests. There is a not-so-subtle suggestion that being gay means potential infection with the AIDS virus. In fact, not all gay men are infected with the AIDS virus. As lesbians, we need to be careful not to extend our fears of being exposed to AIDS to a general condemnation of gay men and their life choices.

To a large extent, AIDS hysteria promotes homophobia. Homophobia can take many forms. Most commonly, we are seeing it in the discrimination of gay men in employment, housing, and health care. Lesbians are not immune to homophobia and our attitudes may contribute to the homophobic mentality in the culture at large.

WHAT IS AIDS?

AIDS is a disease caused by a virus called the Human Immunodeficiency Virus (HIV). When the virus enters the bloodstream, researchers believe that it attacks certain white blood cells, called T-lymphocytes. This attack on the T-lymphocytes causes a breakdown in the functioning of the body's immune system and leaves the body vulnerable to a variety of otherwise controllable infections known as opportunistic infections. While the opportunistic infections themselves may be treatable, there is no cure for the underlying immune deficiency that causes them. It is not known what percentage of people infected with HIV will go on to develop AIDS or ARC (AIDS-Related Complex). However, some studies have shown that at least 70 percent of people infected with the virus will develop some HIV-related symptoms or AIDS.

WHO IS AT RISK FOR AIDS?

We now know that it is not who you are, but what you do that increases your risk of exposure to the AIDS virus. Therefore, a discussion of risk needs to describe risk behaviors, not risk groups. A lesbian may be at risk for HIV infection if, since 1978 she has:

- shared needles while using I.V. drugs,
- had sexual contact with men who were bisexual or gay, were I.V. drug users, were hemophiliacs, were known to be infected with HIV, or had sexual contact with women

who either use or have used I.V. drugs or have had sex with men known to engage in high risk behaviors,

☐ had a blood transfusion in the United States between 1978 and 1985,

☐ had donor insemination by a donor whose sexual or drug-using history is unknown to her, or who is known to be at increased risk because he is an I.V. drug user, hemophiliac, or gay or bisexual man.

As of September 1988, there have been no documented cases of lesbians infected with HIV through alternative fertilization. However, in 1985, a report from Australia stated that four heterosexual women, who were inseminated with semen from a donor who was later found to be HIV-positive but had no known symptoms of AIDS or ARC, were found to be infected. Since the HIV is known to be transmitted through specific body fluids, principally blood and semen, and because a man can be infected and not have any symptoms, lesbians choosing alternative fertilization may want to follow the screening techniques suggested below with all of their donors.

## SUGGESTED SCREENING TECHNIQUES

1 Do a risk assessment of your donor(s). Gather all the information you can on his health history and sexual activities since 1978. That means asking how he has sex, how often and with whom. Receptive anal intercourse is known to be the riskiest sexual practice. Active anal intercourse, receptive oral sex and receptive anal fisting are also very risky. Find out if he has engaged in these activities and how many partners he has had.

2 Any potential donor should be asked to take an AIDS antibody test. The AIDS antibody test measures the presence or absence of HIV antibodies in the blood. If antibodies are present, the test results are positive and the individual is presumed to be infected and capable of passing the virus on to others through the usual routes of transmission. Many people have faced discrimination in their health insurance, employment, housing, and so on, when it was learned that they had had the antibody test or when the result of their test was revealed. Therefore, anyone taking the test should have it done where anonymity and confidentiality can be protected and guaranteed. If your donor cannot get an anonymous test in his town or city, hopefully he can get one nearby. He must carefully consider all the implications of taking the

213

test and have an opportunity to talk with a counselor prior to taking the AIDS antibody test.

**3** It is recommended that your donor have two AIDS antibody tests, six months apart, before you begin inseminating. If your donor has two tests, six months apart, and both are negative, you have the best assurance that he does not have the virus at this time. Between tests and while you are using his semen for insemination, he should be practicing safe sex with his partner(s).

**4** If you are going through a private physician or a sperm bank, make sure that they have the same guidelines you do for choosing a donor. Talk with them in specific terms about how they choose donors, ask for any and all information they have on your donor and let them know any additional questions you want answered.

For further information about AIDS and/or the AIDS antibody test:

Contact your local health department for any information they may have about the incidence of AIDS in your community.

Contact the National Gay Task Force Crisis Line for the AIDS organization nearest you. In New York, Alaska, and Hawaii: (212) 807-6016. All other states: (800) 221-7044.

Contact the Women's AIDS Network c/o San Francisco AIDS Foundation, 333 Valencia Street, San Francisco, CA 94103 for copies of the pamphlets "Women and AIDS" and "Lesbians and AIDS" and for information about what women are doing to assist in our community's battle against this disease.

## AIDS BIBLIOGRAPHY RESOURCES

Since the first edition of this book, there have been a number of excellent books written on AIDS and some of the legal, political, social, and personal issues of importance to women. Listed below are only a few of the many resources now available.

Loulan, JoAnn, "What Do Lesbians Need To Know About AIDS?" in *Lesbian Passion: Loving Ourselves And Each Other*, Spinsters/Aunt Lute, 1987.

Norwood, Chris, *Advice for Life: A Woman's Guide to AIDS Risks and Prevention*, Pantheon, 1987.

Patton, Cindy and Janis Kelly, *Making It: A Woman's Guide to Sex in the Age of AIDS*, Firebrand Books, October 1987, in English and Spanish.

Richardson, Diane, *Women and AIDS*, Methuen Press, 1988.

# LEGAL ISSUES IN DONOR INSEMINATION

## Donna J. Hitchens

## *Introduction*

During the last five years, the Lesbian Rights Project in San Francisco has been consulted by lesbians who have decided to become mothers through donor insemination. Women have varied as to the time they seek legal advice — for some it has been prior to beginning the insemination; for others, during their pregnancy; and for still others, after a baby has been born and problems have arisen with the donor. The purpose of this chapter is to share the results of our legal research and work with lesbians who are conceiving children through donor insemination. It is our hope that by doing so, we will alert women to potential legal problems that can be avoided through careful planning.

It should be noted that this chapter is *not* a substitute for talking with a lawyer. Because every state has different laws governing parent-child relationships, women considering this procedure should consult with a lawyer in the state where the insemination and birth will take place.[1] In three states, for example, it is against the law for anyone except a doctor to perform an insemination.[2]

## *Is a Donor a Father?*

The legal term for this form of conception is Artificial Insemination by Donor (AID). The legal implications vary from state to state and depend upon the type of donor used. The major concern, of course, is whether a donor will be recognized as the father of the child.

215

Many states do not have any statutes covering AID, nor do they have any court opinions that define the rights of the mother, donor, or the child conceived through AID. In those states that do have laws that address this concern, the law tends to be limited to covering a marital situation or a situation where a doctor performs the insemination procedure. For example, California Civil Code Section 7500 provides:

(a) If, under the supervision of a licensed physician and with the consent of her husband, a wife is inseminated artificially with semen donated by a man not her husband, the husband is treated in law as if he were the natural father of the child thereby conceived

(b) The donor of semen provided to a licensed physician for use in artificial insemination of a woman other than the donor's wife is treated in law as if he were not the natural father of a child thereby conceived.

This statute was adopted from the Uniform Parentage Act. Therefore, other states that have adopted the Act probably have similar code sections.[3] In a state which has a similar law, a woman who uses a doctor to acquire the sperm and perform the insemination is protected from a court later determining that the donor is the father and has parental rights as to the child. A number of other states have passed some type of legislation concerning AID.[4]

In states that do not have a statute or where the woman does not utilize a physician to acquire the semen, it is impossible to predict what the courts might do. It *may* be that the judge will look to the intent of the parties at the time the insemination was done.[5] It is also possible that paying the donor for his semen or entering into an agreement with the donor will result in a court deciding that use of an insemination procedure does not give rise to a parental relationship between the donor and the child. These possibilities are discussed below in "Entering Into an Agreement."

The Board of Directors of the American Fertility Society has proposed model legislation for situations involving "Artificial Insemination with Donor Semen." This model legislation specifically states:

The donor shall have no rights in or liability to any child conceived through artificial insemination with donor semen, whether or not the donor's identity is known to the recipient.

The one problem with the proposed legislation is that it provides that only a licensed physician or a health practitioner working under the direct supervision of a licensed physician may perform an insemination. Anyone else who performed a donor insemination could be guilty of a crime. To the best of our knowledge, no state has yet adopted this legislation.

216

# Legal Implications

If a donor is determined to be a "natural father," he becomes vested with certain rights and responsibilities in relation to the child. The most significant of these are:
• A right to custody of the child if a court determines that it is in the best interests of the child to live with the father.
• A right to joint custody with the mother in many states.
• A right to regular visitation with the child if the child is in the mother's custody.
• A right to custody of the child if the mother dies or becomes physically or mentally unable to care for the child, including the ability to prevent adoption.
• An obligation to pay child support.

In addition, conflicts may arise over whether the donor has a right to have his name appear on the birth certificate; has some authority in decisions concerning the child's name, medical care, and education; and has the ability to prevent the mother from moving to another state with the child.

These are all serious concerns that should be considered in depth by women considering AID and trying to decide the type of donor they want. The first major decision to be made is whether the donor is to be a father. Some lesbians want their children to know their biological roots, have a positive male role model, or simply have a father. In addition, some women believe it is the child's right to have a father, or they anticipate future problems if a child demands to know who her (or his) father is or begins a search for the father. Other lesbians have seen no need for the child to have a father, have wanted to avoid legal or emotional conflicts that might impair, thereafter, their family unit, or have not known any men they consider good father material.

The mother and the donor *may* be able to modify the legal implications by use of an agreement. Although it is accompanied by some risks, an agreement may offer the option of having a donor who will become known to the child, while limiting his legal rights and responsibilities in relation to the child.[6] Agreements are discussed below.

# Selecting A Donor

Once the decision is made about what relationship, if any, the donor will have with the child, the next step involves selecting the donor method. A number of methods are available, each of which has its own benefits and weaknesses. In all probability, none of the methods will be perfect. Each woman has to review the alternatives and decide which method is best for her situation. She also must decide on a method she is willing and able to repeat for several months. The following alternatives should be considered in conjunction with the information presented under "Is a Donor a Father?" and "Entering Into an Agreement."

## USING A KNOWN DONOR

A known donor is a man whose identity is known to the mother and who knows the mother's identity.[7]

*Benefits*: The benefits of using a known donor are that the mother can choose the kind of personal and physical characteristics she desires; she has control over the process; it avoids the hassles and uncertainties of going through a sperm bank or doctor; a more complete family medical history will be available in the event the child has future medical problems; the donor's identity can be made known to the child at some point in the future; and the possibility exists for a meaningful relationship to develop between the donor and the child.

*Weaknesses*: The problems connected with choosing a known donor relate to the probability than he will see and know the child. This may lead to more "paternal" feelings that he expected and, consequently, to more demands to be treated as a father than the mother ever anticipated. There have been a number of cases where donors originally claimed that they wanted no rights or responsibilities, and later began demanding the right to visitation, some control over the child's upbringing, and time with the donor's family — "grandparents." The use of a known donor is accompanied by the possibility of future problems.

*Variations*: Some states have laws that say a donor of semen to a licensed physician is not the father of a child born from an insemination using the donor's semen. These laws do not require the donor to be unknown to the woman, only that a doctor be used as the go-between. It may be possible, therefore, to achieve the benefits of using a known donor without encountering the weaknesses, if a woman can find a doctor who will assist her. A woman in this situation should ask the doctor to request from the donor a signed release form, acknowledging that the donor waives all rights and interests in any child born as a result of the use of his semen.

It may also be possible to use a known donor and still limit his rights and responsibilities through the use of an Agreement. If a doctor is involved and the donor signs a waiver of rights, there may be no need for other agreements. A woman should consult with her attorney as to which agreements are desired in her particular situation.

## USING SEVERAL DONORS

In order to have some choice over the donor and protect against potential legal problems, some lesbians have used several donors at the

218

same time. The reason for using this method is that, in most cases, neither the mother nor the donors know which insemination resulted in conception.

*Benefits*: This method provides the same freedom of choice and avoidance of hassles from medical personnel as does choosing a single known donor. The donors are less likely to have a personal investment in the baby than someone who knows he is the biological male link to the child, and are less likely to pursue a legal parent-child relationship.

*Weaknesses*: The child could look very much like one of the donors which might have an impact on that donor's response to the child and desire to get involved in the child's life. There now exists a blood test, called an HLA test, that can determine paternity with a high degree of accuracy.[8] Many states allow this test to be introduced into evidence in a paternity case.[9] That means that a donor might be able to prove his biological link to the child. Another weakness in using multiple donors is that it can be difficult to arrange over several months.

## USING A SPERM BANK OR MEDICAL FACILITY

Almost all states have doctors or medical clinics that will arrange AID. Usually this method involves contracting a doctor and letting her (or him) know that you are seeking donor insemination. The doctor then arranges to purchase semen and does the insemination. Most sperm banks use both fresh and frozen semen. The number of sperm banks has increased dramatically over the past ten years. Some of these are women-controlled.

However, sperm banks vary, and you will find there are differences in screening techniques, standards for donor selection, record-keeping of medical histories, etc. Before using the services of any sperm bank, find out about their policies, their procedures, and the availability of semen when you may need it (i.e., are they open evenings or weekends, how much notice must you give before picking up semen?).

*Benefits*: There is total anonymity. This method provides the best security against any legal problems in the future. Very few doctors keep permanent records on donors.

*Weaknesses*: Single women are likely to be asked a lot of questions about why they are choosing AID. Some doctors and clinics will refuse to inseminate a single woman, especially if they know that the woman is a lesbian. In addition, the screening of sperm donors is usually based on what the potential donor knows and honestly reports about his genetic and family medical history. Because he is receiving money for his semen, he may not report something that he thinks would disqualify him.

Doctors and clinics tend to charge a lot of money for providing this service. A fee of $100 per insemination is an average figure for fresh, or frozen sperm, and most women want two inseminations per cycle.

Another problem with using medical personnel is that there may

219

be no permanent record of the donor or his medical history. Therefore, if the child later has serious medical problems where information about family medical history or tissue typing is important, it will not be available.

## USING AN UNKNOWN DONOR

Some women have chosen to have a friend select a donor and act as the go-between in transporting the semen from the donor to the woman to be inseminated. The go-between does not disclose the name of the donor to the woman or vice versa. Both the donor and the woman sign documents which state that the donor will not have any rights or responsibilities in relation to the child.

Some women have chosen to use a doctor as the go-between. This is advantageous if the state law requires a doctor to perform the artificial insemination. If a doctor serves as the go-between, a release form signed by the donor, discussed under "Using a Known Donor" is still applicable.

*Benefits*: As long as the donor and woman are really unknown to each other and do not travel in the same social circles, using an unknown donor is one way of providing for anonymity and lowering the risks of future legal problems. The woman retains more control and can still do the insemination at home. Sometimes it is easier for another person to approach potential donors.

*Weaknesses*: A great deal of power is placed in the hands of the go-between. This person must be someone trusted not to reveal the identities of the people involved. There is no guarantee that the identities of the parties will not be made known to each other at some point. Although a remote possibility, the go-between could be sued and forced to reveal the identities. Doctors usually have a doctor-patient privilege that would protect them from being forced to reveal names. Go-betweens do not have that protection. In addition, a woman who uses an unknown donor and does not use a doctor could possibly encounter problems in the future if the donor determines her identity and sues for paternity, and her state statute required the use of a physician in the insemination procedure.

# *Entering Into an Agreement*

To date, no lawsuits have tested the legality of a written or an oral agreement between the donor and the recipient of his semen when no physician is used. In a New Jersey case,[10] a single woman was inseminated with the semen of a known donor. When the donor sued for paternity, the court held that he was the child's natural father. The major reasons given by the judge were: 1) that the parties intended that the donor should be the father when they participated in the insemination; 2) that it is in the best interest of children to have two parents (the judge meant a father); and 3) that had the parties had intercourse, the man would be the father.

The major reasons for entering an agreement would be to clarify the intent of the donor and recipient, and to clarify their relationship. The most important reason for writing an agreement is so that both the known donor and the woman will be clear with each other as to their expectations. We are not aware of any visitation or paternity problems resulting when the parties wrote an agreement.

Some states, as a matter of law, consider parental visitation and child support to be rights of the child; parents may not contract away a child's rights. Although it is a circular argument, it would seem that a court would first be required to determine whether a sperm donor is a father before it could be argued that an agreement between a donor and the mother involved parents contracting away the rights of their child. It is a real possibility, however, that a court might refuse to honor such an agreement.

Some people have suggested that a recipient of semen should pay the donor. If that were done, and described in the agreement, a commercial contract would be involved — a concept with which judges are familiar and more likely to enforce.

Even though the enforceability of donor-recipient agreements is unpredictable, they are strongly recommended. Aside from using an unknown donor, they are the best protection against future legal problems. Judges may be less likely to decide that the donor is the father when the parties have made it clear that they never intended that result. Some lawyers, however, oppose the use of the agreements because they are evidence of the identity of the donor.[11]

When agreements between donors and recipients are developed, they should accurately reflect the discussion and consensus of the parties involved. If, in fact, the parties have decided that the donor will be known and treated as a father, the agreement should so state. The following are clauses that should be included in such an agreement:

• Marital status of each party;
• That artificial insemination was the procedure used;
• The parties' agreement as to the donor's rights and support obligations;
• Who has authority to name the child;
• Whether rights to bring a paternity suit have been relinquished;
• What authority each party has to appoint a guardian or authorize an adoption;
• How the parties will deal with the identity of the donor;
• How the parties will resolve any disagreements that might develop later;

- That the parties understand that the agreement presents legal questions that are unsettled; and
- That each party signed the agreement voluntarily and freely.

A sample agreement is included in Appendix E.

## Some Other Issues That Arise

### BIRTH CERTIFICATES

Most women who conceive through donor insemination are concerned about what to put on the child's birth certificate when they are asked the identity of the father. Unless you intend the donor to have full parental rights, you should not put his name on the birth certificate. You have a choice of putting "unknown," "information withheld," or "artificial insemination by donor." Because the birth certificate is a public document and will have to be provided at various times during a child's life, most women choose to put "information withheld."

### WELFARE OFFICIALS

Women who have conceived children through donor insemination have had serious problems with welfare officials when they applied for Aid to Families with Dependent Children (AFDC) or medical benefits. Whenever a woman receives AFDC, welfare officials try to ascertain the name of the father so that they can go after him for money. It is a crime to provide false information regarding the identity of the father. On the other hand, most women don't want government officials to know that they used donor insemination. There is no correct answer for dealing with this situation. It should be anticipated by each woman, and a decision on how to respond should be made before filing an application for AFDC.

In 1982, a single, pregnant woman applied for medical and other welfare benefits in Wisconsin. She told her caseworker that artificial insemination had been her method of conception. Somehow the information hit the newspapers and there was a huge cry of public outrage against the woman and her doctor. The Wisconsin Legislature passed a bill that would have made it unprofessional conduct for a physician to artificially inseminate a woman who was receiving AFDC or who would be eligible for welfare if the insemination produced a child. Luckily, the Governor of Wisconsin vetoed the bill so it never became law.

In a California case, a donor brought a paternity suit against a mother who had received AFDC for a few months after the child was born. The county then sued the sperm donor for back payments and argued that the donor should be declared the father.

# Legal Rights Of The Mother's Partner

Some lesbians who choose to become mothers through donor insemination make that decision with a partner. Sometimes they assume or hope that the partner will be able to adopt the child and become a legal parent. This is not the case. No state allows an unrelated adult, except in some cases a step-parent, to adopt a child *unless* the natural parent waives all parental rights. In the same vein, this partner cannot become the legal guardian of the child without limiting some of the legal rights of the biological mother.

The only things that can be done to try to protect the parental relationship that exists between the child and the mother's partner are:
• *A Will*: The mother should execute a Will nominating her partner as the guardian of the child in the event of the mother's death. The Will might state, for example:

> "If I am unable to raise my child, I believe that it is in her/his best interest to have the continuity of the loving and supportive relationship already established between (*name of partner*) and herself/himself. This appointment is based upon the fact that said minor child has lived with this adult and looks to her for guidance, support, and affection."

In most states, the surviving parent has a right to custody of the child upon the death of the custodial parent. If the donor is unknown, there will not be a problem. If the donor is known, however, and court decides he is the father, he might be entitled to custody if the mother dies. To try to protect against this, the mother should get written authorization giving her the exclusive right to name a guardian in the event of her death. This could be done in the agreement between the donor and recipient, or in a separate document.

In some cases, other relatives of the mother are assumed to be the people who should care for the child if the mother dies. To try to prevent this result, the mother might include a provision in her Will stating that she has specifically not named her parents, brothers, or sisters to be the guardian of her child becaused she does not believe that it would be in the child's best interest to be placed in their custody.
• *A Nomination of Guardianship/Conservatorship*: In order to make her wishes clear and to underscore the importance of the relationship that exists between the mother's partner and the child, the mother should execute a Nomination of Guardianship or a Nomination of Conservatorship. Like many of the legal procedures recommended in this chapter, the legal enforceablility of such a document has not been tested. Furthermore, whether the document should be called a Nomination of Guardianship or a Nomination of Conservatorship, and what specific

clauses the document must contain varies from state to state depending upon the state statutes. But because the possibility exists that such a Nomination will be enforced, it is best to have one as protection. A sample Nomination is attached in Appendix E.

A guardianship/conservatorship gives the care and custody of the child to a responsible adult in cases where the parent is physically or psychologically unable to provide for the care of the child.

• *An Agreement Between the Mother and Her Partner*: In the event that the mother and her partner dissolve their relationship after the birth of the child, the partner will probably find herself in the position of not having her parental relationship with the child legally recognized. That is, she will not have a right to custody and/or visitation, nor will she be legally obligated to pay child support. Regardless of her closeness to the child and the parental care, security, and support she has provided, she may find herself precluded from ever seeing the child again.

To try to protect against this result, it is recommended that the women enter into an agreement that recognizes the parental role, affection, and responsibility that develops between the child and the mother's partner. A sample agreement has been provided in Appendix E. Once again, this document has not been tested in the courts.

• *Medical Consent Form*: A sample medical consent form has also been provided in Appendix E. The purpose of this form is to give the co-mother the authority to deal with medical problems.

*Footnotes*

1. The LESBIAN MOTHER'S NATIONAL DEFENSE FUND has a good national referral list of sympathetic lawyers. They can be contacted by writing to: L.M.N.D.F., P.O. Box 21567, Seattle, Washington 98111. (Phone number: (206)325-2643) They also have an "Artificial Insemination Packet" available that includes information on medical, "how to," and legal aspects of donor insemination. The packet costs $3.00.

2. Georgia Code Ann. 74.101.0 (felony); Idaho Code 39-5401 *et seq* (misdemeanor); and Or. Rev. Stat. 667.360, 667.990 (misdemeanor). Fourteen other states require a physician to perform A.I.D. but provide no sanctions when A.I.D. is performed by someone other than a doctor. (Alaska Stat. 20.20.010; Cal. Civil Code 7500; Colo. Rev. Stat. 19-6-106; Conn. Gen. Stat. Ann. 45-69f; Minn. Stat. Ann. 257.56; Mont. Code Ann. 40-6-106; Nev. Stat. Ann. 126.061; 17 N.J.P.L. No. 7; N.Y. Dom. Rel. Law 73; Okla. Stat. Ann. Art. 10 ch. 24 551-533; Va. Code 64.1.7.1; Wash. Rev. Code Ann. 26.26.50; Wis. Stat. Ann. 891.40; and Wyo. Stat. 14-7-106.)

3. The artificial insemination clause of the Uniform Parentage Act has been adopted in California, Colorado, Minnesota, Montana, Nevada,

New Jersey, Washington, Wisconsin, and Wyoming. Minnesota, Montana, Nevada, and Wisconsin only address the situation where a married woman is being inseminated; none deals with the situation where the insemination is done by someone other than a doctor. This Act is concerned only with the issue of how paternity is determined. Its provisions do not discuss custody.

4. Alaska Stat. 20.20.010; Ark. Stat. Ann. 61-141(c); Conn. Gen. Stat. Ann. 45-69f *et seq*; Fla. Stat. Ann. 74-2.11; Ga Code Ann. 74.101.1; Idaho Code49-5401 *et seq*; Kan. Stat. Ann. 23-128; La. Civ. Code Ann. Art. 188; Md. Est. & Tru. Code Ann. 1-206(b); Mass. Gen. Laws Ann. ch. 46 4B; Mich. comp. Laws Ann. 333.2824(b); N.Y. Dom. REl. Law 73; N.C. Gen. Stat. 49A-1; Okla. Stat. Ann. Art. 10 ch. 24 551-553; Or. Reb. Stat. 109.239, 667.355-70; Tenn. Stat. 68-3-307; Tex. Fam. Code tit. 12 03; and Va. Code 64.1-7.1.

5. In C.M v. C.C., 152 N.J. Super. 160, 337 A.2d 821 (1977), the only reported case involving AID by a known donor in a non-marital situation, the judge looked to the intent of the parties at the time the insemination occurred.

6. Attorneys should by aware of Roland v. Superior Court, 111 Cal. App. 3d 234, 168 Cal. Rptr. 438 (1980). In Roland, a heterosexual woman became pregnant as a result of sexual intercourse. The woman and man entered a contract whereby she released him from any paternity claims. The court held that the contract could not bar the child from bringing a paternity suit. Because this case did not involve artificial insemination, it is impossible to predict whether it would have any affect in a donor insemination case. It could, however, prove to be relevant at some time.

7. If a known donor is used, it is strongly suggested that he be gay. If a heterosexual man is used, there is greater probability that future legal conflicts might develop and that the woman's lesbianism would be used against her. Whether the woman uses a gay man or a heterosexual man, it is imperative that all health precautions be taken and that the man be screened for any possible health problems.

8. The H.L.A. test involves a tissue typing analysis done on blood samples from the mother, child, and alleged father. It has been determined to be 96% accurate in proving that a certain man is the father of a child.

9. So far, 14 states allow the results of this test to be introduced into evidence in a paternity suit. Those states are: Arizona, California, Florida, Illinois, Iowa, Massachusetts, Michigan, Minnesota, New Jersey, New York, North Carolina, Oregon, Washington, and Wisconsin.

10. See footnote 5.

11. It is true that such an agreement might, in fact, become evidence of the identity of the donor. If, however, the donor already knows the identity of the recipient of his semen and if the woman is in a state that recognizes the H.L.A. test, the agreement may provide more protection than it presents problems.

---

Donna J. Hitchens wrote this article while the Directing Attorney for the Lesbian Rights Project in San Francisco. Reprints of this article are available ($4/copy) from the Lesbian Rights Project, 1370 Mission St., 4th Fl., San Francisco, CA 94103

# Appendices,
# Bibliography,
# and Index

# APPENDIX A: GROUPS FOR LESBIANS CONSIDERING PARENTHOOD

This section is for lesbians who want to organize a group to use the materials in this book, for therapists who want to offer groups for lesbians considering parenthood, for community health centers that want to provide this kind of group as a community resource, and for educators who may already do training about this topic and may want to use these exercises with both lesbians and heterosexuals. This section reflects my purpose and objectives in leading these groups for lesbians considering parenthood, as well as my format, my process-oriented approach, and personal style. Take what you want, expanding on it and shaping it to meet your own style, skill level, orientation, and interests. As you work with these materials, you will develop your own style.

I have found the group format to be an exciting and stimulating one in which to encourage discussion of the issues surrounding the choices being made by lesbians considering parenthood. The groups provide lesbians with a safe place in which to talk about their feelings, concerns, and questions. Everyone learns from the discussion, whether she is a vocal participant or not.

I have listed my objectives in leading these groups in a way that educators commonly use to be deliberate in planning their programs. I hope seeing them this way will be helpful.

The purpose of these groups is:

- To help lesbians understand their decision-making and problem-solving processes.
- To help lesbians establish a support group to meet with on an on-going basis.
- To begin identifying the issues necessary to consider in making this decision.

- ▶ To provide a look at all sides of an issue.
- ▶ To talk with lesbians who are now parents.
- ▶ To hear others' viewpoints, experiences, questions, and perspectives.
- ▶ To provide lesbians with a forum in which to share their thoughts and to listen to the opinions of others, and hopefully get some questions answered.
- ▶ To explore feelings in a non-threatening environment.
- ▶ To learn new things to think about in relation to this decision.
- ▶ To obtain resources.
- ▶ To prepare lesbians for the ups and downs of parenthood and how this choice may effect them in the many avenues of their lives.

## Format of the Groups

The groups last for six weeks, meeting once a week for two hours. The six weeks timeframe gives everyone a significant length of time to begin integrating their thoughts and ideas and to process their decisions. The women have a chance to get to know one another, build trust, and become comfortable talking about the more intimate and difficult aspects of their thinking and decision-making process. One of my goals in leading the groups is to help lesbians establish on-going support groups to talk about these and related topics, give one another support in their decisions and create an information network. I encourage each group to continue meeting on their own, without me, after the six sessions are over.

### SIZE OF THE GROUP

Size is a critical factor in facilitated groups. You don't want them too large or too small. I generally keep them between six and 15 participants. More than 15 is simply too many people for the leader to manage. It is also too large for each participant to have an adequate chance to talk and be an active group member. I have found between 11 and 12 to be an ideal size. Small groups (fewer than six) are definitely more intimate; however, having a few more women increases the possibility of more varied viewpoints.

Leaderless groups are a different story. Three lesbians constitute a group. You don't need any more than that to get your own group going. Having a few more women would increase the range of perspectives, but you can start with as few as three people and add others as you go along.

## TIME COMMITMENT

It is important for everyone in the group to make a time commitment to the group, the minimum being six weeks. The commitment is especially important so that people have a chance to build relationships and learn to trust one another. With an understanding that everyone has made a commitment to be at the group for a designated length of time, a feeling of closeness and camaraderie can be established.

## EXERCISES, HOMEWORK, AND READINGS

Each session focuses on a particular topic. The schedule of topics is determined by the group's members during the first session (see the first session outline that follows). There are exercises for each topic. In my groups, I either do an exercise in the group or give one as homework; then I begin the next session with a discussion of the homework assignment (along the line of the "Things to Consider" and "Questions to Ask Yourself" in this book).

I never do more than one exercise per session. The exercises are meant to get everyone thinking and then stimulate guided and spontaneous discussion. They are not designed to serve as the entire structure for the session.

The readings are from books and/or articles I have collected over the years. Some are included in the bibliography in this book. Others are copies of articles from women's newspapers and local newspapers which have had stories on lesbian mothers.

Over the years, I have found that almost everyone does the homework and the readings. They serve as a pivotal basis for discussion. I explain that doing the work outside of the group will contribute significantly to group discussion and to individual learning.

## SCREENING

I have handled the process of screening in a number of different ways since I began doing these groups. When I first started, I was careful to talk with each interested participant prior to the first group meeting, usually by phone. I would ask her what she wanted to know about the groups, where she was in her process of making a decision, and why she was wanting to do this group now. This initial screening gave me an introduction to each woman and it gave her a chance to talk with me and ask me any questions. I always assured each woman that she could come to the first meeting and if she decided she did not want to be in the group, for any reason, that would be okay. I liked having contact with each woman before the group started, because it helped personalize my contact with her right from the start.

In later years when I offered the groups through local women's health centers, I did not talk with each woman first unless she wanted additional information about the group and called me directly. Occasionally there would be a woman who had expectations the group could not meet, or someone hoping it was a lecture class or wanting to be told what she should do and how to do it.

If you are a group leader, you will want to find the screening technique that is most comfortable for you.

## GROUND RULES

I like to set certain ground rules by which I expect everyone in the group to abide. I feel that these reassure people that there are certain boundaries in this group and that I will take responsibility to see that they are respected. Here is a list of the ground rules I have established:

- Everyone is expected to attend each session. If you can't come or won't be at a meeting, please let someone in the group know if at all possible.
- The group will start and end on time each week.
- As the group leader, I am a facilitator, not a therapist. This is not a therapy group. That does not mean that therapy issues don't come up or may not be brought up. But, if and when they do, we will not explore them as might be done in a therapy group. Instead, I will be glad to talk over these issues privately with each member and make an appropriate referral if necessary.
- As the participants, you will determine the topics, and as the facilitator I will then be responsible for structuring each session, bringing in materials for discussion, and facilitating the discussions.
- This will not be a didactic class. Instead, it will be a place where each of you will have a chance to discuss these topics actively.
- I believe that there is a kind of "participation continuum" onto which everyone falls. Some people learn best by talking a lot; others learn by sitting quietly and listening. Still others are somewhere in between those two. Wherever you are on the continuum is fine with me. Simply be responsible for yourself. If you are someone who talks easily, be sure to take a break and give others a chance to talk. If you are someone who is generally quiet in groups, be sure to speak up when you have something you want to say.
- *I consider this ground rule to be the most important:* In order to develop a safe environment and build trust, I ask that anything shared in the group not be discussed or repeated to others outside of the group. I do tell participants that they may talk about the topics and issues

we discuss, but because each group member needs to feel that what she shares in the group will not be repeated to others, I ask that no names be mentioned. You might say, "One woman talked about . . . ," or "We all discussed how we felt about . . . ."

## Suggested Outline for the First Session

The first session is generally structured so that the people in the group can learn something about one another — why each person decided to come to the group at this time; what she hopes to get out of the group; where each woman is in the process of making her decision. In addition, it gives group members a chance to see if they like each other, the group leader, and the planned group format.

As the group leader, I begin by introducing myself, talking about how I came to be doing these groups, what I hope each woman will get out of being in the group, and the work I have been doing in the past few years. I then ask each woman to take a few minutes to describe what brought her to the group now, where she is in trying to make a decision, and whatever other information she feels is relevant for us to know at this time.

The group leader or a group member may want to tie together the situations the women are in and the choices they are struggling with. Certainly, not everyone will be coming from the same place or be in the same place in their decision-making process. But different experiences can be complimentary; women who are just beginning to consider parenthood may raise questions that others had previously chosen not to deal with or had not thought to raise for themselves. I have led groups in which women were at all stages of the process — already pregnant, starting adoption procedures, beginning to inseminate, or not having even started to think about their decision.

It is crucial that you structure each group to meet the participants' needs, as identified in that first session. I have found that the following way of doing this works well. After the initial introductions, I ask all group members to talk about what they want to make sure is covered in the next six weeks, including topics they want discussed, and information they want to get. I encourage them to name everything that would be helpful to them. All this information may not be covered in the six weeks, but we do get a list going; what is not covered in this group could be information that the group continues to explore on their own after the six weeks. The group leader or a group member should take notes of the topics suggested.

If you are a group leader, you can organize these different topics into blocks and use them to create a schedule for the next weeks. If you

233

are a group of women, you might want to have two or three people spend a few minutes putting the information into a weekly schedule and then have the others agree upon the schedule.

One group I did recently happened to be made up mostly of single women considering parenthood on their own. Their primary concerns were around issues of money and work, as well as finding willing and interested friends to assist with childrearing. Another group of couples spent a considerable amount of time talking about their relationships and how having a child might affect the relationship. Still another group, in which only two of the members had come out to their families, wanted to focus their discussions around talking with families about their sexuality, their interest in becoming mothers, and the consideration process.

The option to choose *not* to parent needs to be intertwined throughout the sessions. There is often an implicit assumption that everyone coming to the group is considering choosing parenthood. That is not necessarily true. I like to devote a part of one session to discussing what it will be like if you choose not to be a parent. Group members do not always bring this up as a topic, so the group leader may have to offer this.

At the first session we also usually do the "Lifeline" exercise that you will find in the "Timetables and Life Planning" chapter. Follow those instructions, using the "Questions to Ask Yourself" as a jumping-off point for your discussion.

Before the first session is over I assign the "Pie Exercise" from the "Timetables and Life Planning" chapter (both parts of that particular exercise) as homework, explaining that it can take between 30 minutes to an hour to complete.

Finally, I make sure everyone knows what is scheduled for the next week and check to be sure that this group is being designed to meet the needs of the individual group members. I give everyone a chance to give me feedback about how they liked the session and if it met their needs.

## MONEY

I always charge a fee for my groups on a sliding scale. I reassure each woman interested in attending that if she does not have the money to pay, I would be glad to negotiate the fee with her. *No one* is turned away for lack of funds.

I discuss the fee with people on the telephone before the group gets started, and I discuss it early during the first session. I collect the money at the end of the first session, so people can decide if they want to do the group and also how they want to pay me. Some pay all at once; others half in the beginning and half at the middle. I ask that people pay me in either one or two payments.

Getting the word out about the groups is usually the easiest step in the publicity realm. Begin publicizing the group at least four to six weeks before your projected starting date. This should be done whether you are a group leader or a lesbian considering parenthood hoping to find others like yourself for a support group. Have a date, place, and time for your first meeting, with the understanding that future meetings can be on different days, at a different place, and at a different time.

If your community has a women's newspaper, you may find placing an ad will be all you need to generate interest in the group. You may also want to make up a flyer announcing the group and send it to be posted in places lesbians frequent, as well as putting it up in key locations yourself.

As a group leader, I found that being affiliated with an agency that was co-sponsoring the group helped to increase my visibility. The agency took responsibility for the publicity – placing the ads, making the flyers, etc. – and would talk to all interested women who called. I have done my groups at women's health clinics, the local women's center, and a birthing resource center. As part of affiliating with these groups, I split any money I made with them on a 60/40 basis.

Once you have done the initial publicity, word-of-mouth will begin to advertise the group.

Be resourceful. Publicizing the groups can be frustrating. One woman told me she ran an ad for two months in her local women's paper and got one call. She knew there were more lesbians interested, but she didn't know how to reach them. You may have to talk to a lot of people and encourage them to talk to others. Be sure to give yourself enough lead time.

Some women are more interested in coming to a one-evening information meeting than to a six-week group. Often from these one-evening events there are enough interested women to start a group. You may want to have one large initial meeting to get a sense of the interest in your community. In Cambridge a number of years ago, the women's center organized a large community meeting in conjunction with a local health center beginning insemination services. Out of that meeting a few smaller groups developed. In other cities, women have come together by word-of-mouth through friends and acquaintances.

## Some Possible Problems

Although I have never had any big problems while leading these groups, I have had some small, but managable ones. Below is a list of situations which have proven problematic for me. Some I anticipated; others took me by surprise. I did not always handle each of these problems well. However, I did get better at it over time.

- *Women who are not lesbians wanting to be in the groups*
    I always have a firm "no" on this one. My reason is that heterosexual women have different issues (see the "Introduction") and more privilege. Also, there were more services available to straight women, so I would refer them to the organizations that offered a similar service.
- *Lesbians parenting with a heterosexual woman and wanting that woman to be in the group*
    This situation happened to a friend of mine during her first group. This was a tough one. She consulted me and we decided that the group leader would offer private counseling to these women and invite the lesbian partner to the group sessions.
- *Group members who come sporadically to the meetings*
    I call each woman who misses more than two consecutive meetings to find out why she has not been there. Sometimes the material in the group was too painful, or a woman may have decided she does not want to participate. Other times, there is simply a scheduling problem she hadn't told us about and she planned to come to the next meeting.
- *Group members with psychological problems beyond the limits of the group or the abilities of the individual group members or the group leader*
    I take that member aside before or after a group and arrange a time to talk privately. I explain that I feel she needs additional help beyond what I am able to offer in the group setting. I suggest therapists in the community if she is interested in a referral. No one is ever asked to leave the group, simply to seek additional help elsewhere.
- *The low energy group*
    As a group leader it is always harder work to have a group with very low energy — that is, the group members don't actively involve themselves in discussion. In these cases I have to raise many of the issues that members in other groups raise by virtue of their interests.
- *A group in which you do not like many of the participants or they do not like you*
    This can be tricky. When I have been faced with the first situation, I must struggle to have the same kind of energy for each person in the group. There are always people you don't like for one reason or another, but as the group leader, I feel a certain responsibility to providing participants with a rich and full experience.
    When I feel that individuals in the groups do not like me, or more exactly, do not like my style, I have to let it go. I simply continue being myself. I tell people that if they are having any problems with me or the group, they could bring them up in the group sessions or speak with me individually. Occasionally, women talk with me after a group or call me on the phone. This gives me a chance to respond to the problem and try to resolve it.

- *Dealing with conflicts among group members*

This is probably one of the most difficult problems. How this is managed depends upon the group and the style of the group leader (if there is one). I acknowledge differences among group members right from the start. When conflicts arise (generally differences of opinion about how to think about certain topics, how to respond, attitudes on specific issues), I am careful to highlight the differences and recognize them as differences of opinion. I view them as a way in which to get another perspective on a particular issue. Sometimes conflicts arise as a result of personality clashes between group members. I intervene only if I feel it is absolutely necessary for the benefit of the other group members. Otherwise, I let the individuals involved work it out for themselves.

Leading the groups has been an enormously rewarding and enriching experience for me. I have learned a great deal from the women in my groups — they have taught me about the fine points of considering parenthood. The groups are a place to learn more about oneself and how different women think about the same topic. What each group member takes away from the groups has a lot to do with a story that someone told, or a phrase said almost off-handedly, or the relationships made with the other members. The groups offer a place to bring concerns and questions related to considering parenthood. They are valuable in building support in our communities, both for women who are choosing and not choosing to be mothers.

# APPENDIX B: A PRELIMINARY INFERTILITY EVALUATION*

A typical preliminary evaluation for infertility includes:

• Semen analysis for the man.
• Physical examination, PAP smear and Chlamydia culture for the woman (including blood work — CBC, VDRL, Sed Rate, and rubella titer).
• Hormonal blood test, i.e., serum progesterone, prolactin, thyroid panel and, if necessary, FSH level, LH level and other blood and urine tests.
• Endometrial biopsy to document ovulation.
• Hysterosalpingogram (HSG) or dye x-ray of the uterus and tubes.

## MALE TESTING

## SEMEN ANALYSIS

The initial test done on the man is a semen analysis. The man is asked to abstain from ejaculation for 48 hours. A semen specimen is collected by masturbation and must be in the lab within one hour. The motility (activity or movement of the sperm) is the most important factor in the test. The number of sperm and the shape of the sperm are also determined. If the test is not normal, it should be repeated at least once because of the great differences in semen quality from day to day.

---

*This Appendix was taken from an informational article written by Esther Levine, R.N., N.P., an Infertility Specialist with the Bay Area Services Infertility Clinic in Oakland, California.

## FEMALE TESTING

The work-up for the woman involves a series of tests, each evaluating a different function. In order for a woman to become pregnant, she must be ovulating (releasing an egg), and have fallopian tubes that are open and unattached to any pelvic organ due to scarring or adhesions. Her uterus should be normal in size and shape and free from significant abnormalities, such as fibroid tumors (uterine muscle growths) or polyps (sacs filled with fluid or blood). The uterus must also prepare the proper endometrium (lining of the uterus) which allows for implantation of a fertilized egg. The glands in the cervix must produce a clear, stretchy, alkaline fluid (like raw egg whites) that will transport the sperm through the cervix and up the uterus to the outer third of the fallopian tube where fertilization takes place. Evaluation of this complicated process can be done in one cycle if a woman has regular periods.

## UTERINE AND TUBAL FACTOR

A dye x-ray known as the Hysterosalpingogram (HSG) will demonstrate that the uterine cavity looks normal and also reveal if the fallopian tubes are open. The HSG is done when menstrual bleeding stops and before ovulation occurs, usually between days seven to ten of the cycle. The procedure involves passing a small catheter (tube) into the uterus and injecting a water- or oil- based dye. Women experience some discomfort with this procedure. This discomfort can vary greatly depending upon the material used and the practitioner performing the HSG. Some practitioners medicate their clients to prevent tubal spasm during the HSG. (There is a remote chance of infection any time a foreign object is put into the uterus. It is important to be aware of the symptoms of infection, i.e., pain, heavy foul-smelling vaginal discharge, or fever, so that you can receive treatment if necessary.) The HSG not only has a diagnostic value, but many practitioners feel it has a definite therapeutic effect. There is a high rate of pregnancy in the months following an HSG and it is thought that flushing the dye through the tubes is the reason for this.

If the HSG is not normal, the next procedure is a diagnostic laparoscopy. This is a minor surgical procedure done to visually assess the problem and to determine whether or not it can be corrected by major surgery. The only treatment for tubal problems is surgery or (more recently) in-vitro fertilization. If the uterus is abnormal, the only medical solution is intervention through surgery.

## CERVICAL FACTOR

The test to evaluate the cervical mucus is done mid-cycle or approximately two weeks before the next period is due. The timing of this test is very individual. It is done at the only time in the cycle that a woman can get pregnant. The cervical mucus is examined just before ovulation to determine whether or not sperm can survive in it. The test is called a post-coital test (PCT) by most infertility specialists. It is painless and the results are known immediately. The woman is asked to inseminate or have sexual intercourse two to eight hours before her appointment. The mucus is then checked for motile sperm.

## OVARIAN FACTOR

One week before the period is expected, a practitioner can evaluate your ovulation. The record keeping of basal body temperatures (BBT) is one indication of whether or not ovulation has taken place. And, as was discussed in the "Alternative Fertilization" chapter, this record-keeping also helps to determine the fertile time. If you are having difficulty determining the time of your ovulation, consulting a practitioner or a fertility awareness teacher/counselor can be helpful. You can also have a more definitive test for determining the time of your ovulation. This is a simple blood test known as serum progesterone.

The *most* definitive test and the test of choice to document ovulation is the endometrial biopsy. In the endometrial biopsy, a small amount of the uterine lining (endometrium) is removed approximately one week before it is normally shed during the woman's menstrual period. The tissue is analyzed and can clearly indicate an ovulatory problem. The procedure is uncomfortable and may require medication to help you relax.

A small instrument is inserted into the uterus and you will experience a moderate to severe cramp at the time of insertion. The cramp lasts from 15 to 30 seconds and should be completely gone in one to two minutes. The procedure takes only a few minutes and should not affect usual activities for the rest of the day. There is always a small risk of infection because the instrument was inserted into the uterus. Watch for any symptoms of infection (see HSG above), and call your practitioner immediately if any of these develop.

All these tests can be done in one menstrual cycle. Expect to complete the testing in six to eight weeks.

Finally, remember that the emotional impact that accompanies infertility also needs attention. When anyone experiences infertility, the choice of having a child when you plan to has been taken away. People cope with this loss in different ways. You may want to find a support group or counselor with whom to talk.

# APPENDIX C: AIDS

## AIDS IN WOMEN

As of September 1988, over 70,000 people have been diagnosed with AIDS in the United States, and the number of new cases continues to grow. Almost 9 percent of the people with AIDS in the U.S. are women. Slightly over half of these women are or were I.V. drug users. At least 29 percent of the women report having had sex with men who may have been at risk of HIV infection. The numbers in this heterosexual transmission category have more than doubled since 1985. Eleven percent of the women with AIDS have had blood transfusions. The remaining cases are placed in the "undetermined" risk category, meaning that they either have no known risk factor, that they died before they were interviewed, that they did not want to say what their risk was, or that they did not know what their risk could have been.

Of the total number of women with AIDS, current statistics indicate that 50 percent are Black, 23 percent are Hispanic, and 24 percent are White. Three percent are classified as "other" or ethnicity unknown. The vast majority are between 20 and 40 years old. Most of the women have Pneumocystis Pneumonia or other opportunistic infections, with only a handful having Kaposi's Sarcoma. Of the total AIDS cases, over half of the women are in New York City or Newark, New Jersey, and the rest are scattered across the country. Overall, half of the women diagnosed with AIDS have died.

It is not known how many women with AIDS are lesbians, though it is likely that some are. However, there is very little data on the sexual orientation of the women diagnosed with AIDS and even less on lesbian transmission. Although this might suggest an actual low risk for lesbians, it might also be in part due to the lack of documentation of lesbian health concerns. What we do know about the lesbians with AIDS is that they most likely contracted HIV infection through sharing needles for I.V. drug use. To date, there are only a handful of cases of *suspected* lesbian sexual transmission of the AIDS virus. A few case descriptions have appeared in the medical literature. However, as many women health workers will tell you, lesbians may be at risk for AIDS.

Lesbians have been known to pass a variety of infections back and forth between vaginas, clitorises, and tongues. It makes sense, then, that we could pass on the AIDS virus in such a manner, since it is found in blood, including menstrual blood, vaginal and cervical secretions, breast milk, urine, and feces.

Women who are infected with the AIDS virus may pass it on to their children during pregnancy, at birth, or through breast milk. In addition, it has been suggested that pregnancy may increase a woman's risk of developing AIDS or an AIDS-related illness if she is infected with the AIDS virus, due to the added suppression of the immune system during pregnancy.

We are learning new information about AIDS and HIV infection on a daily basis. I suggest you check periodically with the your local health department or AIDS information resources in your area. Check the chapter on AIDS in this book for further readings on AIDS and women.

# APPENDIX D:
# MEDICAL INFORMATION AND
# HEALTH FORMS

## MEDICAL INFORMATION FOR DONORS

Age_____ Height_____ Weight_____

Do you have (or have you had): Read each item and check *each* answer below.

|  | Yes | No |  | Yes | No |
|---|---|---|---|---|---|
| **Cardiovascular:** | | | **Gastrointestinal:** | | |
| Shortness of breath on | | | Indigestion | __ | __ |
|   exertion | __ | __ | Hemmorrhoids | __ | __ |
| High blood pressure | __ | __ | Gastric ulcers | __ | __ |
| Hardening of arteries | __ | __ | Frequent nau- | | |
| Dizziness/fainting | __ | __ |   sea/vomiting | __ | __ |
| Chest pain/pressure | __ | __ | Difficulty in | | |
| Leg cramps | __ | __ |   swallowing | __ | __ |
| Varicose veins | __ | __ | Painful urination | __ | __ |
| Heart murmur | __ | __ | Pain in testicles | __ | __ |
| Heart attack | __ | __ | Blood or other | | |
| | | |   discharge | __ | __ |
| | | | Kidney disease | __ | __ |

Medical information
Page two

|  | Yes | No |  | Yes | No |
|---|---|---|---|---|---|
| **Respiratory:** | | | **Muscle/skeletal:** | | |
| Persistent cough | — | — | Arthritis | — | — |
| Sore throats | — | — | Rheumatism | — | — |
| Hay fever | — | — | Muscle pain | — | — |
| Nose bleeds | — | — | Backaches | — | — |
| Asthma/wheezing | — | — | | | |
| Pneumonia | — | — | **Eyes/ears/mouth:** | | |
| Pleurisy | — | — | | | |
| Bronchitis | — | — | Hearing loss | | |
| Frequent colds | — | — | (partial/full) | — | — |
| Frequent sinus | | | Color blindness | — | — |
| infections | — | — | Double vision | — | — |
| Emphysema | — | — | Glaucoma | — | — |
| | | | Earaches | — | — |
| **Skin:** | | | False teeth | — | — |
| | | | Tonsils removed | — | — |
| Hives | — | — | # cavities_____ | — | — |
| Rashes | — | — | | | |
| Moles | — | — | **Other:** | | |
| Allergies:_____ | — | — | | | |
| Cancer | — | — | Cancer or lumps | — | — |
| | | | Rheumatic fever | — | — |
| **BLOOD TYPE:**_____ | | | Polio | — | — |
| | | | Tuberculosis | — | — |
| | | | Thyroid disease | — | — |
| | | | Diabetes | — | — |
| Gall bladder disease | — | — | Numbness in | | |
| Liver disease | — | — | legs/arms | — | — |
| Syphilis/VD | — | — | New skin growths | — | — |
| Malaria | — | — | Bleeding/bruising | | |
| Headaches | — | — | easily | — | — |
| Hepatitis | — | — | Anemia | — | — |
| Fits or convulsions | — | — | Balance problems | — | — |
| Nervous breakdowns | — | — | Yellow jaundice | — | — |
| Depression | — | — | Lymph node | | |
| Other brain/nerve | | | enlargement | — | — |
| problems | — | — | Kidney stones | — | — |
| Hernia | — | — | Insomnia | — | — |
| Circumcision | — | — | Others_____ | — | — |
| | | | _____ | — | — |
| | | | _____ | — | — |

Give details of "yes" items and include any injury, deformity, or illness not listed: _____

_____

_____

_____

_____

_____

Operations (list type and year): _____

_____

_____

_____

List childhood illnesses: _____

_____

_____

_____

Psychiatric illnesses: _____

_____

_____

Do you wear: glasses_____; contact lenses_____

Are you allergic?_____

_____

Please describe your general eating habits:_____

_____

_____

Do you regularly use alchohol Yes_____ No_____;
How much daily?_____

Do you smoke cigarettes: Yes_____ No_____;
 How many packs daily?_____

Other habits of addiction: Drugs Yes_____ No_____; Which ones and
 how often?_____

_____

Date:_____

## PERSONAL INFORMATION

Why are you willing to donate your sperm to women you don't know?

_____

_____

_____

Sun sign_____ Moon sign_____ Rising_____

Ethnic background:_____

Father's family:_____

Mother's family:_____

Are your parents alive? Yes_____ No_____; If no, what did they die of at
   what age?_____

_____

Your eye color:_____ Hair color:_____

Number of brothers:_____ Number of sisters:_____

Have you ever had children before? Yes_____ No_____; If yes, # female
_____ # male_____.

Interests/hobbies/sports you do:_____

_____

_____

Any other information you think might be of interest:_____

_____

_____

_____

_____

# BASAL TEMPERATURE CHART

**Name** _____  **Shortest Previous Cycle** _____

**Month(s)** _____  **Longest Previous Cycle** _____

**Year** _____  **Length of this Cycle** _____

**DAY OF**

| Mo. | | | | | | | | | | | | | | | | | | | | | | | | | | | | | | | | | | | | | | | | | | |
|-----|--|--|--|--|--|--|--|--|--|--|--|--|--|--|--|--|--|--|--|--|--|--|--|--|--|--|--|--|--|--|--|--|--|--|--|--|--|--|--|--|--|--|
| Wk. | | | | | | | | | | | | | | | | | | | | | | | | | | | | | | | | | | | | | | | | | | |

**TEMPERATURE**

1 2 3 4 5 6 7 8 9 10 11 12 13 14 15 16 17 18 19 20 21 22 23 24 25 26 27 28 29 30 31 32 33 34 35 36 37 38 39 40 41 42

99.5
99.4
99.3
99.2
99.1
99.0
98.9
98.8
98.7
98.6
98.5
98.4
98.3
98.2
98.1
98.0
97.9
97.8
97.7
97.6
97.5
97.4
97.3
97.2
97.1
97.0

1 2 3 4 5 6 7 8 9 10 11 12 13 14 15 16 17 18 19 20 21 22 23 24 25 26 27 28 29 30 31 32 33 34 35 36 37 38 39 40 41 42

## MUCUS AND OTHER OBSERVATIONS

1. _____   22. _____
2. _____   23. _____
3. _____   24. _____
4. _____   25. _____
5. _____   26. _____
6. _____   27. _____
7. _____   28. _____
8. _____   29. _____
9. _____   30. _____
10. _____   31. _____
11. _____   32. _____
12. _____   33. _____
13. _____   34. _____
14. _____   35. _____
15. _____   36. _____
16. _____   37. _____
17. _____   38. _____
18. _____   39. _____
19. _____   40. _____
20. _____   41. _____
21. _____   42. _____

# APPENDIX E: LEGAL FORMS

## *Donor Agreements*

This AGREEMENT is made this _____ day of
_____, 198X, by and between _____,
hereafter DONOR, and _____, hereafter RECIPIENT,
who may also be referred to herein as the parties.

NOW, THEREFORE, in consideration of the promises of each
other, DONOR and RECIPIENT agree as follows:

1. Each clause of this AGREEMENT is separate and divisible from
the others, and, should a court refuse to enforce one or more clauses of
this AGREEMENT, the others are still valid and in full force.

2. DONOR has provided his semen to RECIPIENT for the purpose
of artificial insemination.

3. In exchange, DONOR has received from RECIPIENT _____.

4. Each party is a single person who has never married.

5. Each party acknowledges and agrees that, through the procedure
of artificial insemination, RECIPIENT has become pregnant.

6. Each party acknowledges and agrees that DONOR provided his
semen for the purposes of said artificial insemination, and did so with the
clear understanding that he would not demand, request, or compel any
guardianship, custody, or visitation rights with any child born from the
artificial insemination procedure. Further, DONOR acknowledges that

he fully understood that he would have no paternal rights whatsoever with said child.

7. Each party acknowledges and agrees that RECIPIENT has relinquished any and all rights that she might otherwise have to hold DONOR legally, financially, or emotionally responsible for any child that results from the artificial insemination procedure.

8. Each party acknowledges and agrees that the sole authority to name any child resulting from the artificial insemination procedure shall rest with RECIPIENT.

9. Each party acknowledges and agrees that there shall be no father named on the birth certificate of any child born from the artificial insemination procedure.

10. Each party relinquishes and releases any and all rights he or she may have to bring a suit to establish paternity.

11. Each party covenants and agrees that, in light of the expectations of each party, as stated above, RECIPIENT shall have absolute authority and power to appoint a guardian for her child, and that the mother and guardian may act with sole discretion as to all legal, financial, medical and emotional needs of said child without any involvement with or demands of authority from DONOR.

12. Each party covenants and agrees that neither of them will identify the DONOR as a parent of the child, nor will either of them reveal the identity of the DONOR to any of their respective parents or relatives.

13. Each party acknowledges and agrees that the relinquishment of all rights, as stated above, is final and irrevocable. DONOR further understands that his waivers shall prohibit any action on his part for custody, guardianship, or visitation in any future situation, including the event of RECIPIENT's disability or death.

14. Each party covenants and agrees that any dispute pertaining to this AGREEMENT which arises between them shall be submitted to binding arbitration according to the following procedures:

a. The request for arbitration may be made by either party and shall be in writing and delivered to the other party;

b. Pending the outcome of arbitration, there shall be no change made in the language of this AGREEMENT;

c. The arbitration panel that will resolve any disputes regarding this AGREEMENT shall consist of three persons: one person chosen by DONOR; one person chosen by RECIPIENT; and one person chosen by the other two panel members;

d. Within fourteen calendar days following the written arbitration request, the arbitrators shall be chosen;

e. Within fourteen days following the selection of all members of the arbitration panel, the panel will hear the dispute between parties;

f. Within seven days subsequent to the hearing, the arbitration panel will make a decision and communicate it in writing to each party.

15. Each party acknowledges and understands that there are legal questions raised by the issues involved in this AGREEMENT which have not been settled by statute or prior court decisions. Notwithstanding the knowledge that certain of the clauses stated herein may not be enforced in a court of law, the parties choose to enter into this AGREEMENT and clarify their intent that existed at the time the artificial insemination procedure was implemented by them.

16. Each party acknowledges and agrees that she or he signed this AGREEMENT voluntarily and freely, of his or her own choice, without any duress of any kind whatsoever. It is further acknowledged that each party has been advised to secure the advice and consent of an attorney of his or her own choosing, and that each party understands the meaning and significance of each provision of this AGREEMENT.

17. This AGREEMENT contains the entire understanding of the parties. There are no promises, understandings, agreements or representations between the parties other than those expressly stated in this AGREEMENT.

IN WITNESS WHEREOF, the parties hereunto have executed this AGREEMENT, in the City and County of San Francisco, California, on the day and year first above written.

_____        _____
            DONOR                                    RECIPIENT


*Note: This AGREEMENT was drafted for the situation where conception has already occured. It may be preferable to have the AGREEMENT signed prior to conception. If that is done, paragraphs 2, 3, and 5 should be modified accordingly.*

# Nomination of Guardian for Minor

I, ___(name of mother)___ , the natural mother of the minor child ___(name of child)___ who was born on ___(child's birthdate)___ , am hereby declaring my wishes as to those individuals to be appointed the legal guardian of the person and property of my ___(daughter/son)___ in the event I am unable, physically or mentally, to care for my child.

## I.

I nominate ___(partner/other adult)___ , currently residing at ___(home address of partner/other adult)___ to be the legal guardian of the person and property of my minor child ___(child's name)___ . This nomination is based on the fact that a loving and parental relationship exists between ___(name of guardian)___ and my ___(daughter/son)___ , ___(name of child)___ . Furthermore, my ___(daughter/son)___ has lived with this adult and looks to her for guidance, support and affection. It would be detrimental to my ___(daughter/son)___ to deprive ___(her/him)___ of this established relationship at a time when I am unable to provide the security and care necessary to my child's healthy development.

## II.

In the event ___(name of guardian)___ is unable to serve as guardian or is disqualified by a court of law from serving, I nominate ___(name an alternate)___ to serve as the guardian of the person and property of the minor child ___(child's name)___ .

## III.

Both the identity and whereabouts of the minor child's natural father are unknown to me.

or

The minor child was conceived through artificial insemination by donor and has no natural father.

or

The minor child was conceived through artificial insemination by donor, and said donor has waived, in writing, any and all rights he may have to object to my nomination of a guardian.

## IV.

I have purposefully not nominated my parents or siblings to be the guardians of my child in the event of my disability because they lack an established, close and warm relationship with my child, and I believe it would be detrimental to ___(name of child)___ to remove ___(her/him)___ from ___(name of guardian)___ and place ___(her/him)___ with adults who are, for all practical purposes, strangers.

Dated:_____                    ___(signature of mother)___
                                         (print name of mother)

STATE OF CALIFORNIA ) ss. _____
COUNTY OF SAN FRANCISCO)

On _____ before me, the undersigned, a Notary Public in and for said State, personally appeared ___(name of mother)___, known to me to be the person whose name is subscribed to the within Nomination of Guardian of Minor, and acknowledged that she executed the same.

WITNESS my hand and official seal.

_____

# *Authorization for Consent to Medical Treatment of Minor*

I, ___(name of biological mother)___, being the parent entitled to the legal and physical custody of my minor child ___(child's name)___, born ___(date of birth)___, do hereby authorize _____(name)_____ into whose care the child has been entrusted, to consent to any X-ray examination, anesthetic, medical or surgical diagnosis or treatment and hospital care to be rendered to said child under the supervision and upon the advise of a physician or other medical care provided licensed to practice medicine in any state of the United States. I further authorize _____(name)_____ to consent to any X-ray, examination, dental or surgical diagnosis or treatment and hospital care to be rendered to said minor child by a dentist licensed to practice dentistry in any state in the United States.

This authorization shall be valid from _____(date)_____ to _____(date)_____ .

DATED: _____ at _____, California.

_____

STATE OF CALIFORNIA) ss. _____
COUNTY OF SAN FRANCISCO)

On _____, 198X, before me, (name of notary), a Notary Public for the State of California, personally appeared, known to

255

me to be the person whose name is subscribed to the within CONSENT TO MEDICAL TREATMENT and acknowledged that she executed the same.

WITNESS my hand and official seal.

_____
NOTARY PUBLIC
for the State of California

# *Partnership Agreement*

This AGREEMENT is made this _____ day of _____,198X, by and between _____ and _____, hereafter referred to as the parties.

NOW, THEREFORE, in consideration of the promises of each other, the parties agree as follows:

1. Each party acknowledges, and agrees that (biological mother)'s decision to conceive and bear a child was actually a joint decision of the parties and based upon the commitment of each party to jointly parent the child.

2. On  (child's birthdate) , the minor child  (name of child)  was born

3. Each party acknowledges and agrees that both _____ and _____ will equally share in providing their child, _____, with the necessary food, clothing, shelter, medical, or any other remedial care that may be needed by the child until the time she/he is 18 years of age.

4. Each party acknowledges and agrees that if _____ and _____ are no longer living together in the family home they will both continue to provide for their child _____ in the manner described in paragraph 3 above.

5. Each party acknowledges and agrees that even though _____ is not the biological (or adoptive) mother, that she is a de facto parent

who has provided ___(child's name)___ with a stable environment and has formed a psychological parenting relationship with _(child's name)_ . _____'s relationship with ___(child's name)___ should be protected and promoted to preserve the strong emotional tie that has developed between them.

6. Each party acknowledges and agrees that if _____ and _____ decide to stop living together in the family home, the following will serve the best interests of the child and will occur:

a. The parent-child relationship that has developed between _____ and the child will be respected and fostered.

b. _____ will have reasonable visitation rights with the child.

c. _____ will continue to provide financial support for the child in the amount of _____ per month.

7. Each party acknowledges and agrees that all major decisions regarding physical location, support, visitation, education, etc. affecting ___(child's name)___ shall be made jointly by the parties and that ___(child's name)___ shall be involved in the decision-making to the extent she/he is able, by maturity, to do so.

8. Each party acknowledges and agrees that both parties will make a good faith effort to remain in the county of _____ until ___(child's name)___ is in high school.

9. Each party acknowledges and agrees that in the event that ___(biological/legal mother)___ is no longer able to care and provide for the child because of death or legal disability, it would be in the best interests of the child to remain with _____ because of the strong psychological parent-child relationship that has developed between the child and _____.

10. Each party covenants and agrees that any dispute pertaining to this AGREEMENT which arises between them shall be submitted to binding arbitration according to the following procedures:

a. The request for arbitration may be made by either party and shall be in writing and delivered to the other party;

b. Pending the outcome of arbitration, there shall be no change made in the language of this AGREEMENT;

257

c. The arbitration panel that will resolve any disputes regarding this AGREEMENT shall consist of three persons: one person chosen by _____; one person chosen by _____; and one person chosen by the other two panel members;

d. Within fourteen calender days following the written arbitration request, the arbitrators shall be chosen;

e. Within fourteen days following the selection of all members of the arbitration panel, the panel will hear the dispute between the parties;

f. Within seven days subsequent to the hearing, the arbitration panel will make a decision and communicate it in writing to each party.

Each party acknowledges and understands that there are legal questions raised by the issues involved in this AGREEMENT which have not been settled by statute or prior court decisions. Notwithstanding the knowledge that certain of the clauses stated herein may not be enforced in a court of law, the parties choose to enter into this AGREEMENT and clarify their intent to jointly provide and nurture their child _____, even in the event that they are no longer living together in the family home.

12. Each party acknowledges and agrees that she signed this AGREEMENT voluntarily and freely, of her own choice, without any duress of any kind whatsoever.

13. This AGREEMENT contains the entire understanding of the parties. There are no promises, understandings, agreements or representations between the parties other than those expressly stated in this AGREEMENT.

IN WITNESS WHEREOF, the parties hereunto have executed this AGREEMENT in the City and County of San Franciscio, California, on the day and year first above written.

| _____ | _____ |
| (signature) | (signature) |
| _____ | _____ |
| (print name) | (print name) |

# ANNOTATED BIBLIOGRAPHY

### ADOPTION/FOSTER CARE

Arms, Suzanne *To Love and Let Go,* Knopf, 1983. $14.95
This is a series of stories about people for whom the issue of adoption is central to their lives — women who have given up their children at birth, people who have been adopted, adoption lawyers, and adoptive parents. The stories are told with great compassion, and form a carefully woven argument for private non-traditional adoptions where sensitivity to the biological mother is the rule. An excellent book, highly recommended.

Bolles, Edmund Blair *The Penguin Adoption Handbook,* Penguin Books, 1984. $8.95
In the first chapter, the author tells us that adoptions by homosexuals "are less common than moonwalks," and that you will have to "pioneer your own strategy." Although Bolles does not provide any information specific to prospective gay or lesbian parents, he does offer important information on adoption law and possible channels to pursue in locating a child for adoption.

Morrison, Grace *To Love and Let Go,* Pillar Press, 636 Tarryton Isle, Alameda CA 94501, 1983. $7.95
A first-hand account of a family that provides a home for a series of foster children, *To Love and Let Go* gives a good introduction to the realities of being a foster parent. Despite the fact that the parents are straight, white, and reflect middle-class values, including a dose of homophobia, this book would still be useful to lesbians considering becoming foster parents.

## DECISION-MAKING

Dowrick, Stephanie and Grundberg, Sibyl, editors *Why Children?*, Harcourt Brace and Jovanovich, 1980. $6.95

    This is a collection of writings by 18 women concerning their decision to have or not have children. *Why Children?* is refreshing because it gives equal weight to the decision not to have children, and does not focus on heterosexual coupling as a prerequisite for childbearing. Dowrick and Grundberg assert that "partnership with a man may contribute to but does not define or delimit [a woman's] decision whether or not to have a child." Lesbians and bisexual women are given a voice here. One drawback of this book is that most of the women are artists or writers, and all but one are white. In this way, their testimonies cannot be considered representative.

Whelan, Elizabeth M. *A Baby?. . . Maybe. A Guide to Making the Most Fateful Decision of Your Life,* Bobbs-Merrill, 1975. $8.95

    An excellent book to use in deciding whether to parent in spite of its heterosexual bias. Dr. Whelan looks at the reasons for having children and for deciding not to parent. She brings to this discussion an even-handed evaluation of the advantages and disadvantages of both decisions. Her brief, but interesting, chapter with older parents and non-parents discussing their decision, adds another perspective to this decision.

## LESBIAN/GAY

Anonymous, Sarah and Mary *Woman-Controlled Conception,* Union Wage, 1979.

    Although this book is now out-of-print, you may still be able to find it at women's centers or women's bookstores. Written by two women who had children by Artificial Insemination by Donor, this book is a personal account of their experiences. They share their trial and error process of choosing various methods of insemination, giving the reader a realistic sense of the available options and the advantages and disadvantages of each. This was the first booklet to address woman-controlled conception.

Feminist Self-Insemination Group *Self Insemination,* Feminist Self-Insemination Group, 27 Clerkenwell Close, London WC1, England, 1979.

    *Self Insemination* is an excellent resource for lesbians who want to be more aware of the feelings they may experience while self-inseminating. This book might be of particular comfort to women who are having trouble becoming pregnant, as several members of this group inseminated for a long time before succeeding. Although the technical information is covered thoroughly, this book is most interesting for its personal perspective and its information on the emotional aspects of trying to conceive through self-insemination.

Hanscombe, Gillian E. and Forster, Jackie *Rocking the Cradle; Lesbian Mothers: A Challenge in Family Living,* Alyson Publications, 1981. $5.95

A good portion of *Rocking the Cradle* is based on intensive interviews with lesbian parents, many of whom became parents as lesbians, through Artificial Insemination by Donor, adoption or sexual relations with a man. The chapter entitled, "Where There's a Will There's a Way," describes the methods lesbians have used to bring children into their lives, and the emotional and political issues surrounding insemination as a method of conception.

Jullion, Jeanne *Long Way Home: The Odyssey of a Lesbian Mother and her Children,* Cleis Press, 1985.

This moving autobiographical saga chronicles the long custody battle of a lesbian mother for the custody of her two sons. Jullion takes the reader through her struggles and experiences from loss in a hostile courtroom in Oakland, California to organizing public support, and from marches in San Francisco to her solitary pursuit of her children in Europe. This book is a mother's story of endurance and love of her children in the face of entrenched anti-gay prejudice and overwhelming odds. Highly recommended.

Loulan, JoAnn *Lesbian Sex,* Spinsters Ink, 1984. $8.95

A lesbian mother herself, JoAnn Loulan has included an excellent chapter on "Sex and Motherhood" in this well-written, easily readable, and very informative book. She discusses many of the stresses inherent in lesbian motherhood including topics such as time, privacy, and jealousy. Each subject is approached in a realistic and supportive manner. Believing both that "motherhood and active lesbian sexuality are not incompatible" and that "there is not enough support available in the culture for a pregnant lesbian," Loulan provides many helpful ideas on how to successfully walk a difficult path.

Santa Cruz Women's Health Collective *Lesbian Health Matters!,* Santa Cruz Women's Health Center, 250 Locust St., Santa Cruz, CA 95060, 1979. $3.95

The chapter on "Alternative Fertilization" clearly describes the physical and emotional aspects of alternative conception for lesbians. The authors have included the advantages and disadvantages of various sources for sperm donation, useful medical questions to ask potential donors, and some of the emotional issues surrounding the choice of self-insemination. This chapter would be a good choice for a brief overview of lesbian insemination. The entire book is an excellent health care resource for the lesbian community.

Saphira, Miriam *Amazon Mothers* Papers, Inc., P.O. Box 47-398 Ponsonby, Auckland, New Zealand, 1984. $6.00

Aimed at social workers, teachers, and psychologists, *Amazon Mothers* offers an analysis of seventy questionnaires completed by lesbian mothers in New Zealand. Most interesting are excerpts from interviews with lesbian mothers and co-parents.

Vida, Ginny *Our Right to Love — A Lesbian Resource Book,* Prentice-Hall, 1978. $11.95

"Sharing Your Lesbian Identity with Your Children," by Betty Berzon, pages 69-77 and "Lesbian Mothers in Transition," by Mary Stevens, pages 207-211.

These two articles in *Our Right to Love* will be of interest to lesbians considering parenthood. The first contains a section by a therapist, offering suggestions on coming out to your children and two testimonies by lesbian mothers on their relationships with their children. Although this is addressed primarily to women who have children from previous heterosexual relationships, the insights offered will be of interest to any lesbian parent. Particularly helpful are the experiences dealing with schools and childcare centers. The second article provides good background information on lesbian custody battles. It is clear and well-written. Because case law on this subject is rapidly expanding, the article is not up-to-date, and does not include Artificial Insemination by Donor cases.

## DISABILITY

Browne, Susan; Conners, Deborah; Stern, Nanci, editors *With the Power of Each Breath: A Disabled Women's Anthology,* Cleis Press, June 1985. $9.95

The first comprehensive book about the lives of disabled women. One section specifically explores parenting issues for disabled women and contains both theoretical and personal articles by and about disabled mothers. This thoughtful anthology is intended as a tool for examining and challenging ableism both in the mainstream and in the women's community. It is also one of the first books to bridge the gap that separates disabled women from each other.

Corbett, Katherine; Cupolo-Carrillo, Ann and Lewis, Vicki, editors *No More Stares,* Disability Rights Education and Defense Fund, Inc., 2212 Sixth Street, Berkeley, CA 94710, 1982.

Written by disabled women, this is a role model book for young women with disabilities. It combines a series of quotes and photographs of disabled girls and women and focuses on the issues that affect their lives. Throughout the book is the fictional narrative of a young disabled woman. There is also an excellent resource section.

# GENERAL BIRTH INFORMATION

Ashford, Janet Issacs, editor *The Whole Birth Catalog — A Sourcebook for Choices in Childbirth,* Crossing Press, 1983. $14.95

This is an excellent resource. Designed in the same format as the *Whole Earth Catalog* this sourcebook reviews resources, books, organizations, and products relating to childbirth. Comprehensive, well-written, and beautifully designed, this is an invaluable tool for women who have made the choice to parent. Edited with a strong feminist perspective, *The Whole Birth Catalog* contains a section on lesbian mothers, covering books, films, and organizations addressing the specific needs of lesbian parents.

Ashford, Janet Issacs, editor *Birth Stories: The Experience Remembered,* Crossing Press, 1984.

These stories have been gathered together specifically for women who are about to give birth for the first time and for women who have had a difficult birth and feel isolated in that experience. All thirty-three stories are first person, non-fictional accounts. They take place over a span of seventy years and include multi-generational stories. Although most of the women are white, Ashford has some representation by women of color and from different occupation groups. She has included "A Lesbian Birth Story" by Cathy Cade, one of the first lesbians to use donor insemination. Written in the form of journal entries, Cathy Cade's account emphasizes the loving community of friends and lovers that contributed invaluable support during her son's birth.

Baldwin, Rahima *Special Delivery: The Complete Guide to Informed Birth,* Celestial Arts, P.O. Box 7327, Berkeley CA 94707, 1979.

This is a useful book for women considering homebirth. *Special Delivery* includes sections on prenatal care and nutrition, as well as newborn care, however the bulk of the information presented concerns birth. The step-by-step birthing guide sections are clear and complete, as is the chapter on complications and emergencies. There is a strong heterosexual bias in this book, however it is an excellent resource on home birth preparation.

Bert, Diana, et al.; *Having A Baby,* Dell, 1984. $9.95

This book is a collection of comments on a variety of topics from conception to post-partum depression from seven women who were part of an exercise class for pregnant women. Unfortunately, all the women are professionals and married to professionals. In some ways, the class bias is more overwhelming than the heterosexism. If first person narrative appeals to you, this book could be helpful.

Brackbill, Yvonne; Rice, June; Young, J.D. and Diony, B.A. *Birth Trap:*

*The Legal Low Down on High-Tech Obstetrics,* C.V. Mosby Company, 1984. $9.95

An update of Suzanne Arm's *Immaculate Deception, Birth Trap* extrapolates on her condemnation of modern hospital obstetrical practices. The authors outline the latest in high-tech intervention, compare out-of-hospital birthing to in-hospital delivery, and provide a clear guidelines to use in making your own benefit/risk decision about intervention. Appendices provide information on questions you might want to ask about hospital practices, suggestions for finding a midwife, and listings of films, books, and organizations of interest to pregnant women. Highly recommended, especially for those planning a hospital birth.

Cassidy-Brinn, Ginny; Hornstein, Francie and Downer, Carol *Woman-Centered Pregnancy and Birth,* Cleis Press, 1984, $11.95

This is a truly feminist birthing book written by women who work with the Federation of Feminist Women's Health Centers. It includes references to lesbians as mothers throughout, and addresses insemination in the chapter on becoming pregnant. It is also an excellent sourcebook for information about medical interventions, where they are indicated and where they are not. Excellent, highly recommended.

Cohen, Nancy Wainer and Estner, Lois J. *Silent Knife: Caesarian Prevention and Vaginal Birth After Caesarian,* Bergin and Garvey Publishers, 1983. $14.95

This book addresses the dramatic rise in the use of caesarian sections and exposes how unnecessary most of them are. It is the thesis of this book, that sensitive, women-centered pre-birth preparation and delivery can prevent most caesarians and that women who have had one caesarian birth can safely deliver subsequent children vaginally. Thoroughly researched and well-written, *Silent Knife* is highly recommended. Since one out of every four or five women giving birth in the United States ends up having a caesarian, this book is worth reading.


FERTILITY AND INFERTILITY

Adess, Nancy; Brown, Kris; Hackett, Susan and Turiel, Judy *Fertility and Pregnancy Guide for DES Daughters and Sons,,* DES Action National, 2845—24th Street, San Francisco, CA 94110, 1983. $7.25

DES children are at a higher risk of developing several problems which directly affect conception and childbearing. If you are a DES daughter, you will find clear information about potential risks and the treatments available if problems do arise for you. This pamphlet is an excellent resource providing an up-to-date listing of books and medical journal articles which expand further on the issues discussed.

*Fertility Awareness: Its Use in Family Planning,* An Instruction Booklet prepared by Health Center #4

This is an excellent booklet detailing the steps of fertility aware-ness. Although it is written with the idea of using fertility awareness as a means of contraception, the explanations of charting, basic physiology, checking one's mucus, and interpreting one's fertility cycles are excellent. This book must be ordered directly from the address listed above.

Glass, Robert H. and Erricsson, Ronald J. *Getting Pregnant in the 1980's, New Advances in Infertility Treatment and Sex Preselection,* University of California Press, 1982.

Written by two well-known physicians in the field of infertility, this is a valuable handbook of information on infertility treatments. Again, heterosexual bias is present throughout, however, the clear and concise explanations of each treatment make this book worth reading.

Menning, Barbara Eck *Infertility: A Guide for the Childless Couple,* Prentice Hall

Don't be put off by the title. Although this book has a heavy het-erosexual bias throughout, it is well-written, informative, and thorough. The author gives considerable attention to the emotional impact of infer-tility in a sensitive and thoughtful manner.

## OTHER BOOKS OF INTEREST

Brewer, Gail Sforza, Editor *The Pregnancy After 30 Workbook: A Program for Safe Childbearing No Matter What Your Age,* Rodale Press 1978 $11.95

This is a collection of articles written by different people cover-ing several aspects of childbearing. Only the first chapter is specific to women over thirty, the remainder of the book, including articles on nutrition and breastfeeding, are applicable to any woman. The chapter on exercise during pregnancy is particularly well-written. Many lesbians in the groups have mentioned that this book was useful to them. Al-though, be forewarned, all the women pictured are white, and the per-sonal commentary accompanying the articles is from white, heterosexual couples.

Arditti, Rita; Klein, Renate Duelli; and Minden, Shelley, editors *Test Tube Women What Future for Motherhood?,* Pandora Press, 1984.

This book contains an excellent collection of essays from the international feminist community in response to new developments in reproductive technologies. The section entitled "Women Taking Con-trol: A Womb of One's Own", includes articles on self-insemination. One article is an informative overview of the history of donor insemina-tion in the United States by one of the first lesbians in this country to have a child by AID. This is an excellent book and highly recommended given the emergence of these reproductive technologies and they way they will inevitably affect women's lives and bodies.

Friedman, Rochelle and Gradstein, Bonnie *Surviving Pregnancy Loss*, Little, Brown and Company, 1982. $8.95
This book is written primarily for women who have experienced a miscarriage, stillbirth or ectopic pregnancy. It validates the depth of the loss and describes the typical emotional and physical impacts of an unsuccessful pregnancy. The authors use their clinical experience to make suggestions for coping and facing future plans. Explanations of each type of loss are accompanied by women's personal accounts. Beware of the husband/marriage assumptions.

Rich, Adrienne *Of Woman Born Motherhood as Experience and Institution*, Norton, 1976. $12.95 Bantam paperback, $3.95
This is a powerful book, beautifully written with the spare prose of a poet. The author carefully examines the ways in which motherhood has been institutionalized and controlled by patriarchy. She traces the historical roots of this phenomenon and its impact on a woman's sense of herself and her relationships with both daughters and sons. *Of Woman Born* is the perfect antedote to lesbian invisibility, as Rich speaks from and to a consciousness of lesbians as daughters and mothers.

Adair, Margo *Working Inside Out: Tools for Change: Applied Meditation for Intuitive Problem Solving* Wingbow, 1984.
For the past ten years, Margo Adair has led groups on Applied Meditation. In this book, she draws together what she has learned and presents a training course in intuitive problem solving. Her purpose in all her work "is to awaken the creative resources within each of us so that we can take charge of our lives." In the text of each chapter, she helps the reader explore her internal and external realities, and clarifies the interplay between them. Each chapter contains meditations to aid in tapping the power of intuition for guidance and problem solving. Margo Adair stands at the junction of spiritual and political life, and has provided us with a valuable tool for integrating these aspects of our lives.

# INDEX

Environment, and parenting decision, 12

Exercises. *See* list at end of index

Exercises, how to use, 3-5

Expectations
    of children, at different ages, 79
    and co-parenting, 106-107
    of family of origin, 37
    of friends, 33-35, 120
    of having children, 71-79
    of having the perfect family, 72, 77
    of non-biological motherhood, 99-101

Expenditures, 54-56. *See also* Money

Eyedropper, 167, 177-78


Fallopian tubes, 169, 173, 178, 180

Families, lesbian
    building, 71-76, 118-19
    ideal, 75-76

Family background, 12, 61, 70, 73-75

Family form, 71-76, 125

Family of origin
    and coming out, 39-40, 45
    description, 74-75
    and family activities, 74-75
    and non-biological motherhood, 38, 44, 103
    and support, 37-45
    talking to, 37-45
    and telling of parenting plans, 42-45

Father, 85-90, 215-16. *See also* Donor

Ferning test (for mucus), 174

Fertility awareness classes, 170

Fertility concerns, 171, 203-205

Fertility, of donor. *See* Semen analysis

Fertilization, 169

Fetal monitoring, 208

Finances. *See* Money

Flexibility, in parenting, 49, 98, 120

Foreign adoptions, 161-62
    and political implications, 161

Fost-Adopt program, 158, 163

Foster care, 99, 152, 155, 163-64
    and adoption, 158, 163
    and coming out, 16, 164
    and home visits, 164
    *See also* Non-biological motherhood

Friends

and parenting decision, 31-36
and single parenting, 119-21


Gay men, as donors, 211-14, 225n

Genetic counseling, 129-30

Girl children
    and insemination timing, 180-81, 187
    and lesbian community, 82-83

Goals, in life, 23-24

Go-between, in arranging alternative fertilization, 192, 220

Gonorrhea, 186-87, 189, 200

Grandparents, and coming out, 45

Grief, of child, and unknown father, 89

Grief, of mother, in miscarriage/stillbirth, 209-10

Groups, for lesbians considering parenthood, 5, 229-37

Guardianship. *See* Legal guardianship


Hauer, Laurie, 211n, 243

Health care practitioners
    and coming out, 16
    and disabled lesbians, 130-31, 132

Health history forms, 185, 199-200, 245-49

Hepatitis B test, 185, 200

Heterosexuality, of child, 83-85

Hitchens, Donna, 112, 184, 215-26

HLA paternity test, 219, 225n, 226n

Home visits, 158, 159, 164, 166

Homophobia, 13-17, 33, 45, 160, 162
    and AIDS, 212
    internalized, 13, 15, 119
    in workplace, 53
    *See also* Coming out

Homosexuality, of child, 83-85

Hormonal blood test, 239

Hubbard, Ruth, 206

Hysterosalpingogram (HSG), 239, 240


Income, 56-58. *See also* Money

Independent adoption, 159-60

Infertility, 203-205, 239-41
    emotional impact, 241

Insemination, 177-79, 180-81. *See also* Alternative fertilization

271

# EXERCISE LIST

Photo: Lynn C. Campbell

Cheri Pies was born in Los Angeles in 1949. She received her Master's degree in Social Work from Boston University in 1976 and her Master's degree in Public Health from the University of California at Berkeley in 1985. She has been a health activist for the past 15 years in the women's health, reproductive rights and disability rights movements. Cheri has worked in many community organizations, including Planned Parenthood as a health educator and trainer. She is also one of the founders of a shelter for battered women and their children in Oakland.

Since 1977, Cheri has been leading groups for lesbians considering parenthood. In addition, she freelances as a facilitator and mediator, and has served as consultant to legal organizations, gay and lesbian groups, film projects and the mass media. For fun, Cheri enjoys jogging and swimming, spending time with her friends, playing with her three cats — Teddy, Bob and Tinkerbell, and performing as Violet the clown for adults and children. She is currently exploring the social and ethical implications of reproductive technologies and prenatal screening.

And yes, Cheri Pies is her real name.

# ▨ spinsters book company

Spinsters Book Company was founded in 1978 to produce vital books for diverse women's communities. In 1986 we merged with Aunt Lute Books to become Spinsters/Aunt Lute. In 1990, the Aunt Lute Foundation became an independant non-profit publishing program.

Spinsters is committed to publishing works outside the scope of mainstream commercial publishers: books that not only name crucial issues in women's lives, but more importantly encourage change and growth; books that help to make the best in our lives more possible. We sponsor an annual Lesbian Fiction Contest for the best lesbian novel each year. And we are particularly interested in creative works by lesbians.

If you would like to know about other books we produce, or our Fiction Contest, write or phone us for a free catalogue. You can buy books directly from us. We can also supply you with the name of a bookstore closest to you that stocks our books. We accept phone orders with Visa or Mastercard.

Spinsters Book Company
P.O. Box 410687
San Francisco, CA 94141
415-558-9586